Ali Akbar

aka

Horace Pittman

By

R.B. Morris

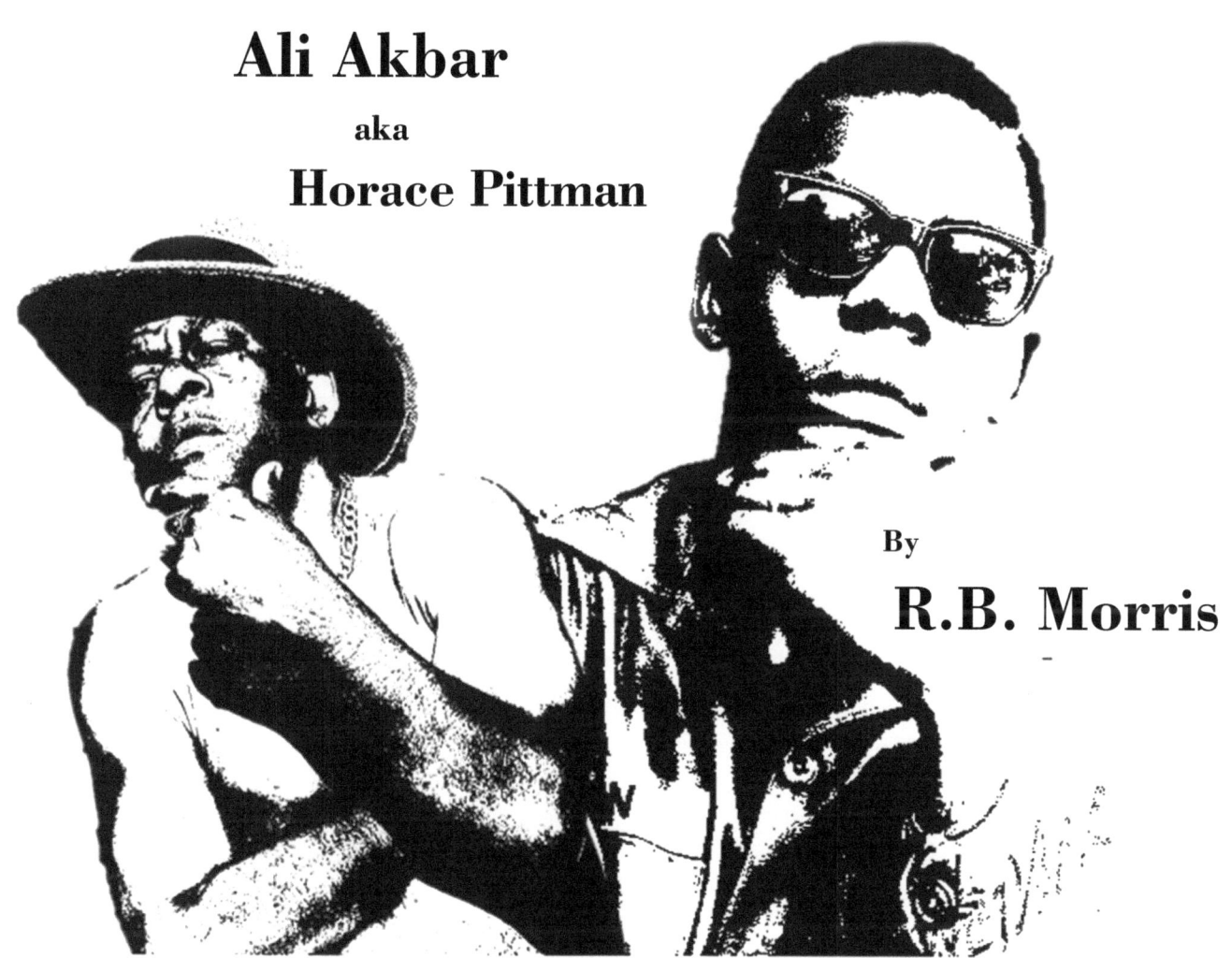

WHO IS THIS MAN?

Published by

RICH MOUNTAIN BOUND

BOOKS
MUSIC
WOODWORK
PHOTOGRAPHY
SCULPTURE

www.richmountainbound.com
www.rbmorris.com
www.imagerap.net

Cover design by Karly Stribling
Title page photo collage by Frances Johanna Morris

ISBN 978-0-692-32424-0

Other works by the author

Poetry

The Mockingbird Poems
Keeping the Bees Employed
Early Fires

Music

Rich Mountain Bound
Spies Lies and Burning Eyes
Empire
Zeke and the Wheel
Take That Ride
Knoxville Sessions
Local Man

Drama

The Man Who Lives Here Is Loony
A one-man play
based on the life and work
of James Agee

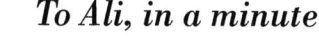

To Ali, in a minute

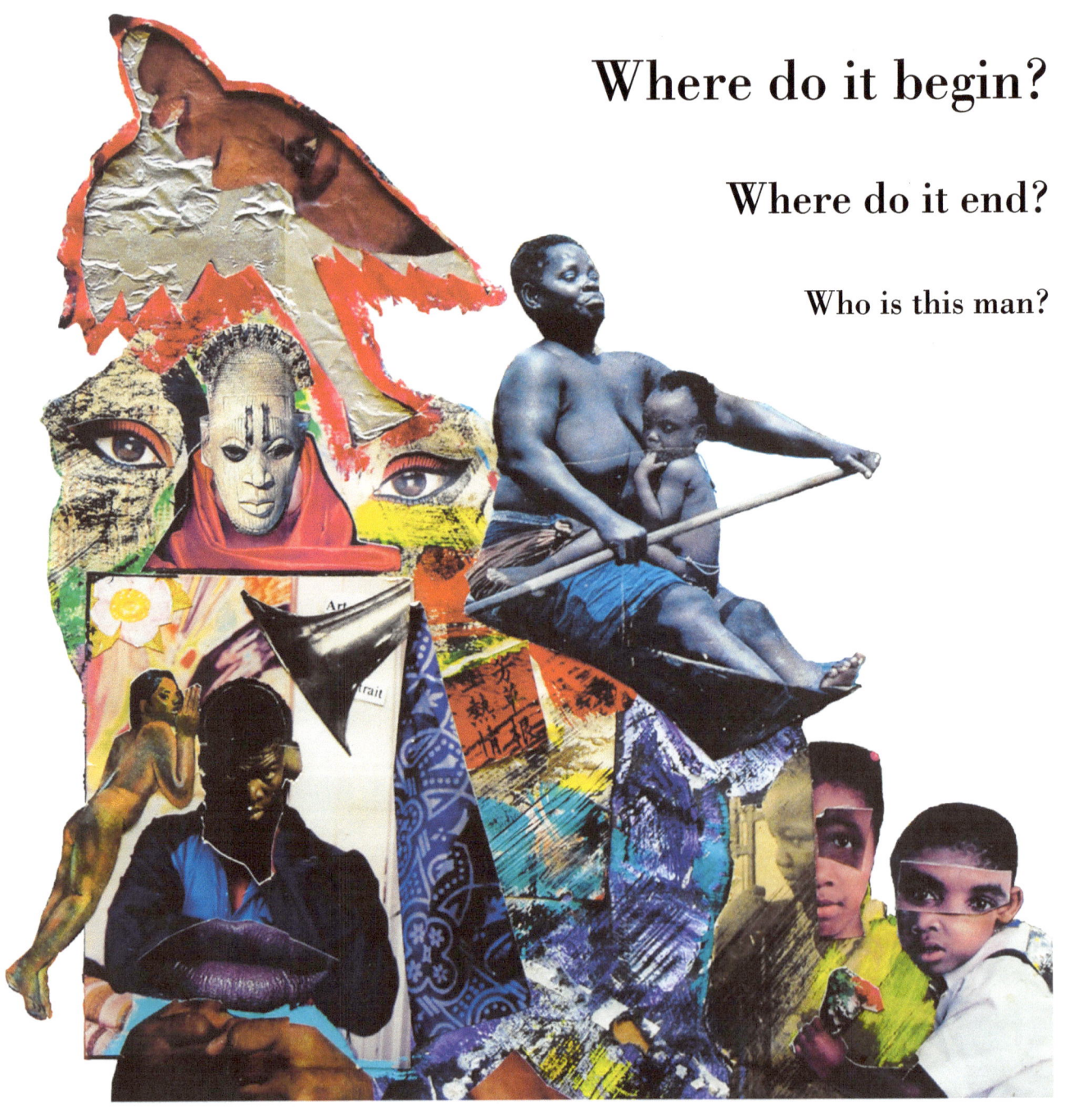

Where do it begin?

Where do it end?

Who is this man?

I seen my face in a mud puddle man
I seen my face
I was just a little bitty boy man
And I seen my face and knowd it was me see
I knowd it was me
But that mud puddle man it scaret me
It was like a MYSTERY
I din't know where it go
I din't know how deep it was
I thought it went on forever man
I thought I might fall in be gone

-Where you come from man?

-Come from Rock Hill, South Cackalackee.

-Yeah? My momma from South Cackalackee.

-Yeah? My momma is too.

-My momma from down in the low country.

-Oh yeah, you a home boy.

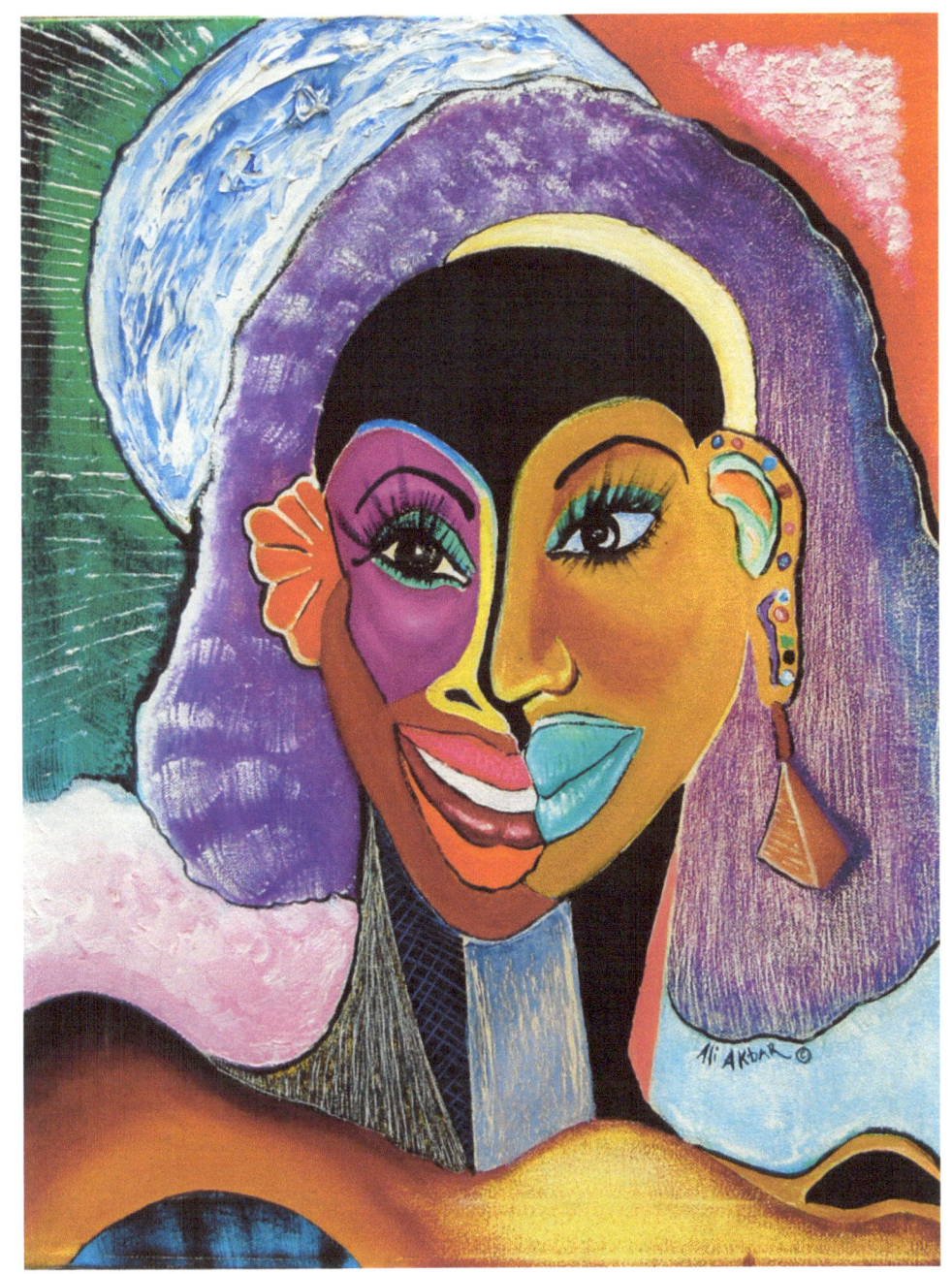

I told my daddy I say
I want to be a artist
He questioned me
He say you be a artist
you got to draw
something from reality
from the world he say
And when he say
from the world
He wave his hand out
like he waving over to
the corner of the room
And I look see the broom
there against the wall
So I drawed the broom
Cause it out there
in the world
I worked hard on
that broom
I worked and worked
and I showed it to him
And he seen it
And he never questioned
Me no mo

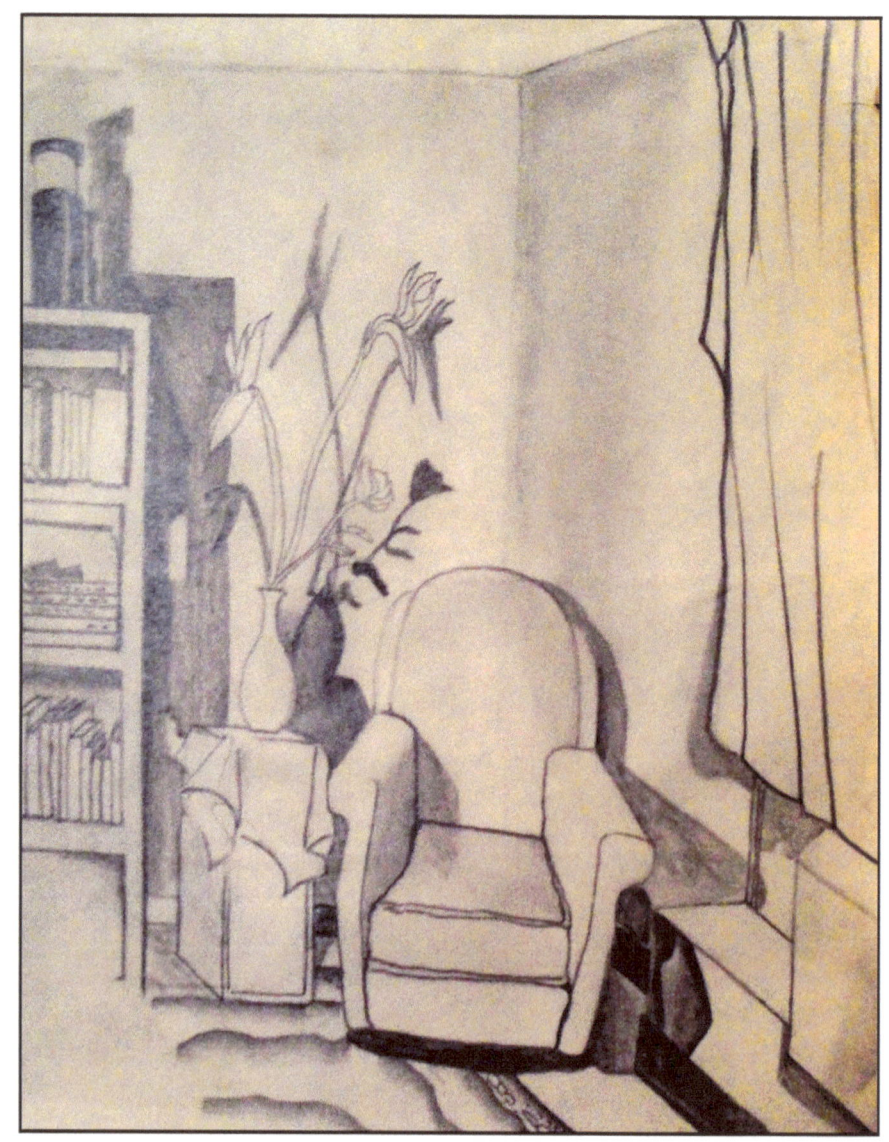

SENIORS

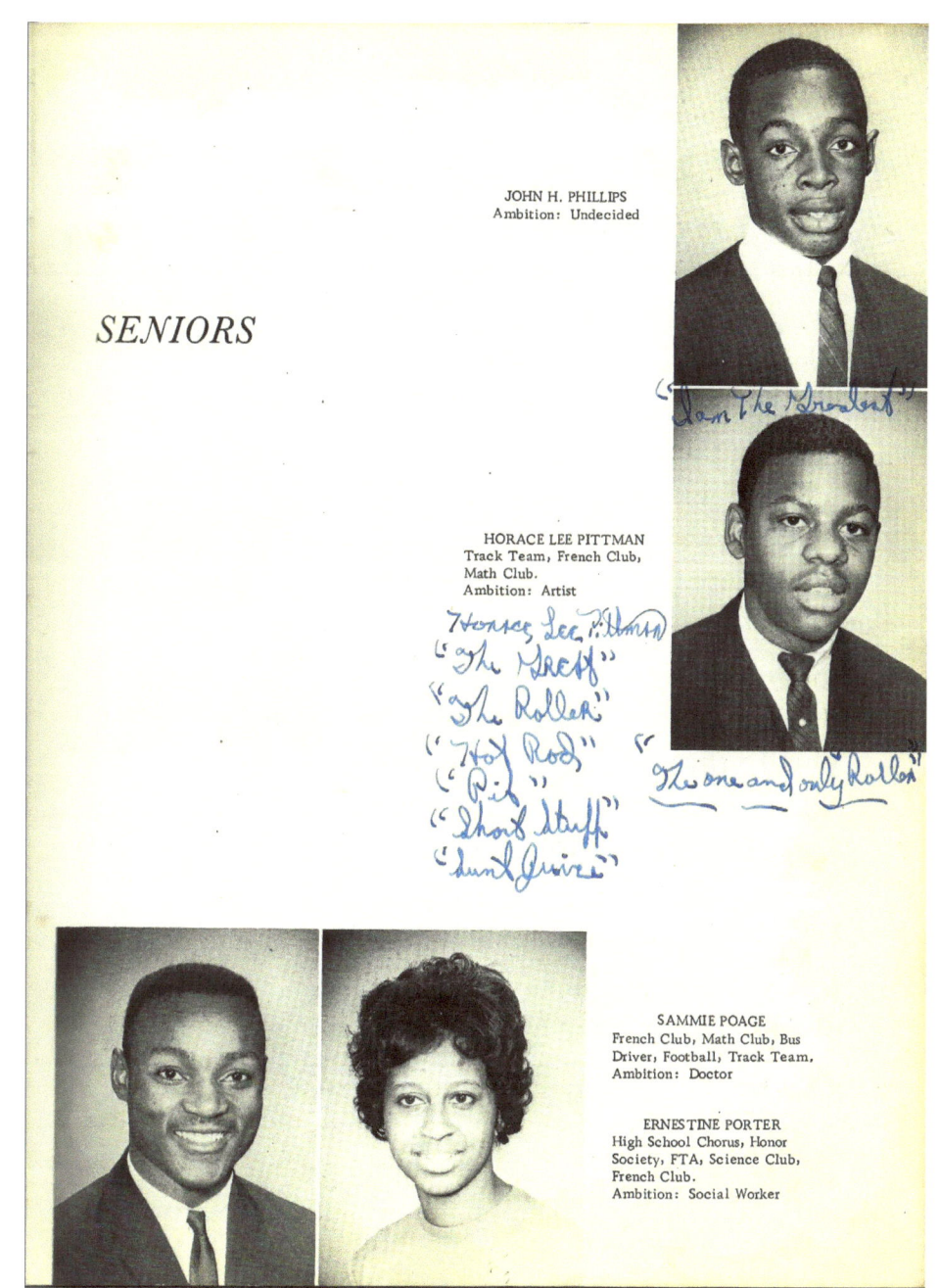

JOHN H. PHILLIPS
Ambition: Undecided

HORACE LEE PITTMAN
Track Team, French Club,
Math Club.
Ambition: Artist

SAMMIE POAGE
French Club, Math Club, Bus
Driver, Football, Track Team,
Ambition: Doctor

ERNESTINE PORTER
High School Chorus, Honor
Society, FTA, Science Club,
French Club.
Ambition: Social Worker

There aint no telling the story man
Cause you can't tell the story.
I don't know the story and neither do you.
Everbody story can't get told man,
You know what I'm saying?
You think you remembered, but you ain't.
You gone. I mean we ALL gone.
We turn over like the grass baby,
Turn over and fold under and be gone.
That's right, gone with the wind.
So there you go.

But hey, our stories going all the time see.
This IS the story man. I am telling the story
And so are you, see. That's what nobody see.
Yeah. But they people man,
People you see and everbody see and
They remembered a little longer by more folk,
You know what I'm saying?
But hey, what's that?

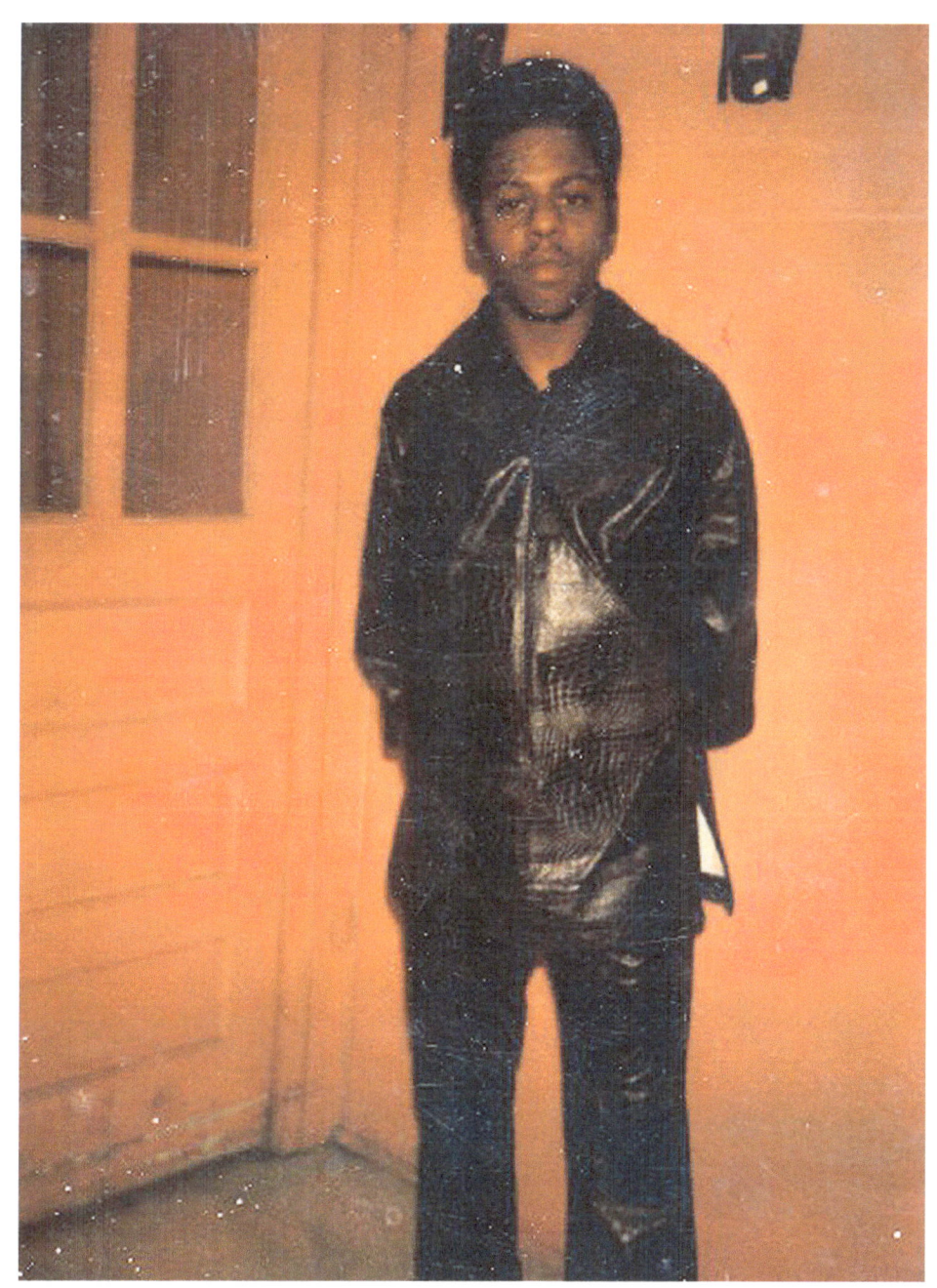

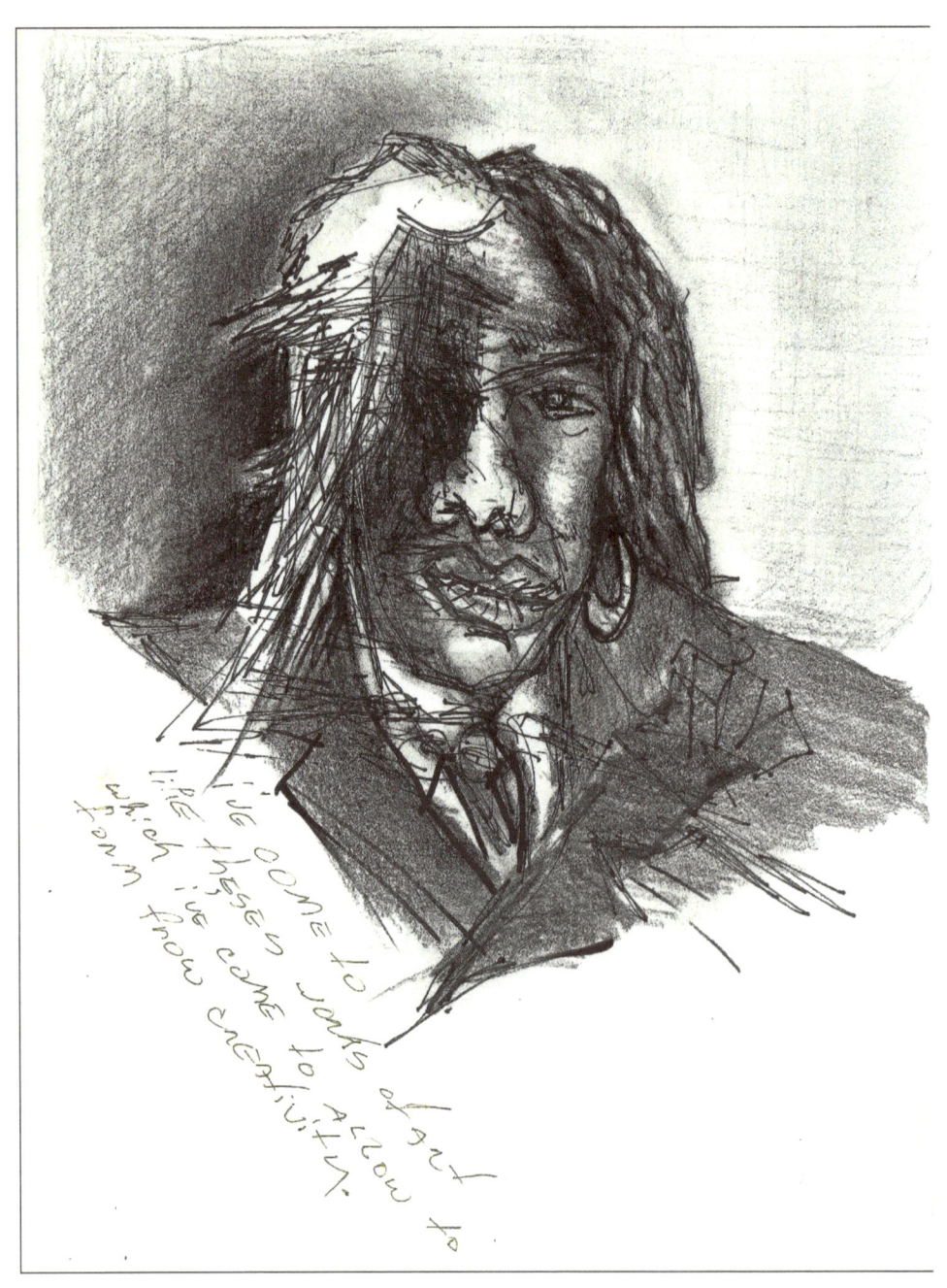

"...ive come to days of art like these ive come to allow to which ive come to allow to form from creativity."

Now a young man get ideas right,
Romantic notions, say bout women,
Music and art, maybe getting rich,
You know maybe be famous.
Maybe be a king, HAH!
But mainly he jus tryin get by and
Get through all what he gots to deal wid.
You may see youself doing something
MAGNIFICENT, you know,
Some glory road for you. But hey
In the meantime you tryin keep you
Ass alive right? You trying eat sleep
Live and make you way with the
World. Am I wrong? No. But see,
You be looking for a way out, or a way
Up, wherever you going. Or whatever
Possibility presents itself see.

-Horace stayed with an uncle in New Jersey for a while.

-*Oh yeah?*

-Not sure if that was before the war or after or both, but I'm pretty sure it was before.

-*Yeah.*

-I remember seeing a photograph or two.

-*Really?*

-Yeah, he told me those was his pimpin' days.

-*Oh yeah.*

-He coulda meant a lot of things by that.

-*Right.*

-But I got the feeling he was learning the street you know and get'n up with all that.

-*Yeah.*

-Learning to project hisself into the world, you know, push it a little, get a feel for what you up against.

-*Right. But then he went to Nam?*

-Yeah, he went to Vietnam.

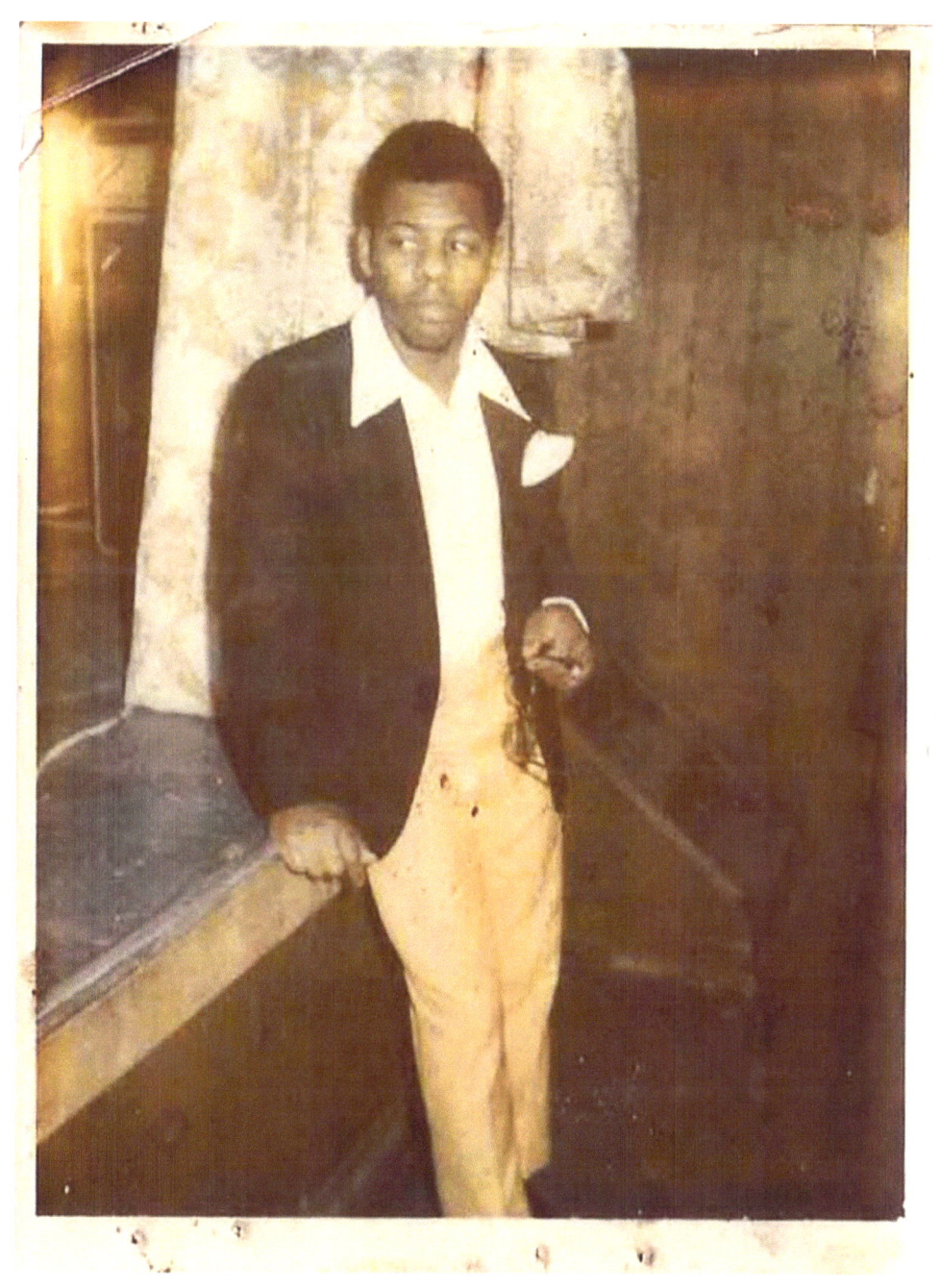

19

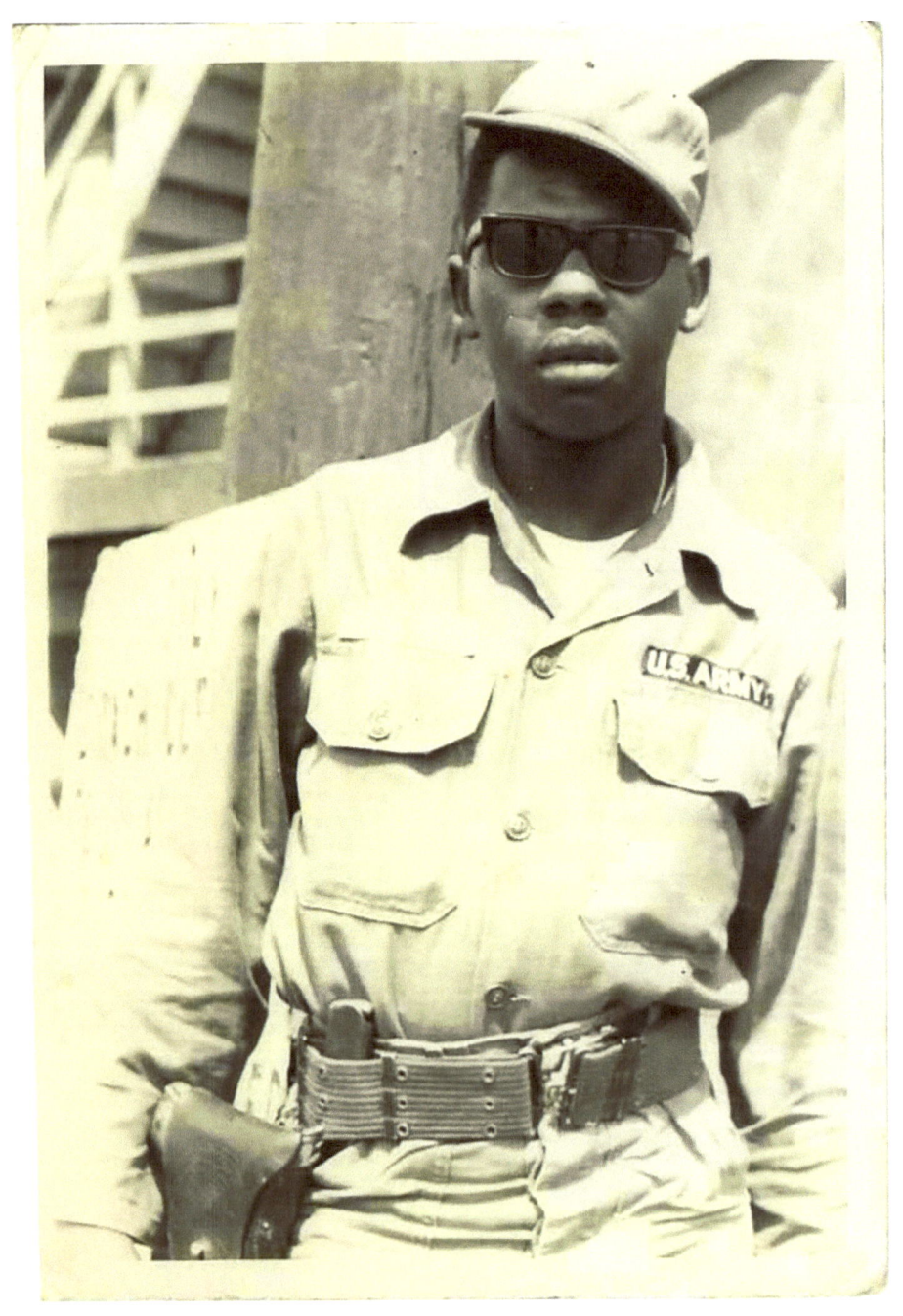

20

-And he come back with shrapnel in his head, and a big scar go halfway round his head right?

-Yeah. He suffer a shrapnel wound some kind, had to have a metal plate put in his head. I never really did see the scar for a while cause his hair cover it you know.

-He ever talk much about all that?

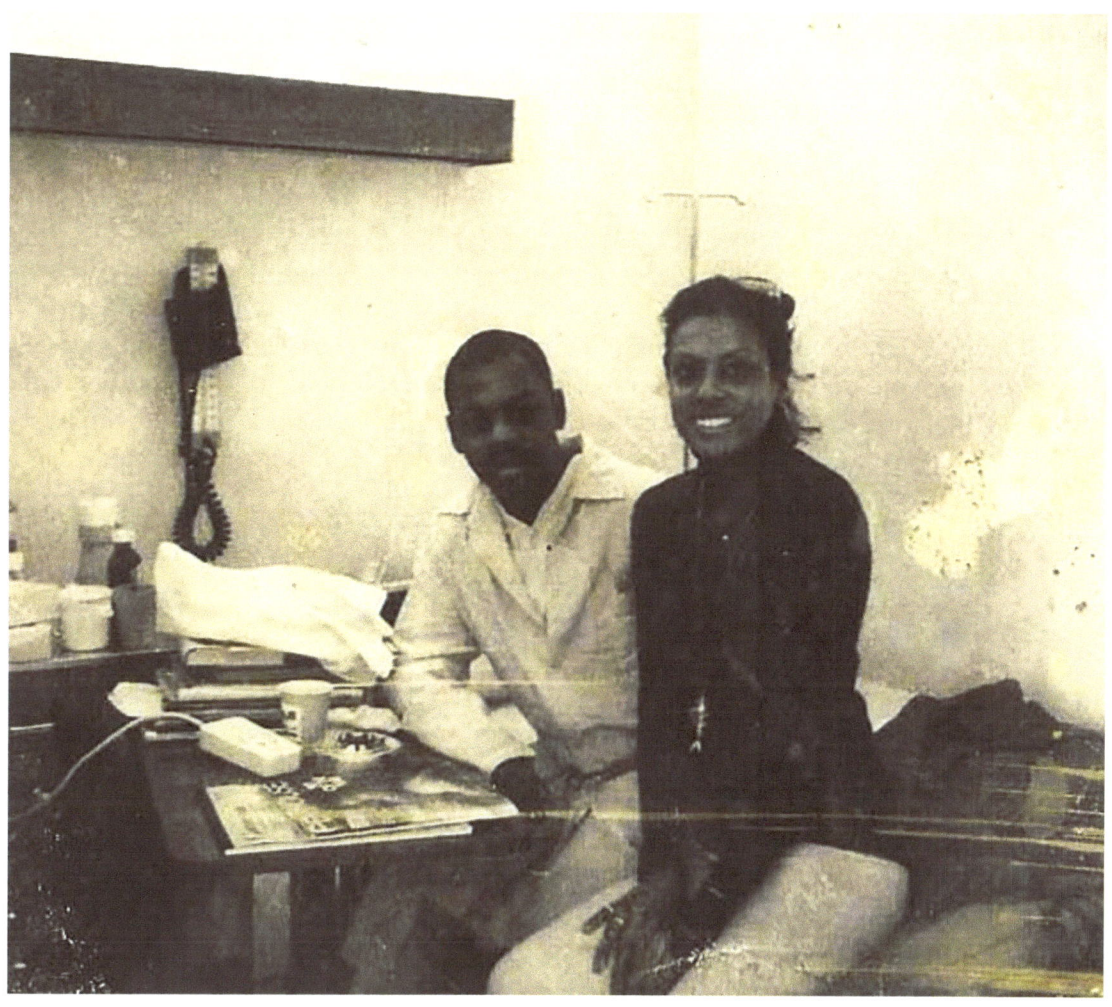

-Not really. I know he seen some shit, but he never really talk too much about it. Oh he mention it some way if he with friends, you know, and it come up. But I don't 'member he ever going into too much a detailed account, you know, or some rant, you know, goin on 'bout any that.

-*Yeah.*

-I'll tell you how he mention Vietnam, like when he told me one night he was in a bar there on Market Square having some drinks and when he left and was walking cross the Square the barkeep and another guy come running over to him like he ain't paid his bill or something, saying this lady done lost her purse or a hat or what it was she lost and saying he took it. He be sitting close to where she was and they all thinking maybe he run off with it right. They not trying to search him but they want him to come back cross to the bar with them and figure it out. He says to me, he says, I toldt them I didn't take nothin from nobody. And they say okay but come back and let's get it straightened out. He says he look at them and then he say okay. And they go to walk back. But one of them is walking behind him see. And he say, no dude you want me to walk back over there wich you okay but you ain't walking behind me. He toldt me, he say, I been Vietnam man and seen how that shit can go. I been trained he say, and he say I told the man you can walk up here beside me but you won't be walking behind me. And so he did, the man say okay and they walks back over.

And I say, well what happen when you get there?

He say, they ax me what's in my bag. I tell'em what's in my bag my bidness. And they say, show us what in you bag or they call the cops. And Horace say he look at them and everbody all round lookin at him and he step up to the bar and empty his bag right there in front of everbody. He say they wasn't much in his bag and everbody see he ain't got no bitch's shit. And Horace say he look at everone a them and say, see I ain't got nothing of this woman's, but you all thought I did. And then he say, and you all cowards ever one of you who's thinking that. And then he tells me the barkeep look under the booth where the lady be sitting and her bag was pushed back under her seat and she just didn't know it. Yeah. Horace took his shit and walk out. Ha, you know what I'm saying? Yeah, he call

22

ever one of them on that shit man. And they knew it. But hey, what I'm saying see is that the way he might mention Vietnam when he talking, 'bout like that.

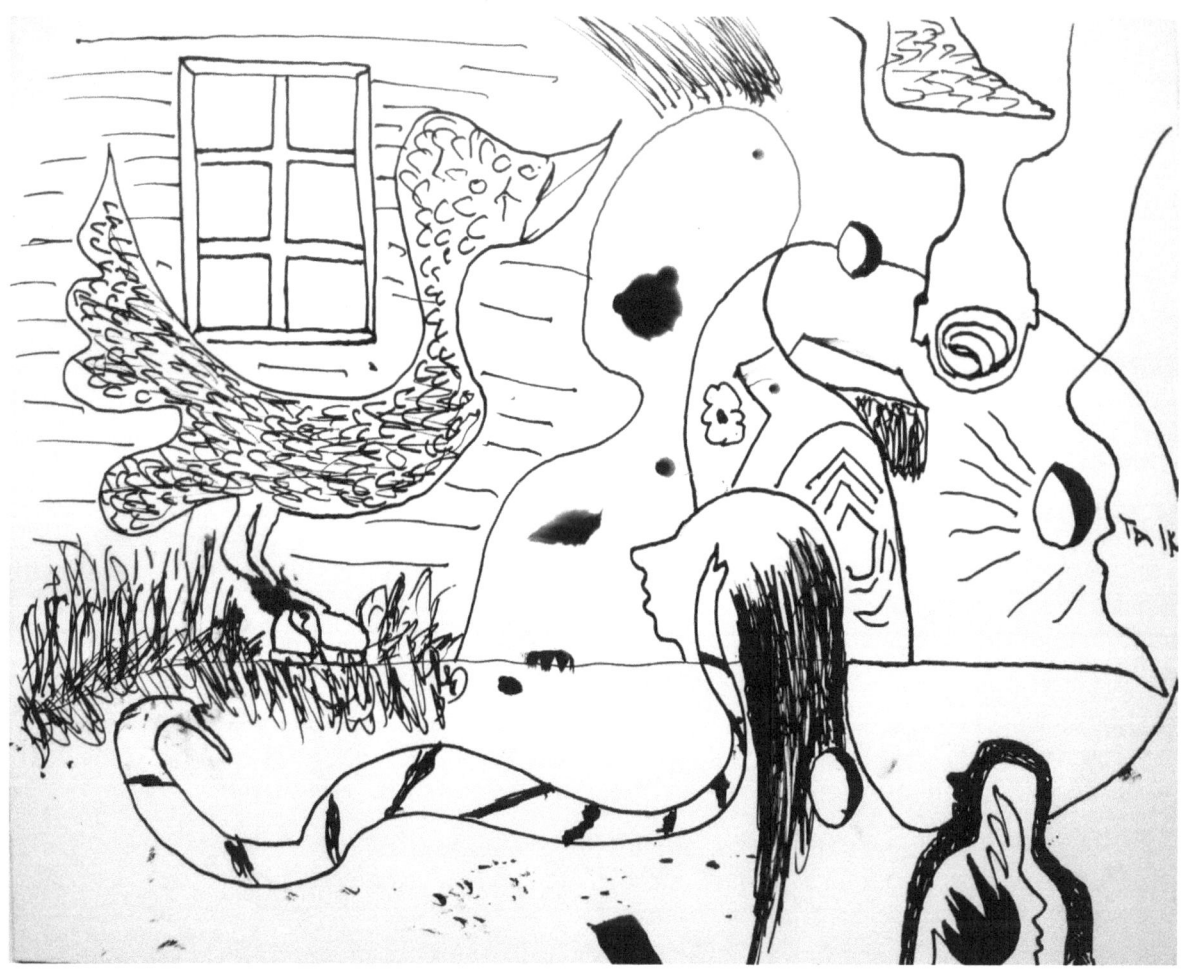

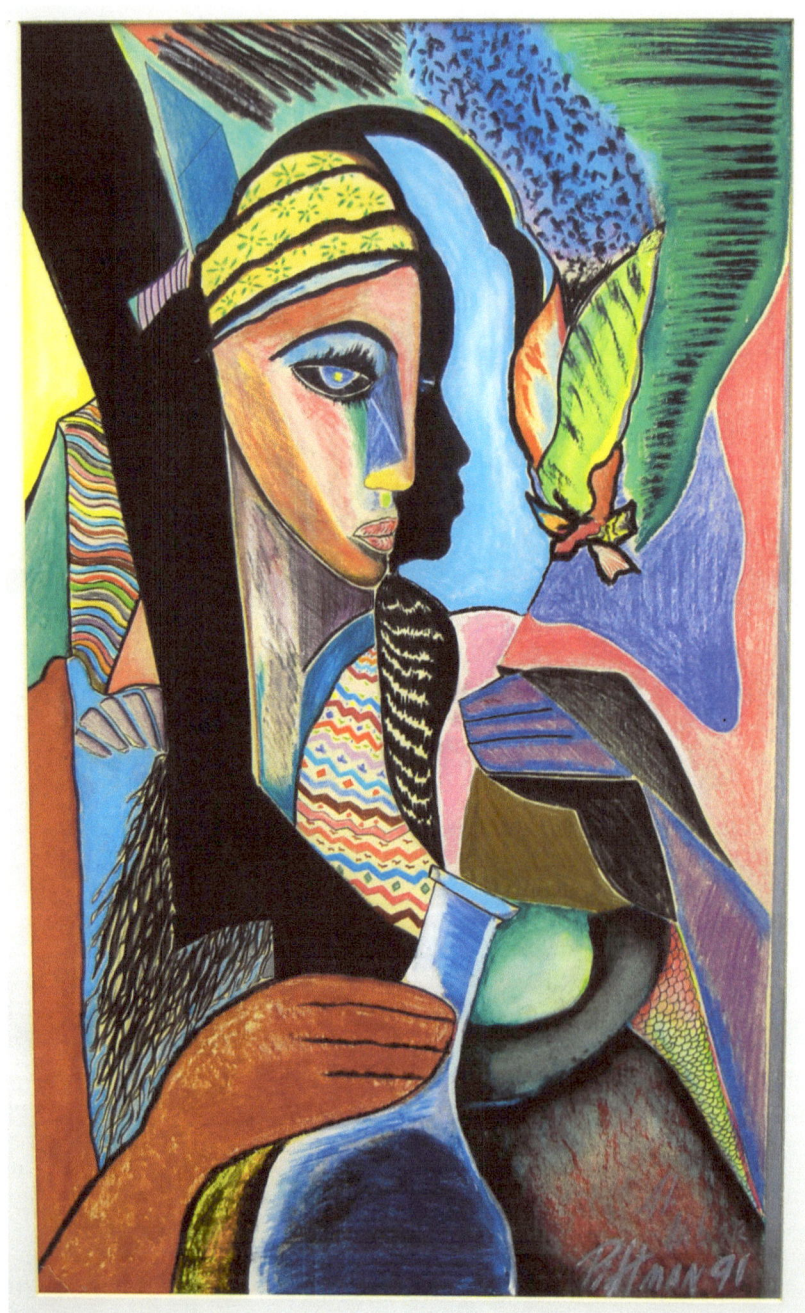

24

Somewhere along the line you
gots to drink the POSHUNT man.
You know what I'm saying?
You can't go to war and smoke
dope with the enemy man and
travel the seas and go to little
villages and big cities and sleep
with the peoples of the world man
and not drink the poshunt.

The poshunt is life man, it's everthing. It's the essence dude and you gots to get it. It's like *duende*, you know what I'm saying? It's the soul of the world man. It ain't black magic, but it magic, it real. And you gots to see how far it go. You gots to know about it. That the only way you can learn man, and that is the only thing to learn. If you living. You scaret but you got to live anyway. What choice you got? Like in the army man you scaret but what you gonna do? You had training man and you gots to use it. But you got to use you *intooishun* too dude. You got to train that too see. Now out in the world you gonna wanna get a taste of everthing right? That only natural. But it natural to fuck up and die too. Yeah. That happen all the time. And it gonna happen to everbody some time if they ain't careful. But see, I don't wanna be no general. And I don't wanna be killin no peoples. They always gots some war going somewheres, and they always gets somebody to fight that war. Maybe that be you some time. Cause that just the way it goes. But some point you gots to say you can have that war, cause you got other fights to fight. You know, some point you have to wander off to the world. Some point you gots to get beyond war and find whatever essence you can man. And hope it ain't war. Yeah. But hey, that a whole 'nother kinda war see. But that the poshunt you gots to drink.

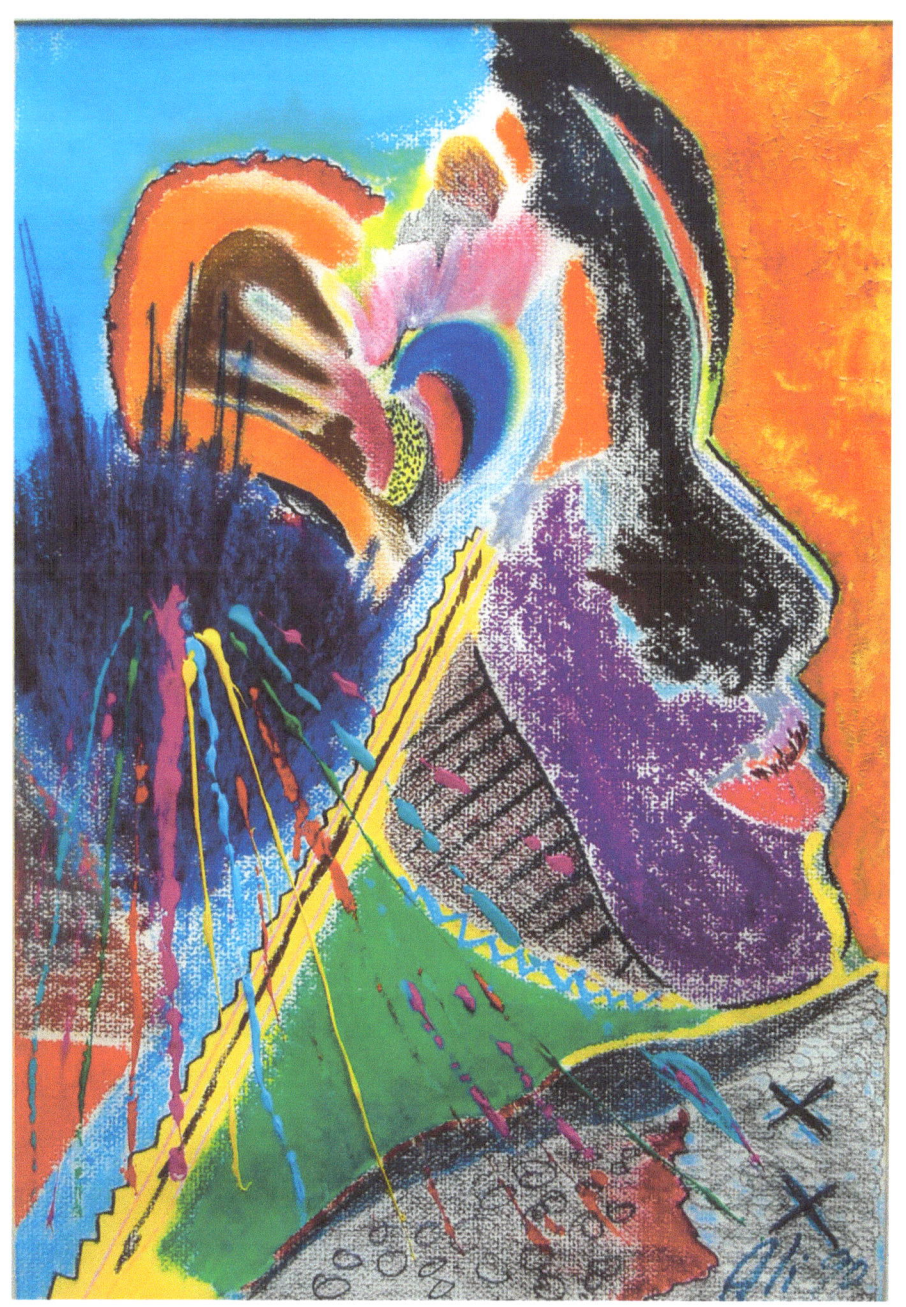

-But it bound to be a wild deal man coming back from the war to America where everthing crazy. You know what I mean? And everbody you know, everbody you see, look different. And who is that man, and who is that man, and who that woman? And everwhere you go it the same thing.

-*Yeah.*

-All kinda shit goin down them days, 'specially in California. You gots social unrest a'all kind. People changing. Got your war protestors and your national guards, got your deserters and your draft dodgers, your fem'nists, your black panthers, got your hippies and your yippies and your 'stablisments, got your ROCK music 'splodin everwhere, got your whole society SHAKIN' from the ground up.

-*That's for sure.*

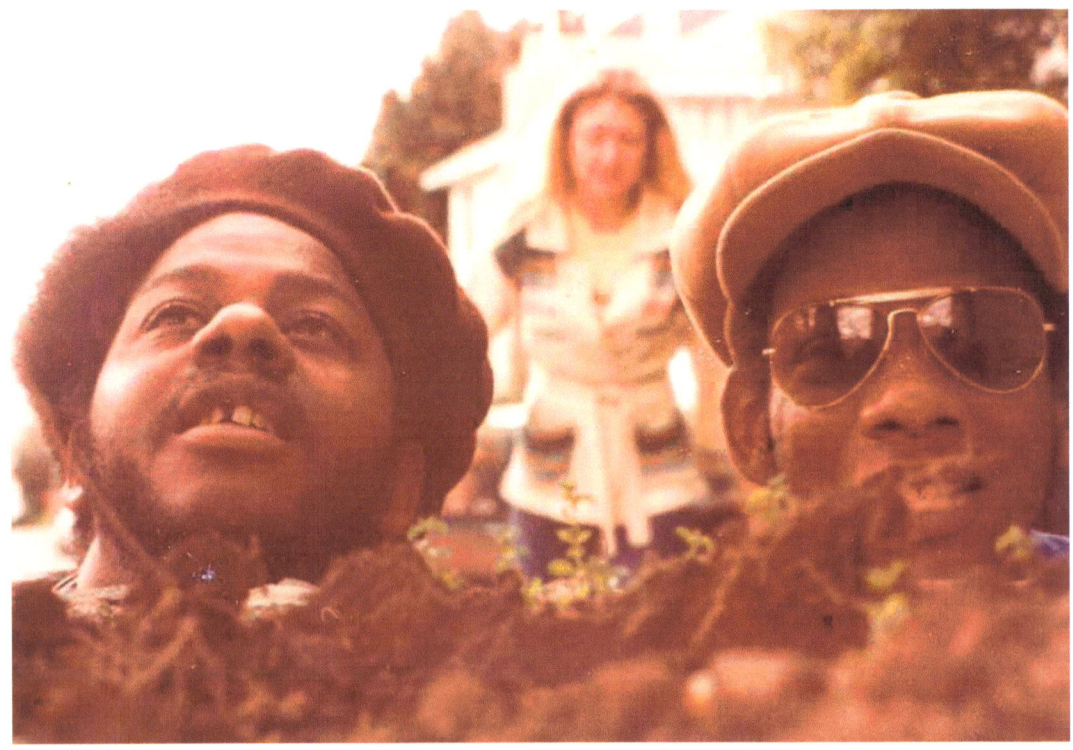

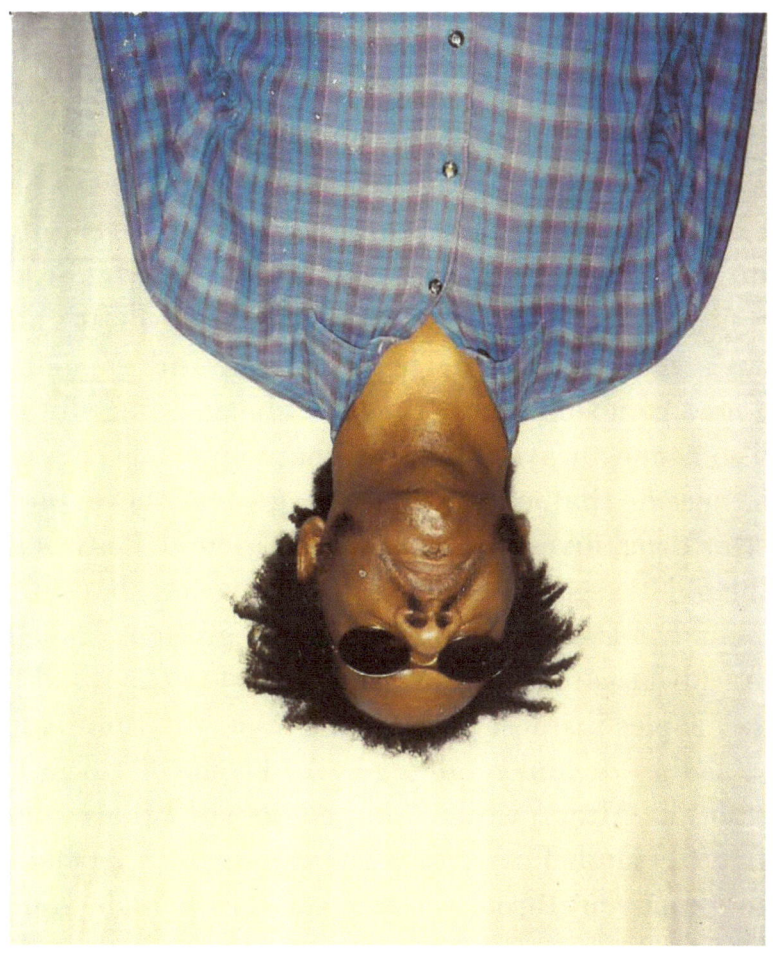

-Talk bout growin pains and changin of the guard man. Everthing upside down. Don't nobody know what happenin and what come next. You know?

-*Oh yeah.*

-And they killin everbody here just like over in Vietnam, all them sassinations and students gettin shot. Is bad man, things is bad, yeah. But you know, it was the best of time too. HAA!

Everwhere you go's an es'splosive landscape man, always have been.
Maneuver with caution. Always. Country was shiftin, country kept
shiftin, country shiftin now. And if you black man, you best be ready
for a rude awakening at all times. They was tellin you it's all new, it's
all new, that's what everbody tryin to tell you. And everbody tryin
something new, goin somewhere they ain't been, doing shit they ain't
done. And someone always tellin you what you needsa do, go here
do this, go there do that, come over here, go over there, try this try
that, take this drug, invest in this, go see this, go to heaven go to hell.
Just like the old day, go to war be a hero get yo ass shot off, same
thing. Somebody OD on some shit somebody give'em, somebody else
get eaten by a bear cause they never camp out in the wood before.
Yeah. Lotta peoples just lost and looking man, you know. Just wanta
find what it is they do and get doing it. And some of'em just lost, ain't
lookin for nothin. After a while lotta peoples start to wonder if they
ain't gettin left behind. They either go crazy or wander back to the
old trip, you know, cut throat rat race get ahead. Yeah, you figure
it out. You a civilian now, if that *what you want to call it.* America
baby, coast to coast, home of the brave. That's right. Now dance
through this mine field sucker. HA! I hear ya.

Hey, I tell you what I do sucker. I am a Artisté.

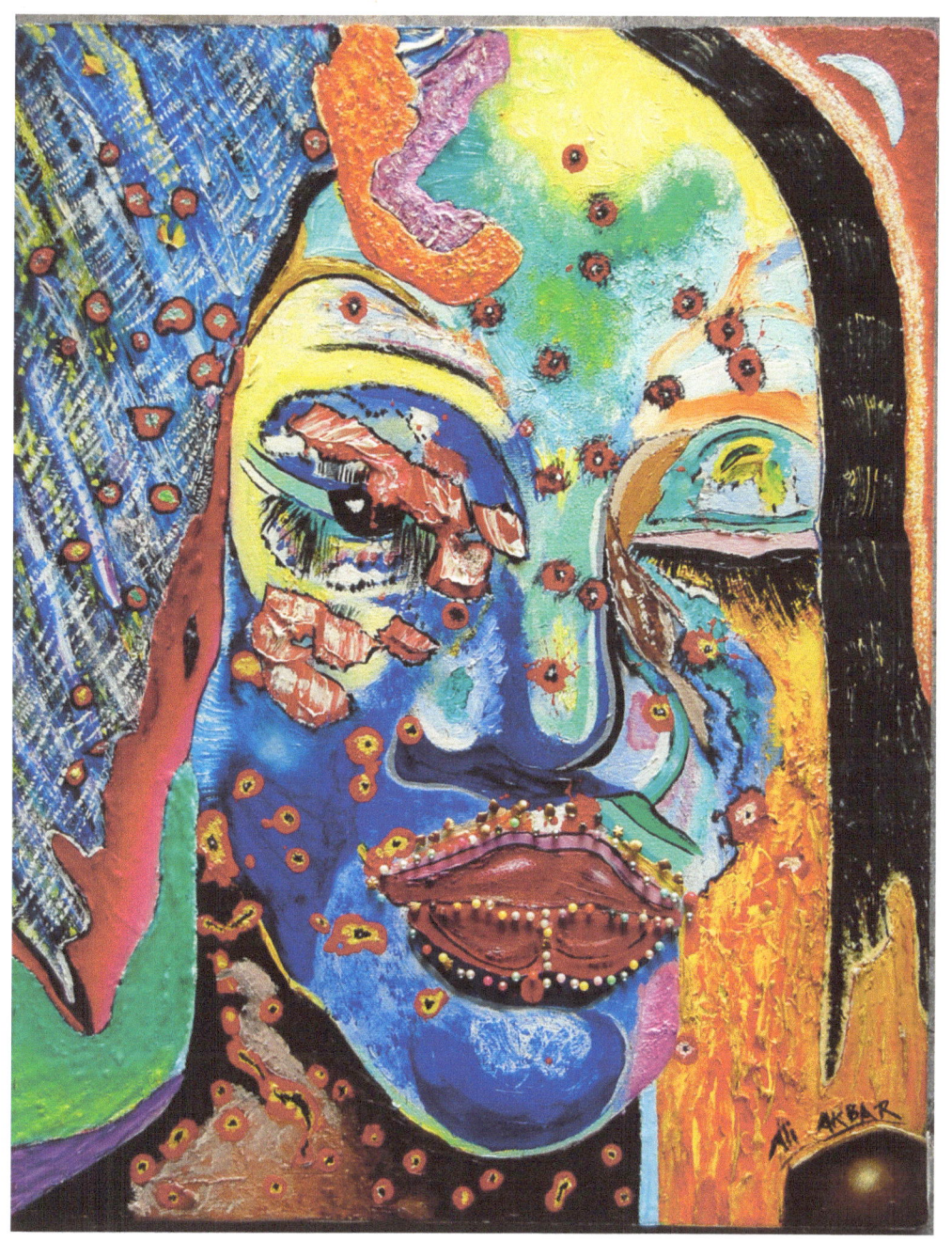

31

-Now he come in from San Francisco.

-*Yeah?*

-Said he studied at the San Francisco State.

-*I guess he was enrolled?*

-I think he was. But he walk up anywhere and say let me in. You know what I'm saying?

-*Yeah.*

-And he got some GI Bill right. He a veteran.

-*Right.*

-He can do some stuff.

-*Yeah. Wonder how that effect his art?*

-What, fighting a war?

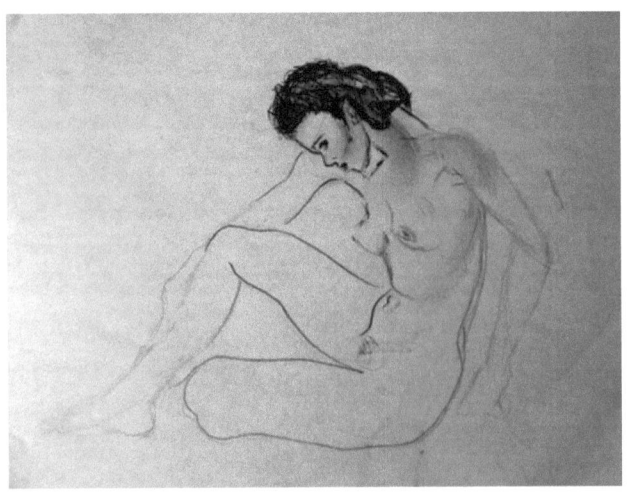

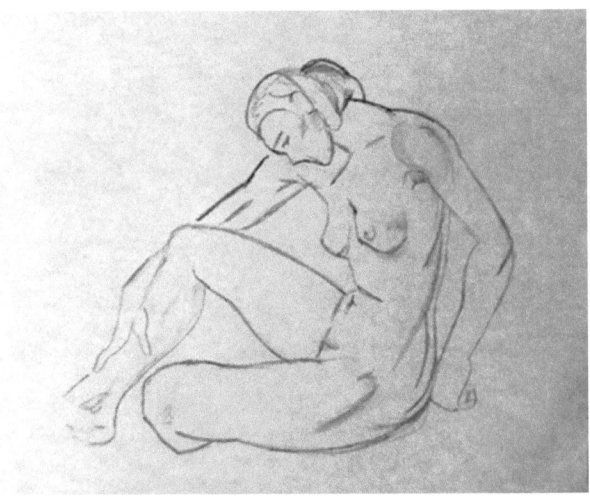

-*Yeah, bound to have some effect.*

-Hell yeah man. You been to war you come back a dfferent person. It may hurt you, it may enable you. It may kill you, but it change you. You ain't got the same perspective as when you went in. You mighta thought you wantsa be a soldier or mighta thought you wantsa be a artist. But now you might not know who you are, what you gonna do. Yeah, everything different. And you be different, too.

-*But he got back into art.*

-Yeah. He a born artist. Had it in him man, had it in the way he PERCEIVE, you know.

-*Yeah.*

-It was his natural sensibility, I say that.

-*Yeah.*

-But after the war he musta got more.

-*More.*

-Got more courage man, more eyes, he SEEN more.

-*Yeah man, he been to Nam, he fought the Cong. He back in the jungle.*

-That's right. He gone into the war see, into the fray. When he talkin to you he see the FLAMES all around you. He got context for all this shit.

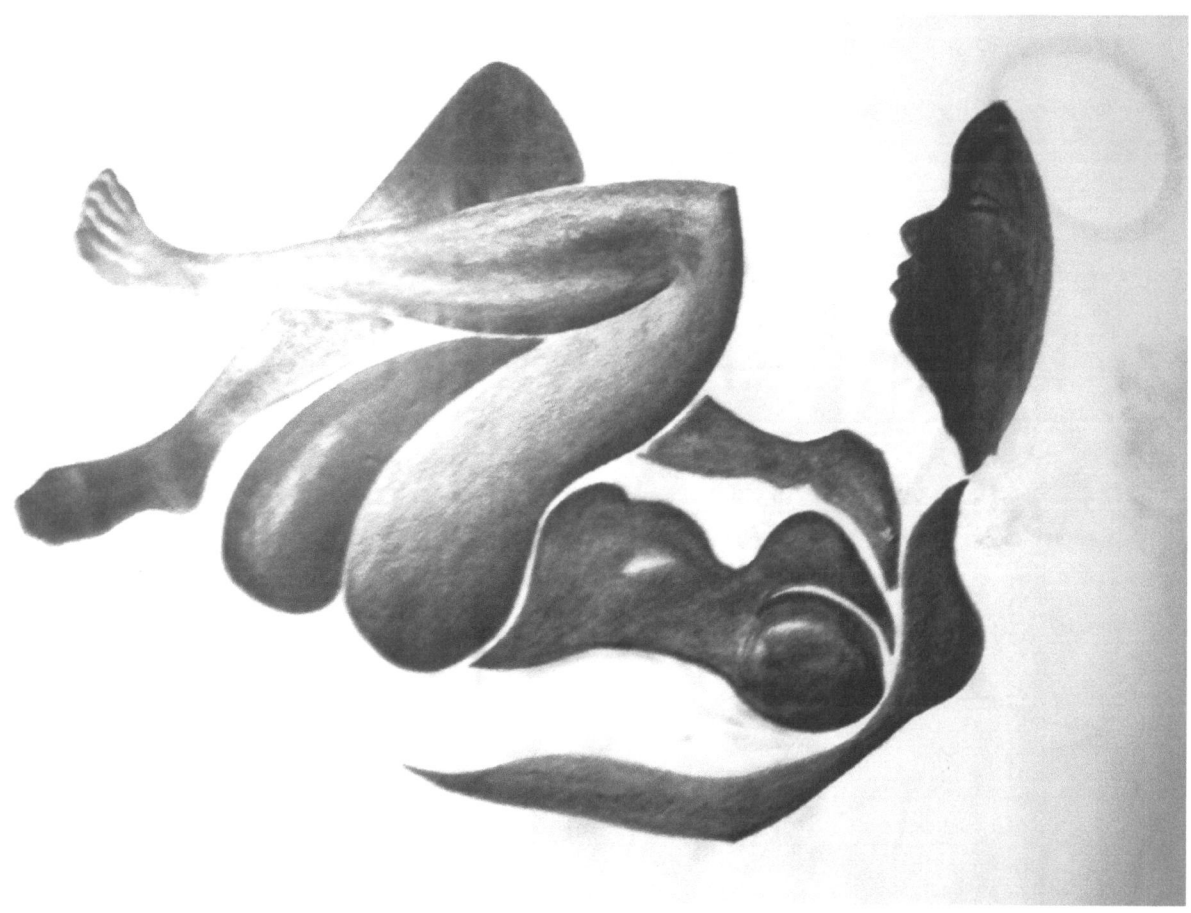

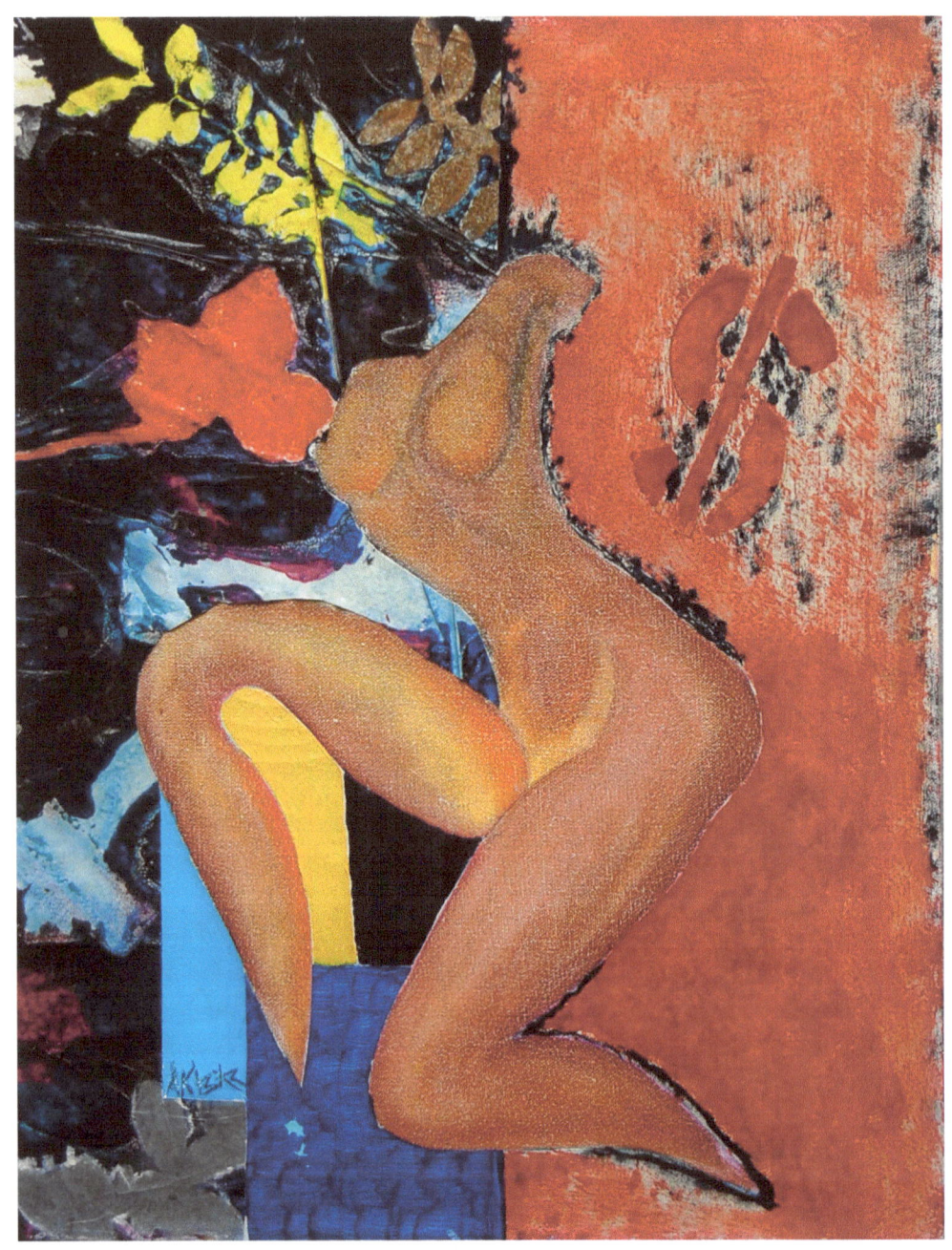

34

Once you out in the world can't nobody find you way but you. Can't nobody live you life and can't nobody make you art. You gots money to go school and study art, that's good, but what if you ain't? You still gots to make you art. And even if you do go school and study art, it be over soon and you be out on the street and still have to make you art. Then you see who a artist and who not. How you goin keep making you art when nobody goin give you no money for it? How you goin to keep doing it? You not. You goin quit brother, you goin quit sister, and do something else get you by. And you just dream about you art, or you get it out a you head. But if you find a way see, you find a way keep doing it and not quit, then you be a artist.

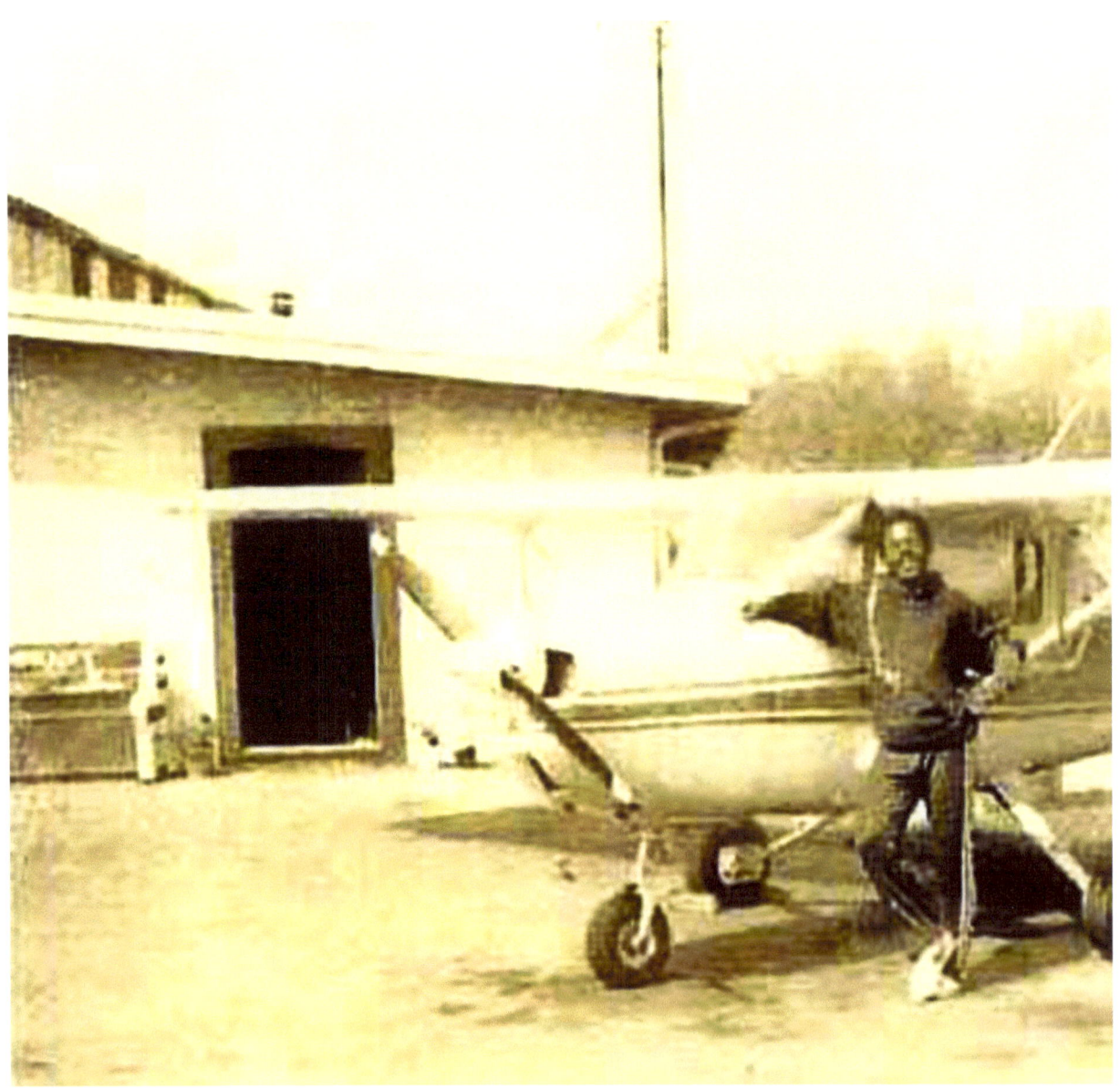

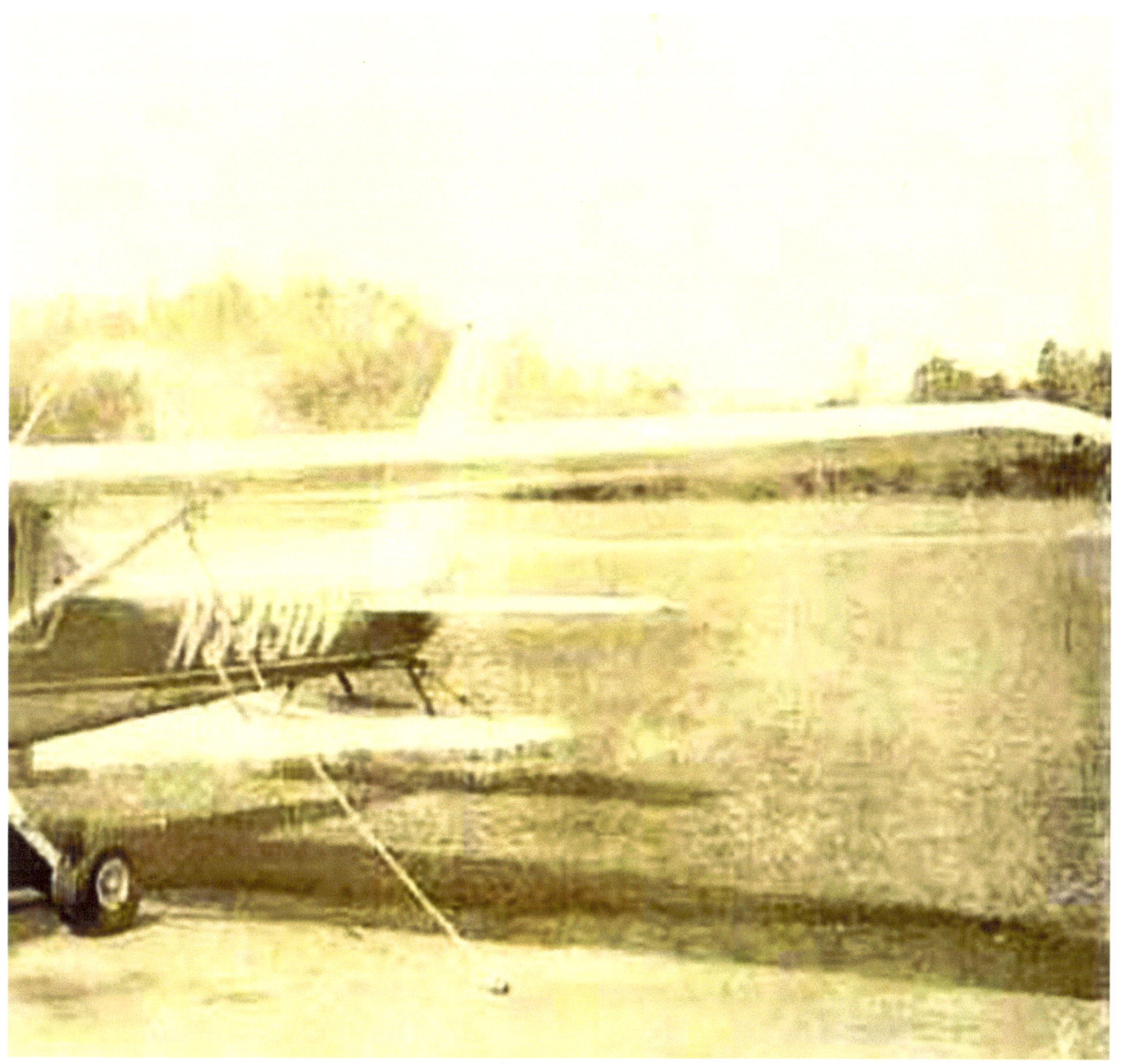

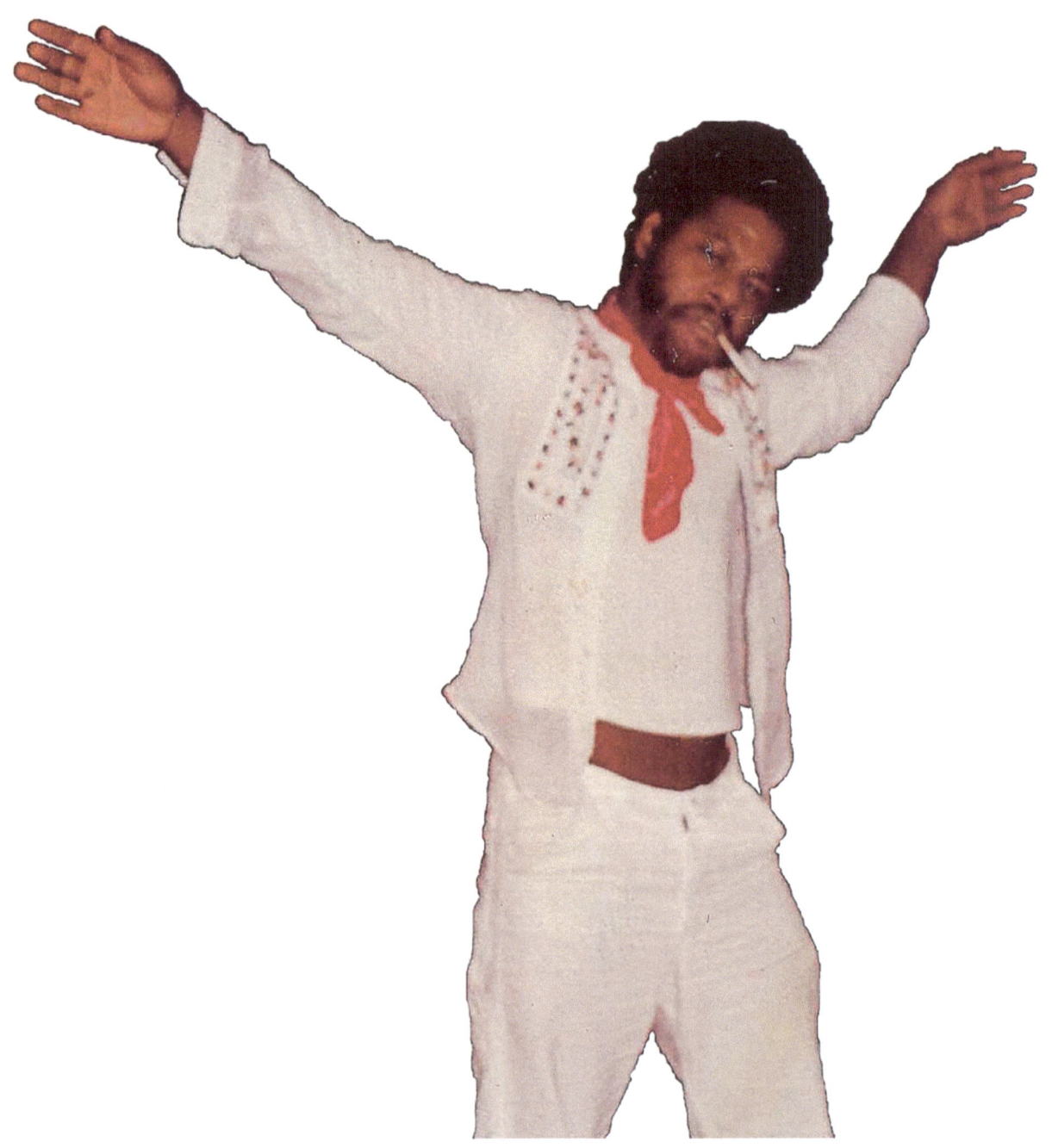

-To live is to fly, ain't that what the man said. Well he living and he flying.

-*Yeah.*

-And you know, he drift a while too. Don't know where all he go. He studied art, he studied people, he really a student of the culture man. Got no wife and family. Ain't ready to roll back to Cackalackee.

-*Yeah, he's living in the new world now.*

-Takin what he know and gettin on. You know, he mighta got lost out there in some INTRIGUE. Mighta gone searchin for one thing and found another. You know, sometime you try chase something down, you finally catch it find out it ain't nothing you want that bad anyway. And he changin all the time, changin and stayin the same. Searchin for whatever. He may be lookin for a soft spot to land, a little mercy, a little slack right, but he also casting his pearls see, he temptin his fate, and he want to be challenged, he want to learn, and he want to show someone what he know. Yeah. I think he gotta lotta that in Knoxville.

Ali enters the city…

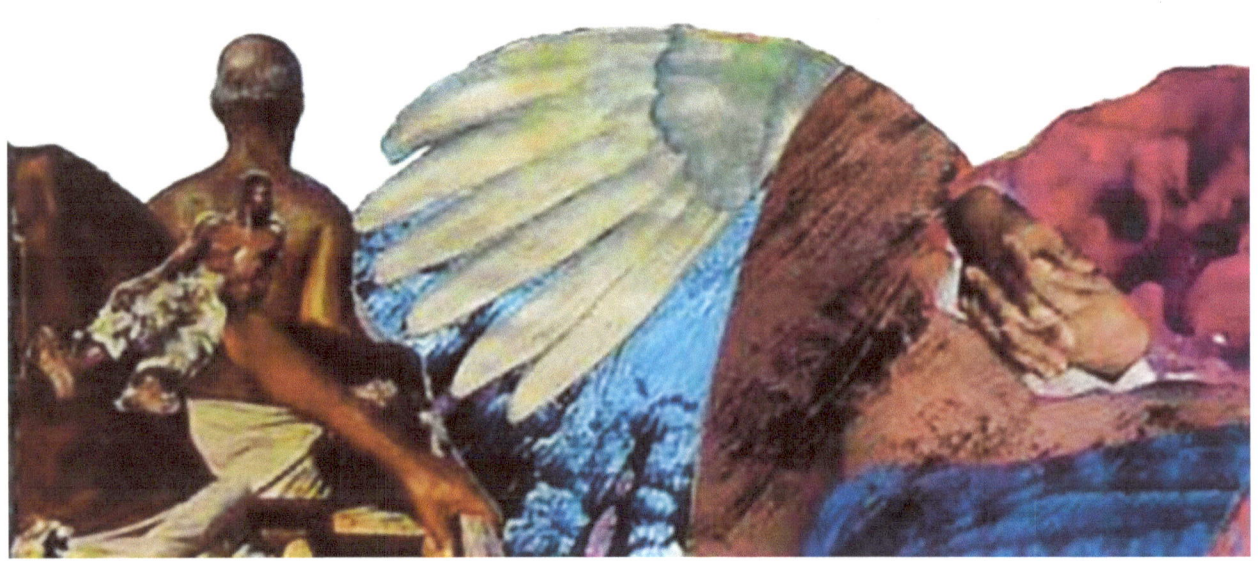

Horace Pittman, the man, the Pittman, Pitt, the Roller, the one and only, the greatest, the gone daddy, gone soldier, lost child, God's child of the wild South, done been to the Far East, done traveled the world rolling over the great seas to the mad cities and madder jungles of faraway lands, seen everything there is to see, seen the tail of the dragon swallowing the sins of man, been changed, been opened up, been made a man and still walking, walked all over the country, all over California, been to the last lip and drank deep the western brew, seen the tits of God's sister shining in the sweet moonlight of modernity, done run with the bums and bummed with the sons and sunned with the golden ones, been radicalized, been pantherized, been free loved, been pushed and shoved and pulled and tugged, been so far inside the music you come out on the other side of the moon, sleep in the stars, wake in the dust of the universe and shake it off, shake off all the blood and shed that skin. He done woke up and started living the dream. And where are we now?

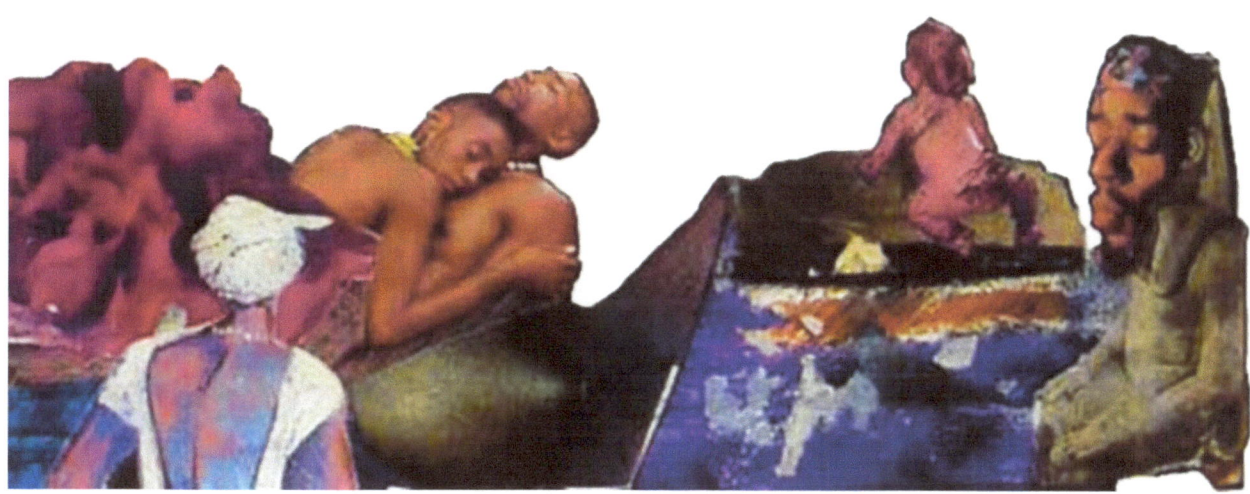

-Didn't I see you on Magnolia Avenue?

-Yeah that was me.

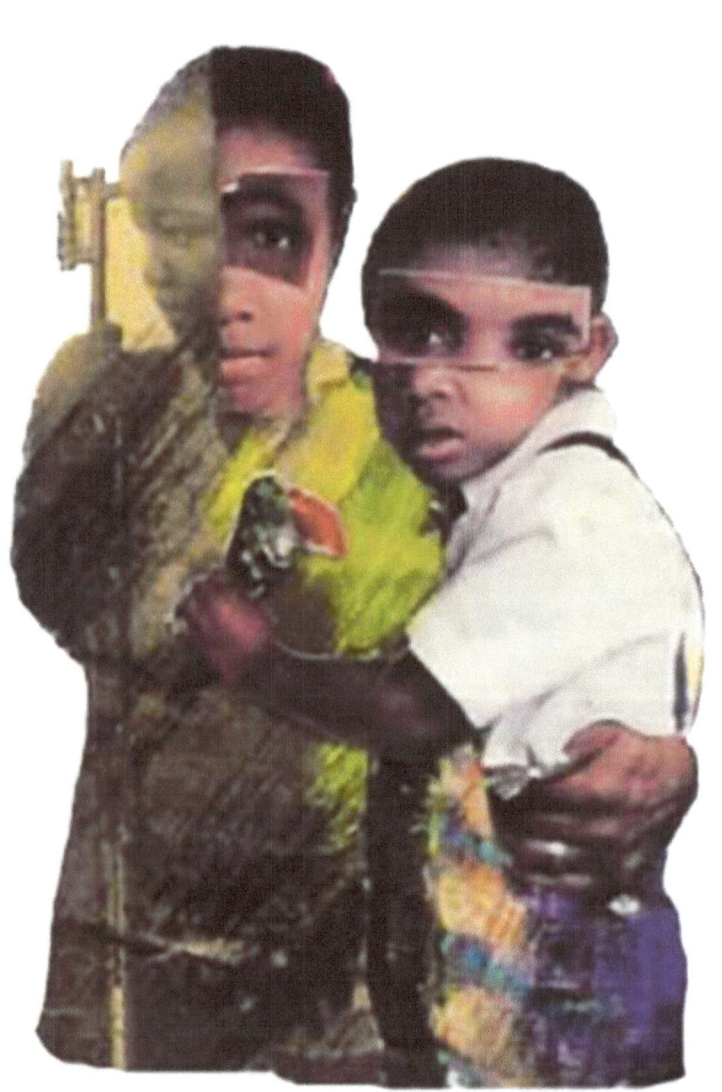

-How'd you ever meet him?

-Met him in Knoxville on Jackson Avenue in the Old City.

-Yeah, when was that?

-Sometime the fall a '82.

-Okay.

-But I seen him first over East Knoxville on Magnolia Avenue.

-Oh yeah?

-I seen him when I was driving by. He was standing on side the road, you know, just standing there by hisself when I drove by. But he had a look about him, something you know, made me wonder who is that man? Yeah something bout him stuck in my head cause it wasn't long after bunch of us was all down to 200 East on Jackson hangin out in this new gallery space they got there on the street, getting it ready for a big art show, and he come in there. I recognize him as the man I seen on the street, and without thinking I say, Didn't I see you on Magnolia Avenue? And he look at me and say, Yeah that was me. I mean, how he know I seen him? How he know I'm talkin bout him? He don't, but he do, see. The whole world revolve around him, the way he see it. And he right, it do. I mean, in a way that's true. And he believe if somebody see him they remember him. He mighta said, no man you must be talkin bout someone else, you know, like I don't know who you be seeing, and you don't know where I been. Lotta people woulda say something like that, you know, just protectin their privacy, their identity. You know, be *cool*. But see he don't need that, he don't have to do that. I say, Didn't I see you on Magnolia Avenue, he say, Yeah that was me.

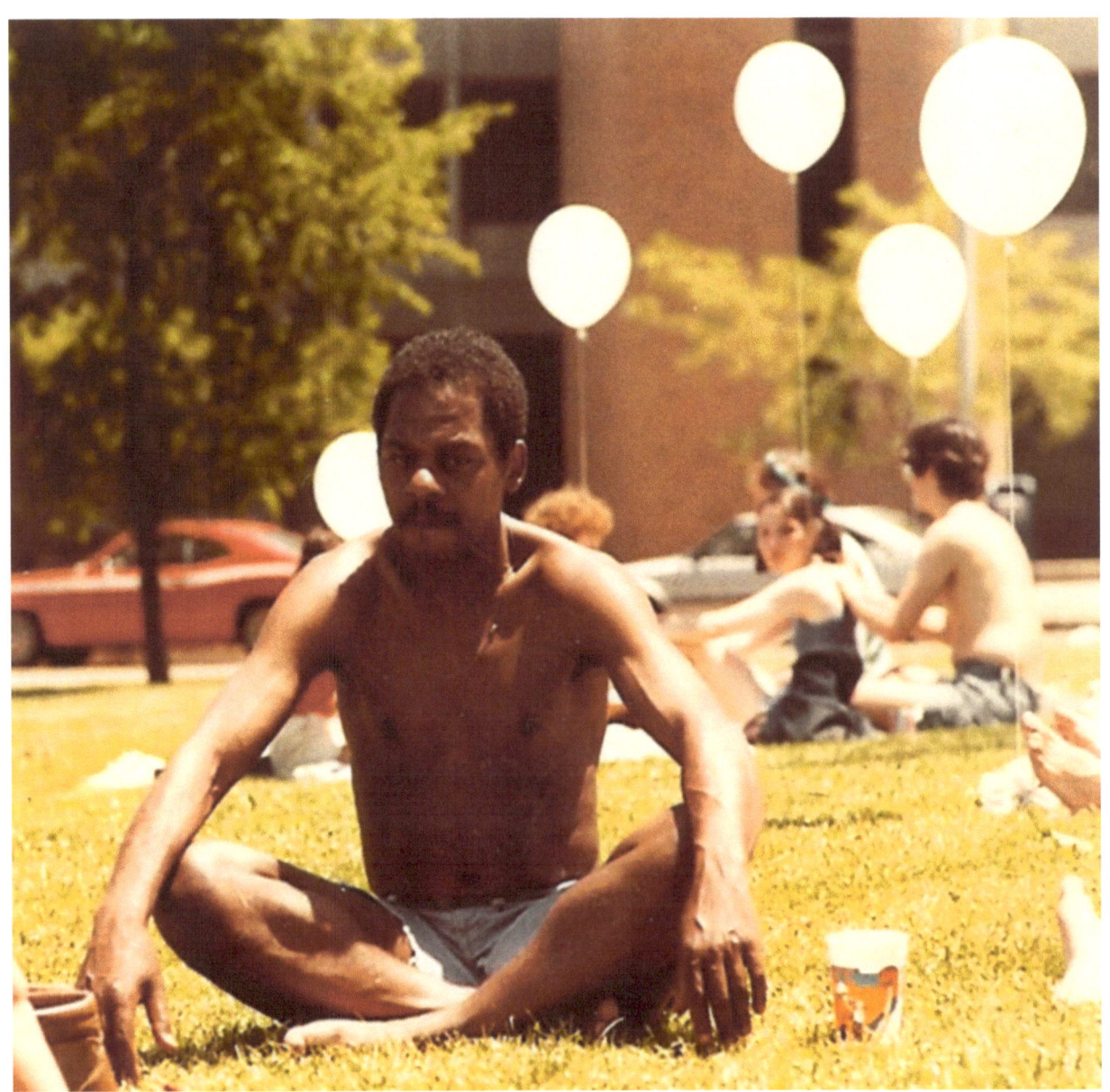

What type person am I, you may wonder.
Would you agree that few people see themselves
As seen by others.

I am no one dimensional person, nor have I ever
been. I don't perceive myself as being ordinary
or just average. Although, I make no claims.

-Then he shows up at that big art show poetry reading at 200 East there on Jackson. He come in there and checkin it out. Theys college professors and authors and poets and all kinda artists right, but theys street peoples and all kinda peoples there too. Cause it's FREE and they gots like free wine and free beers and people coming right on in, and they drinking and all, but they checkin it out too, they listenin, cause they was layin it down you know, and they gots musicians playing while they saying what they saying see. And they right there in the middle of everbody. And it be wild and be good and Horace he see that. And he there watching and encouraging everbody right. He good at that, being one side, you know, and pumpin it up, gettin people excited. I mean he was born to do it. But then, he read too. They have him up, and it's like the last thing, they close with the Pittman. And he go off there for a minute. And I don't mean no hip hop no slam shit, I'm talkin bout he go off on the human body man, the female body, and love man, he talkin bout the sweetness and cosmic aspects of the body electric. You know what I'm saying? Well everbody there know what HE saying and they lovin it. And he the finale man. That was like his introduction to whole lots'a folk. And they cheerin him on and yeah yeah yeah, right. They know they havin one big special night, and that this sorta thing unusual for around here. Shit man, it unusual for anywhere do it like they do it. And they know they's locals there of all kind but they peeps from other places in the country too and in the WORLD man that have found they way there. Yeah. And he one of'em. He was Horace Pittman man, and you had to dig it.

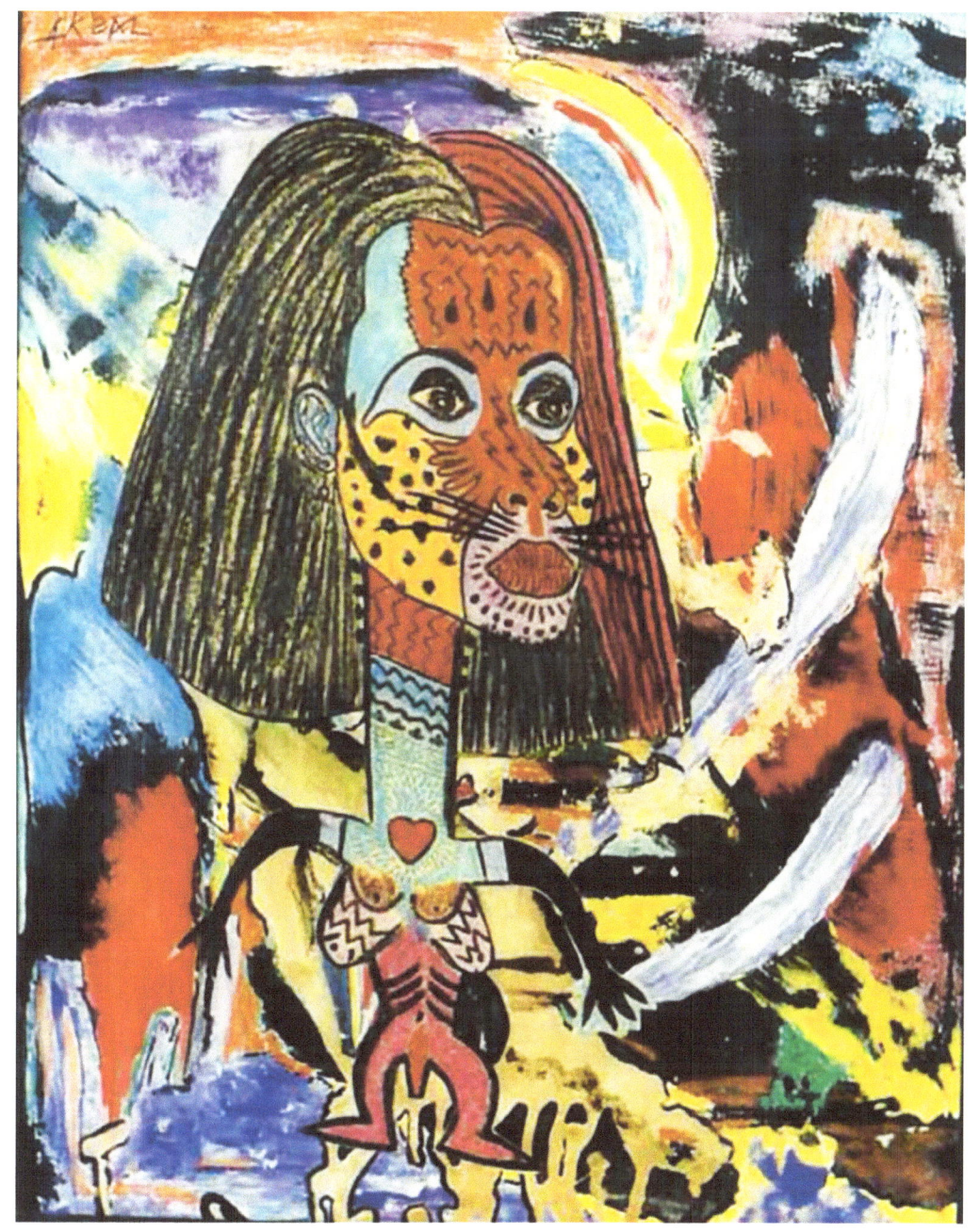

Before the gods took flight
The sun shine bright
Every night
Wisdom blew in the wind
God and the Devil were friends
And the sun shine bright
Every night
The truth was the light
Men and women
Met with their minds
In those times
They uttered no words
And understood the signs
And the sun shine bright
Every night

-I tell you a story. I was with Horace Pittman one night way back not long after I met him and we hook up with some the artists from Oregon and California right, some the ones startin up the 200 East. This back when it first got going and these artists was part of the founding group see. Well, somehow we was all together one night and they wants to do some guerilla art up on Gay Street where they close the Gateway Bookstore. It down there somewhere cross from the Bijou on Gay. And it all boarded up and taped off and been deserted and fixin be tore down and you aint s'pose to be in there. Well nobody like to see a bookstore tore down it not opening up somewhere else and they talkin bout that and IT WAS DECIDED to break in there and do some art or whatever. Well, it not a big building, just a big front room right there on the street with big windows where everbody see in. And well, we breaks in see, me and Horace

49

and bout four others and they start stacking blocks and leaning one thing 'ginst another and doing little things you know just to say they done it. Well, they all nervous cause cops all bout there and they more or less visible to the street and wants to get out of there. Well, me too. But Horace he working on something. He got a long piece of board and some other stuff making like a seesaw or some shit, a balancing thing that drift around of its own see, and on top of one end like some pedestal he got something sitting now look like it somebody or some thing, you know, of great importance, and it just floatin and driftin sideways and anyone can touch it and make it move different ways, you know, like a mobile. And he working on this, and they all nervous and saying come on man we gots to get out a here. And he just gettin it done and it really don't take long, but they all ready to run right. Well Horace not scaret see, and he did what he doing and then showed it to'em. And man, we all seen that he done constructed some kinda intricate wild thang. And whoever come in there next gonna see it too, right. And it was funny and it was cool. And then he say, okay let's go. And we went. Now what I'm saying, round this time 200

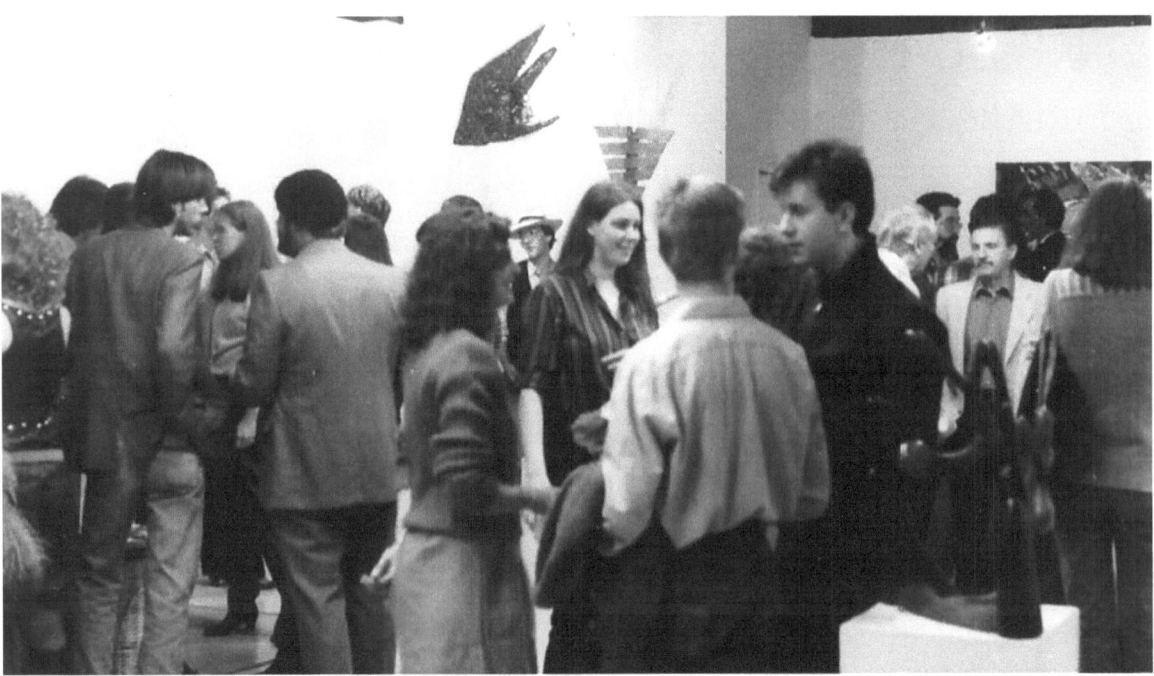

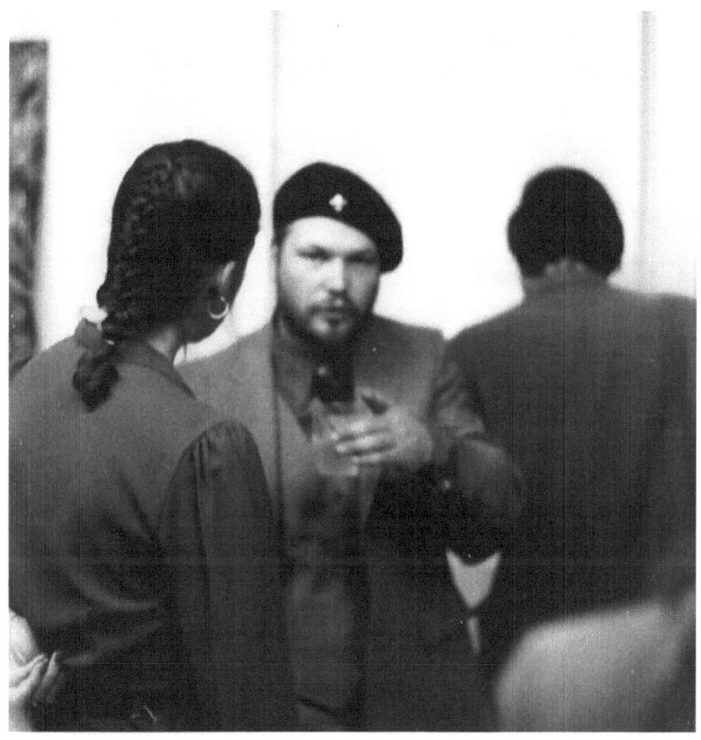

East done their first art exhibition, the opening was on the day the world's fair closed in the fall of 82. It was a show of their members, 'bout a dozen artists and each one putting works in it. That was the first show and a few weeks later on the last day of that show they had the big poetry reading with all the music and shit, and Horace go off at the end, right. Well then the members done another show 'fore Christmas, and Eric de Red brought the telephone pole into the gallery that show. That was the last show of '82, but the first show of '83 that January they have an invitational show, each member of 200 East inviting a artist to exhibit. And Horace was invited by Eric de Red see, be one of the artists. Eric de Red seen the work Horace was going to exhibit but Horace hadn't presented the group no slides of it right, and some them members didn't want him to show. They say we don't want no *pile of junk*. Yeah. That's what they say. Like maybe he want to put something in the show like what he rigged up at the blowed out bookstore right. Well Eric de Red say I seen what he workin on and he my guest.

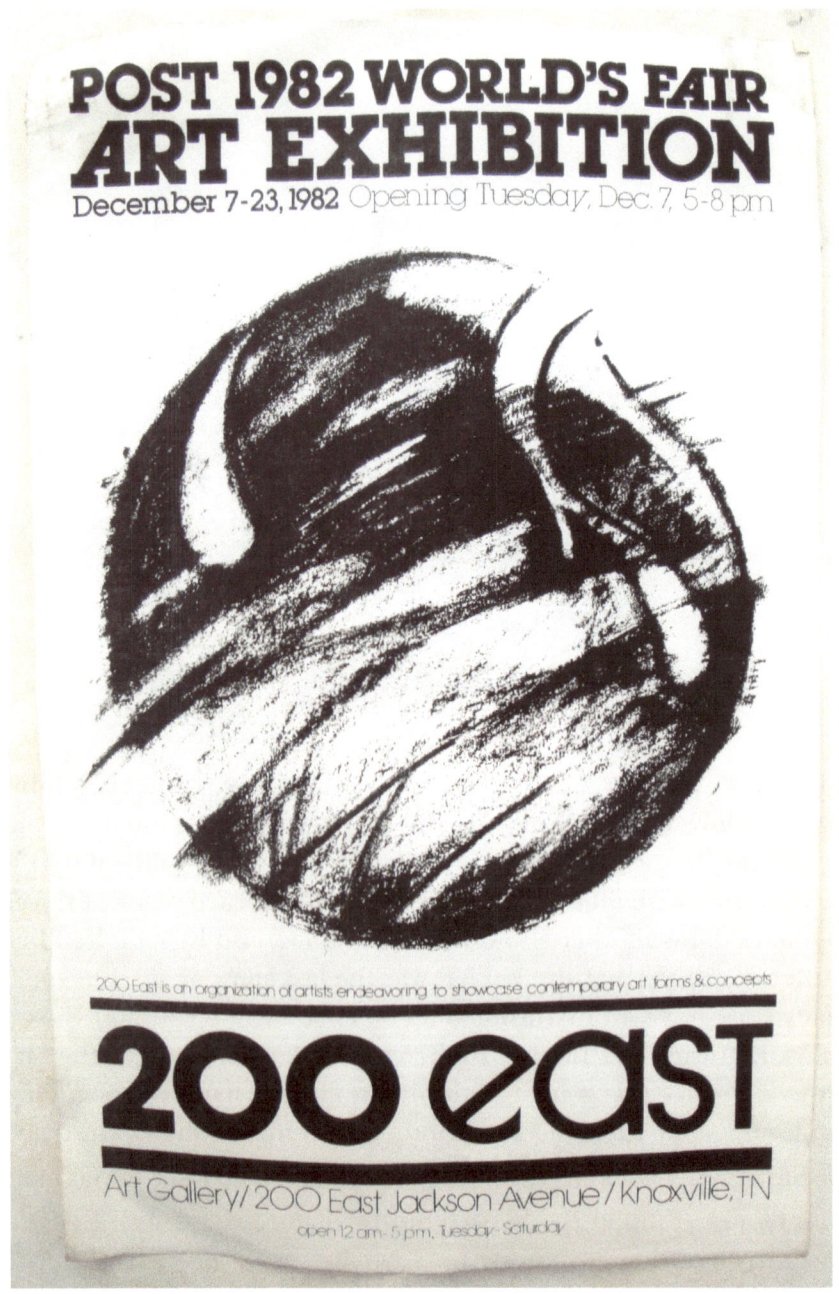

POST 1982 WORLD'S FAIR
ART EXHIBITION
December 7-23, 1982 Opening Tuesday, Dec. 7, 5-8 pm

200 East is an organization of artists endeavoring to showcase contemporary art forms & concepts

200 east

Art Gallery / 200 East Jackson Avenue / Knoxville, TN

open 12 am - 5 pm, Tuesday - Saturday

But some them members pitch a hissy and they have a vote and don't let him show. Now Eric de Red know more bout art than any them, he raised in the art world, it's his blood right, and he tell them they shouldn't do that. He say you invite a artist to an invitational show they show what they want. Well, thing is they have the show and the only work that sold and got all the attention and reviews was Bessie Harvey's work, who wasn't so big a artist then as she gots to be soon after. And she work in roots you know, a root worker, and made all these wild pieces look like they growed that way from the ground with beads and bones and shit. Well Horace's work was most like hers, he different but it like he calling on the same muse and they somehow related. But it just go to show that Horace's work would have been powerful beside her work in that show. And that some these art people full a theyselves and don't know what right in art or protocol. You know what I'm saying? It was a insult how they done him, and it become a rift with Eric de Red and the group. Horace took it in stride but he said it was the *pinnacle of pissitivity*! Yeah, and he right. But Horace find his own tribe then, starting with Eric de Red and Arh Be who done that poetry reading. They his allies now see. And they was always hangin after that. And they was just startin to art off.

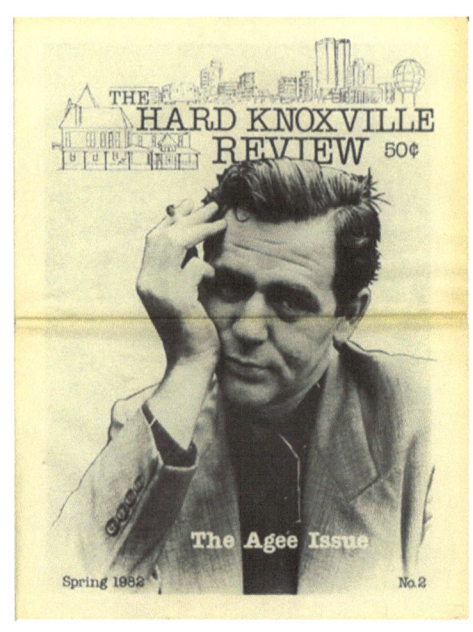

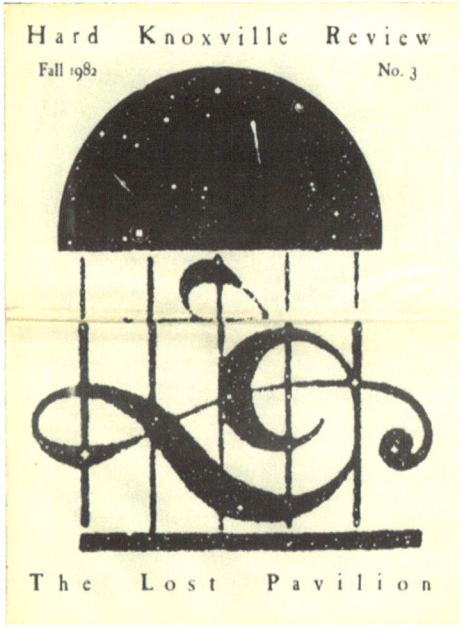

-Eric de Red and Arh Be got this little studio right, where they work, right up there on Clinch Avenue man in the heart of Fort Sanders. Everbody call it the STUDIO and that where they do the HARD KNOXVILLE REVIEW right, a little art paper they puts out. And Horace and others put their work in that.

-The Hard Knoxville Review?

-Yeah. But that little studio, that where everybody hang, you know. People in and out there all the time. It got a little bathroom and stove, and Arh Be he stay there at night, he sleep there on the couch when everbody not sitting on it. He a poet and he got a old typewriter belong to his daddy on the table there where he work. And the Hard Knox gots his work and Eric de Red's and others that they gathers up and puts together see, they the editors. They prints'em up and sells'em or gives'em away, and sends'em off everwhere, you know, in the mails to California, Europe, places like that. It just a little rag, little tabloid news print, you know, only it ain't no news no journalism right.

-Okay.

-It the news but it the news in another way. You know. Ever issue different, got a different theme or whatever, different peoples work, though they's a small group in 'bout all of'em. Eric de Red and Arh Be and artists like Roger Smith who some peoples call Artist X, and Steve Wyatt who Horace always call Eliot, for some reason.

-Oh yeah?

-Horace got names for everbody you know and everthing. He make up words, and he twists words round to sound the way he wants'em sound. You know what I mean? I mean, that part of who he is his VOICE and what he say. I mean, the way he say something give it as much meaning as what he say. He say welcome to the AVANT GRADE, yeah like it some grade school right. He funny the way he turns words round like that. Instead of ambiguity he say AMBINUITY. He make somebody want to correct him, you know, but he make them think too. They be thinking bout language and meaning and how meaning sound, and how it all a living thing man.

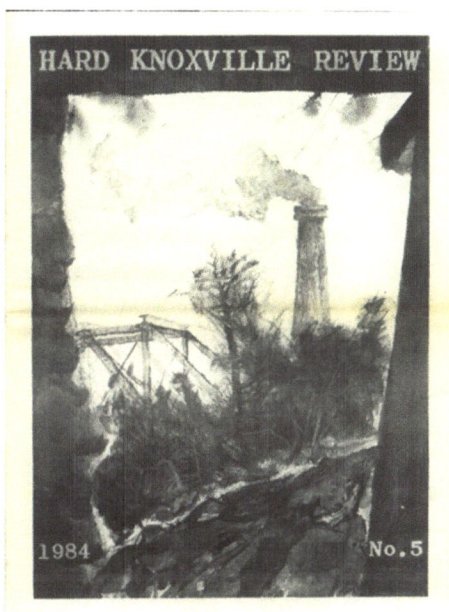

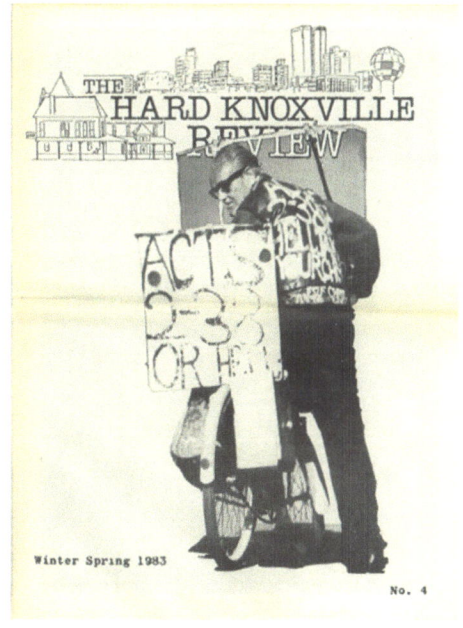

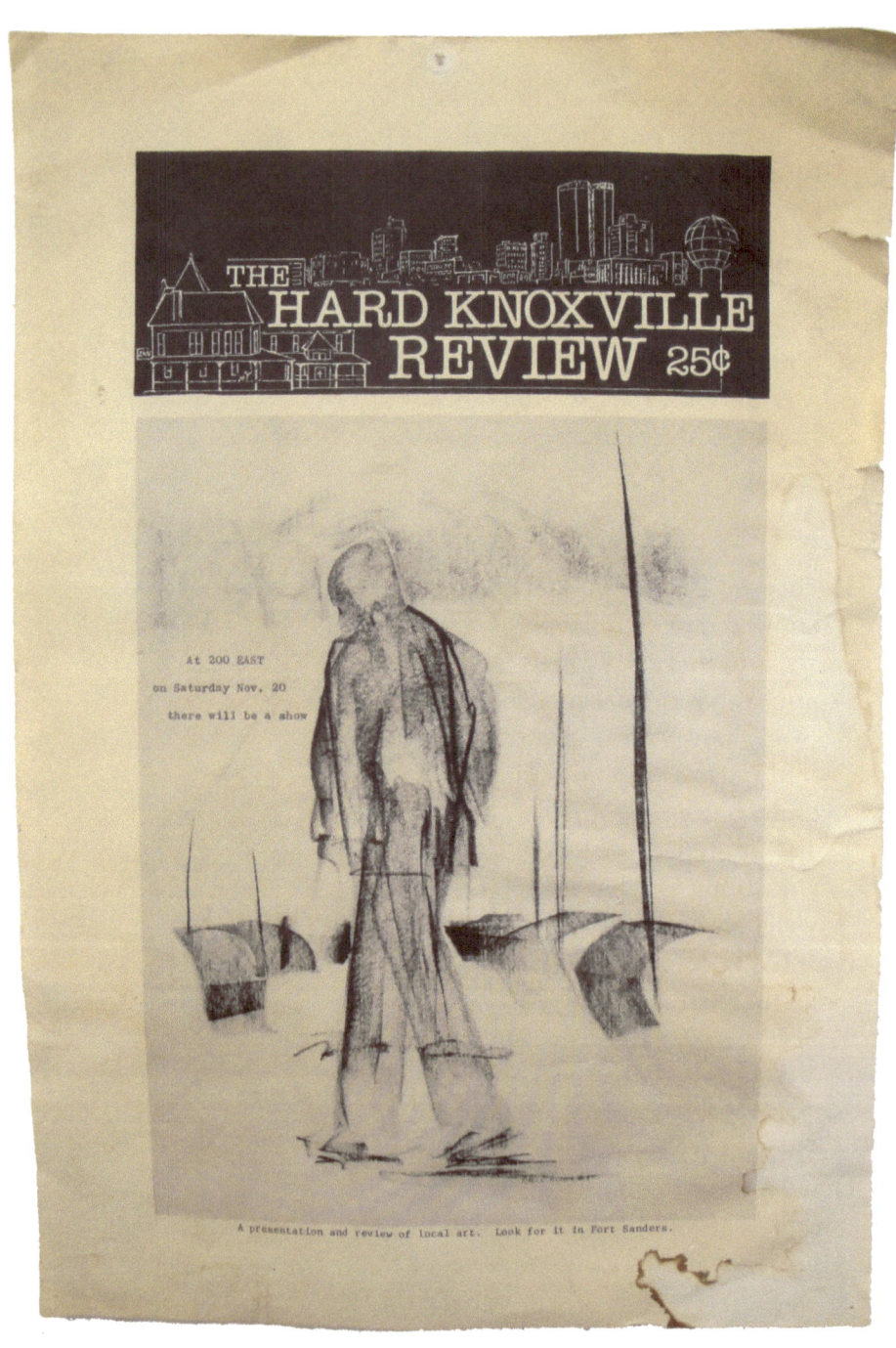

THE HARD KNOXVILLE REVIEW 25¢

At 200 EAST

on Saturday Nov. 20

there will be a show

A presentation and review of local art. Look for it in Fort Sanders.

-Yeah, well the studio be like headquarters for a while, you know. Horace and everbody slide by there all the time. And it all bout the arts man, all bout friends, and everbody collaboratin on something and showin each other what they workin on, you know, and talkin bout it, talkin ideas man, talkin bout everthing in the world, you know, and reading books out loud to one another and… really they was learnin shit, you know what I mean? I mean, I did, I sure did, just hangin round listenin. They expandin they minds and gatherin information all the time. This long before they was anything like a computer right. Maybe the CIA or someone got one, you know, but ain't nobody you know got one those days, nobody really ever heard a such. So everbody just have to get together kinda random like but regular you know, and they learn from each other and gets to know each other, and start working on art together, s'all it was. And they all on the outside anyway right, they all shares that, even if it some of'em hometown.

-*Yeah. So what's this Fort Sanders?*

-That the neighborhood.

-*An inner city neighborhood?*

-Yeah. It's over by the school and the hospital.

-*Why's it called a fort?*

-One time it was a fort. They had a civil war battle there back when.

-*Okay.*

-Yeah, killed bout a thousand people one morning fore anybody could finish they coffee.

-*Okay. That'll leave a bad taste in your mouth.*

-Yeah, I'd say. So a neighborhood grew up around it. I guess back round the turn of the century and most them old houses kinda Victorian, you know, and kinda run down now.

UT and the hospital too always eating away at it. And the city act like it ain't there. But they usually lotta artists and musicians live there, and lotta students too. It right up against downtown with just the world fair park between.

-*Sounds like it is downtown.*

-Pretty much yeah. You know, funny thing, I always remember when we hangin round the studio at night. You know the world's fair be going all that summer '82 right, and ever night when it close they have fireworks.

-*Oh yeah, every night?*

-Yeah ever night they close round 10 o'clock and they goes off with the fireworks BOOM BOOM and you hear it. They just a few blocks down the street man and it shake the house, you know. And we always standing around talking or working or whatever and all sudden the BOOMS kicks in. Yeah you think it the Battle of Fort Sanders all over again. And it like, what you doing or saying or thinking when the BOOMS kicks in, right. It kinda paced the days there for while. I mean the whole city like it under siege anyway with everthing happenin at the fair. They gots the town fenced off different ways round the fair grounds, 70 some'um acres smack in the middle of town, and everthing working round that right. Yeah. So that might be our cue when the fireworks kick in. Eric de Red might say to whoever there, okay time to knock off, let's walk down for a drink, you know, or whatever. It just always some synchronistic moment you know when the BOOM BOOMS start BOOMING.

-*Yeah.*

-But man they all kinda characters round then, and you know Horace he find'em or they find him. People from all over the place be showing up in town. He come in there one night and he gots this man and woman with him. The man look like a Indian right, a native American Indian with long black hair hangin down. And the woman she a white woman and gots this hood on her head. She all mysterious and don't say

Black starrs
Blazin' in the heavens

Black starrs
Shimmerin' day and night

Black starrs
Flamin' out of sight

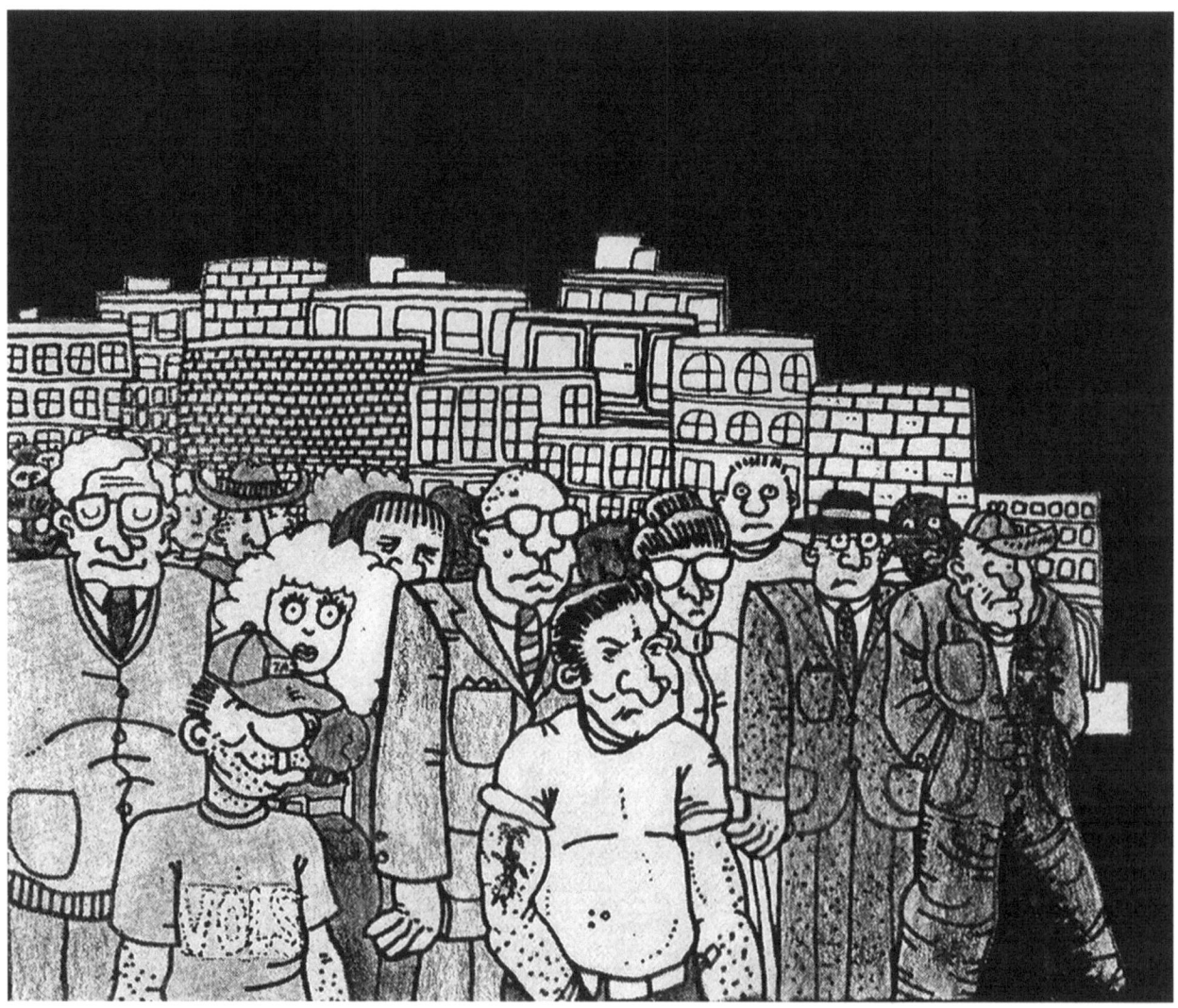

nothing and hangs real close to the dude. And he like some medicine man or something. He gots like these drawings right, they all kinda straight lines crossing over each other and making patterns, ever one of'em different but they all made of lines and lines crossing over different ways and making crazy patterns. And he posts'em up on buildings and places round the city and say this is how he fights the evil forces. He say he on his way to Washington DC cause like some kind of evil thing be going down there right and he gonna post these drawings up all over DC to stop that evil. And that woman of his she don't say nothing, not a word right. She just hang by his side whatever he do, and she got that hood over her head and she look at you like to see if you buyin all this, right. They wild man.

-Yeah. Sounds like a bohemian neighborhood, kinda transitory with students and all. Not unusual right, being near a university?

-Yeah, well they all kinda people live there, not just students and artists. Lots a families and bizness too. It's a mix is what it is, and that's what's good. Theys a lot a people come through there who don't live there too. And that what make it seem different, you know, like it might be in some other town, part of a bigger city. But they just something bout it. We was always taking walks through the Fort and I did love it. And Horace you know he walk right down the middle of the street sometime. Yeah. Well they some soulful streets in that neighborhood. And they always something goin on. That same time few blocks down on Laurel Avenue they done the FREE SOUP, the Hard Times Soup, they done that a few times or more and it was way cool. Fact it was a wonderful thing man. You have two three floors of art in a old house. Art in ever room and art going up the staircases and homemade movies flickerin' on a wall and peoples playin music and crazy poets and performance art or what you wanta call it right, and she gots big pots a soup for everone to eat who come through there. Yeah. All free. And takes lotsa artists workin together to do all that man. That was very happenin. But they wasn't no real places to show then outside the university, no commercial galleries or outlets available see, wasn't no cool salons, wasn't no museum of art back then. Not much opportunity for a local man to get his art on. And that kinda how the Alley des Refusés come 'bout too.

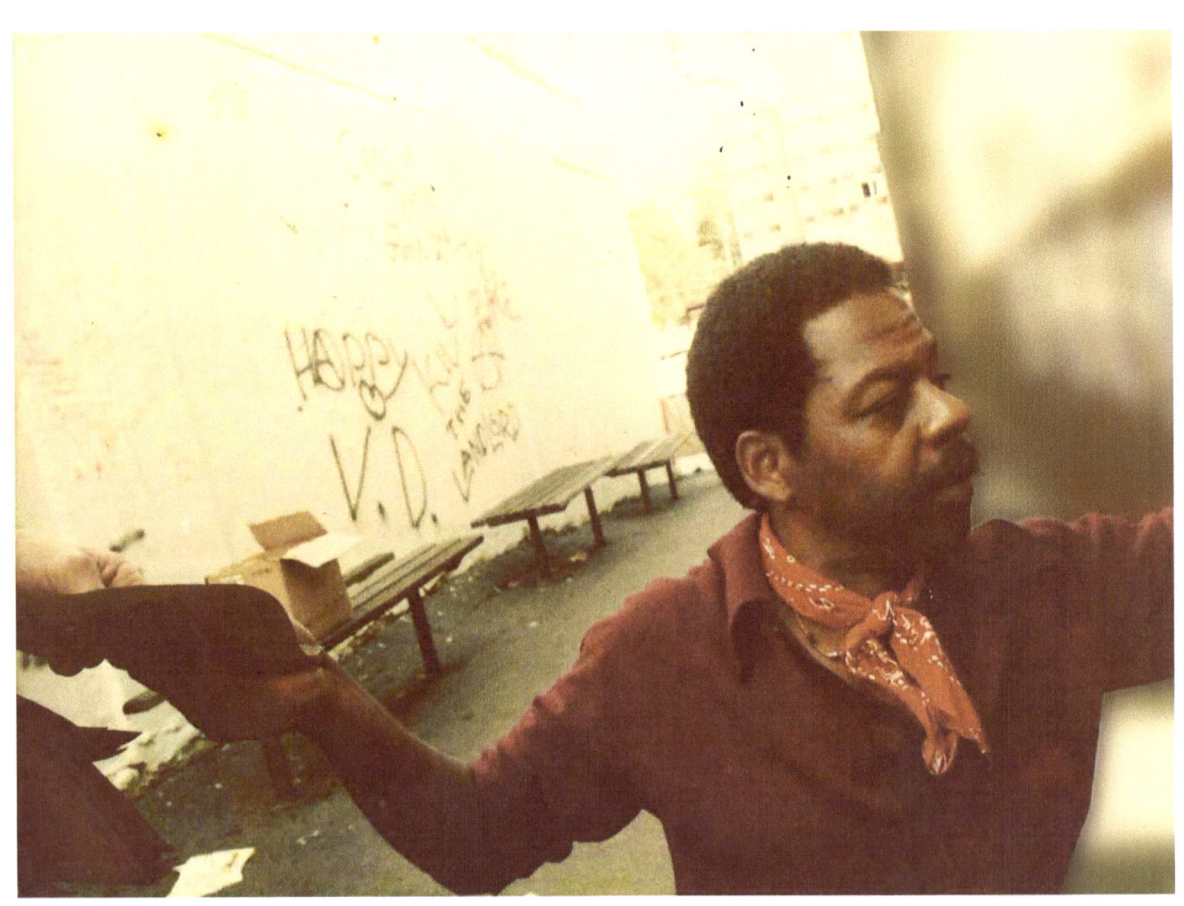

I'm sure it was Eric de Red's idea, cause he got French in his blood anyway, going back to the Huguenots or some them early French peoples. He knew his family tree right. That like back when they was troubadours roaming the countryside and shit. And Eric de Red know all that art history too, and he got his eye on that alley cause it right down there off Cumberland Avenue right, and it connect Cumberland with a big parking lot that back behind all them stores and shops and restaurants, and all kind a peoples come through there all the time. So he gets the big idea of hangin art in that alley. And he call it the ALLEY DES REFUSÉS after the Salon des Refusés in Paris back in the day right. Back when one them Napoleons the II or III or whatever it was declare there be a new salon for all the artists that don't make the cut for the main salon right. And somebody a journalist call it the Salon des Refusés cause those the ones been refused. Turns out you know the ones showed there is the ones remembered, and not the others. The Impressionists and some them. See they on the outside at first. We don't even remember who the others was in the main salon, less you a art history major or something. But what I'm saying, they started doing shows down that alley, Horace and Eric de Red and Peter Artin and others. All kinda shows, and some good art, which they was just giving away. Yeah, just give it away to be able to show it, you know, get it out in front of people. And they posts all the Hard Knox Reviews on that wall too. Yeah ever page pinned up there so peoples walking by can stop and check it out. Just like in China you know where they post up the news or whatever. And that the Ally des Refusés.

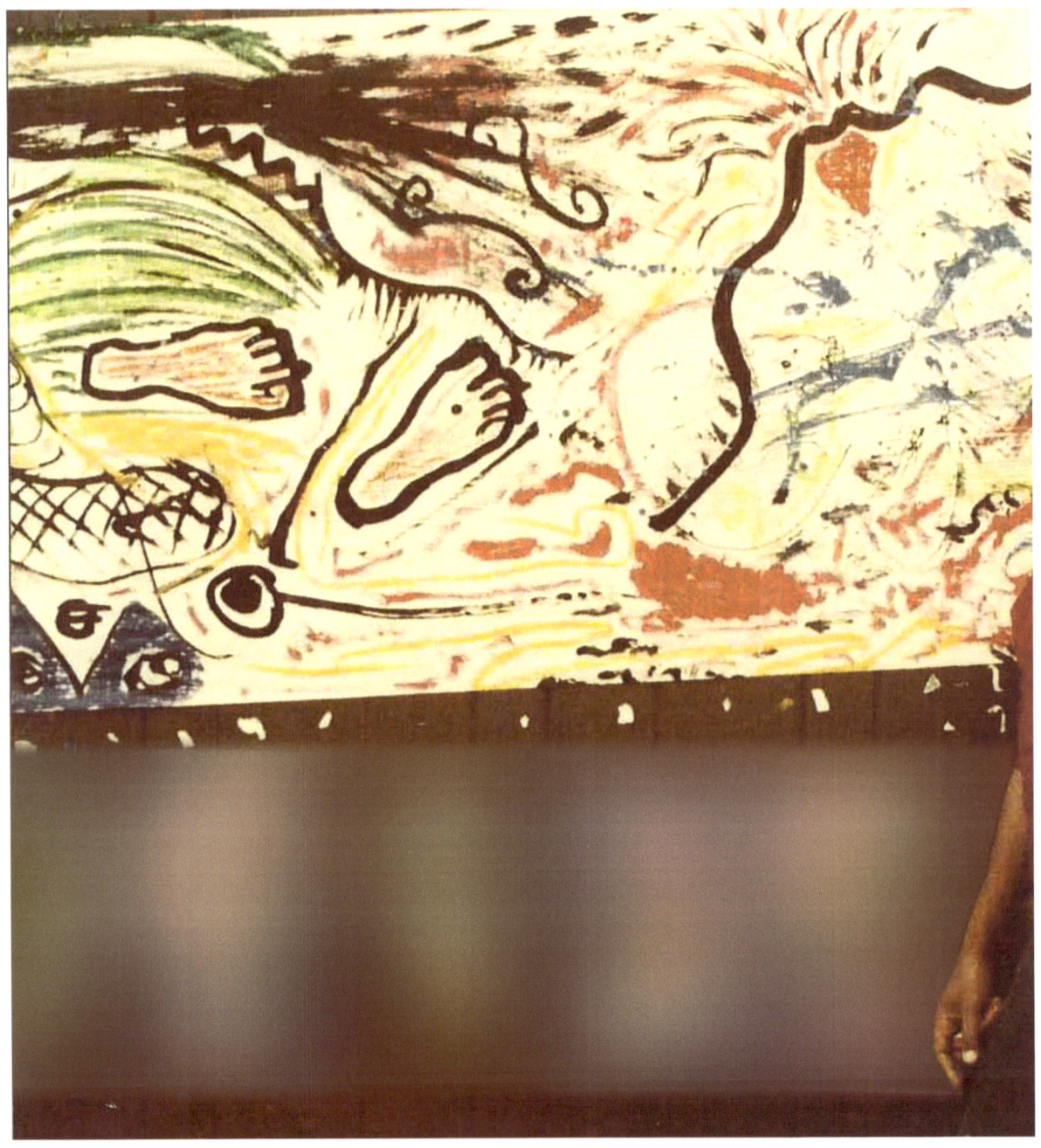

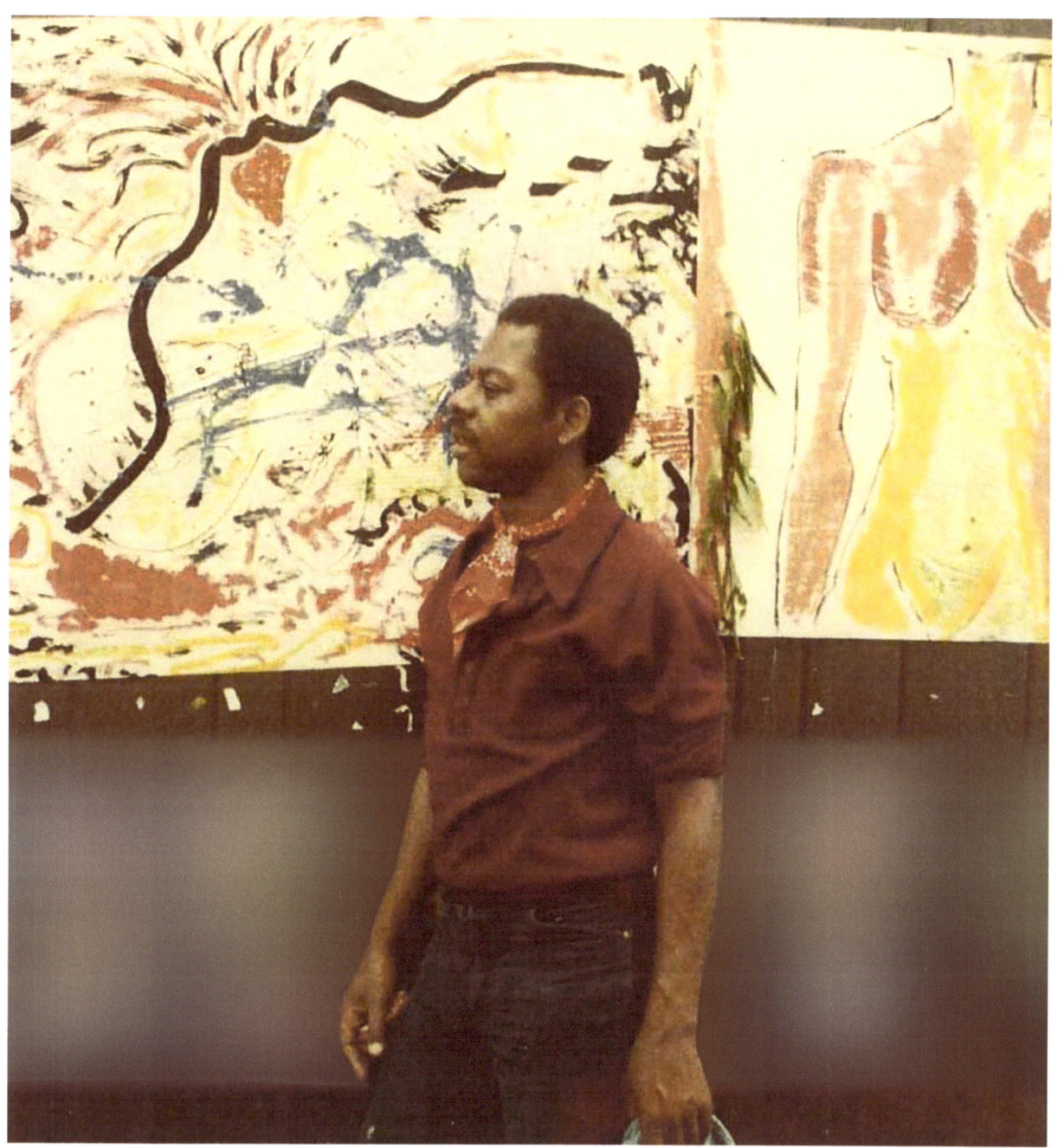

65

But they was a lot of street art. All a'sudden seem like everbody was making flyers and posters and art to put out on the street. Always had been some, a few bands and stuff, but now more and more people was postin all kinda wild shit. Some people would build little signs like billboards and kiosks you know just so's they could post stuff. There was a lot more goin for one thing, activity had picked up. Everbody was looking for a place to show was what it was, place to exhibit. And since there weren't no places they just start exhibitin wherever. People having exhibitions in they houses and studios and all over the streets. Ever telephone pole was a art show man.

-Yeah, okay.

 -And Arh Be he call'em all Enthusiasts, the ones out there hangin shit and postin shit up and givin it away, the ones who really artin off. He call'em the Enthusiasts cause Horace had a painting called *The Enthusiasts.* It was a painting had faces emerging in profile, you know, which was a theme Horace come back to at times. And Arh Be just took that name for all the artists like Horace who out there doing it.

-Yeah.

-But what it was though was GUERRILLA ART. You know what I'm saying? It was illegal for one thing, even the telephone poles.

-Was anybody getting in trouble? Or was business okay with it? The City?

-There was some trouble. But mainly see they was getting away with it. You don't want the law catch you postin' anything but a yardsale or your dog or cat gone missing. And them biznesses don't like none of it. Weren't no one givin permission do no art. And they was laws against it. You had to hit it fast and be gone. And you think about it, you have to want it pretty bad to do it, 'specially a show in the alley.

Cause you have to make all that
art man. And you have to get the
materials to do it too. And you gonna
have to paint and paint some more,
and write out poems and shit,
manifestoes, what it is you saying to
the city and to the world you know.
You have to work do that man, days
sometime. And then you gots to give
it away. Yeah, you go give it away.
And, you gots to know when you can
hang it, when you can put it up
without nobody stoppin you or gettin
in trouble. Yeah, get it up best and
fast as you can. Maybe use tape, 'least
for some stuff. But staple gun, that
you weapon of choice. And you have
to be efficient man. Load and re-load,
keep moving. And once you got it, you
got to tuck that gun in you pocket
and turn a corner. Yeah. Sounds pretty
juvenile, but that just depend on
when and where you living.

-I guess so.

-And most that stuff never was
documented, you know, like they do it
nowdays. But somebody took it home.
Or else it blew down the street and you
have to be okay with that too.

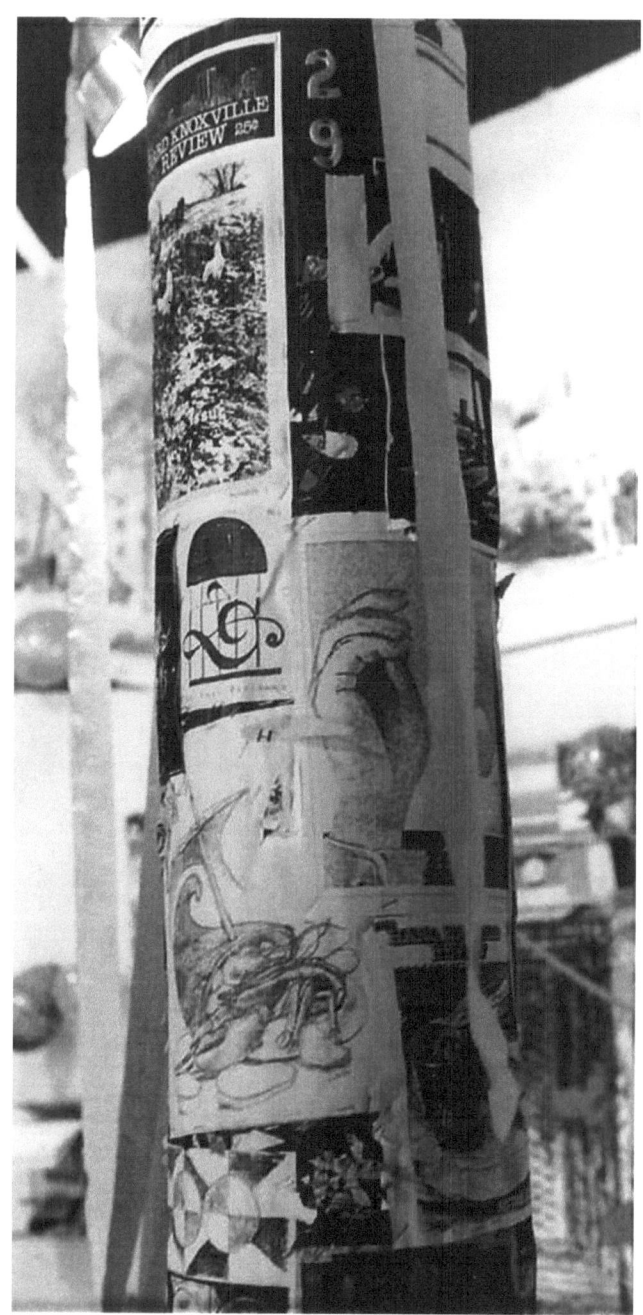

-So where was all this going?

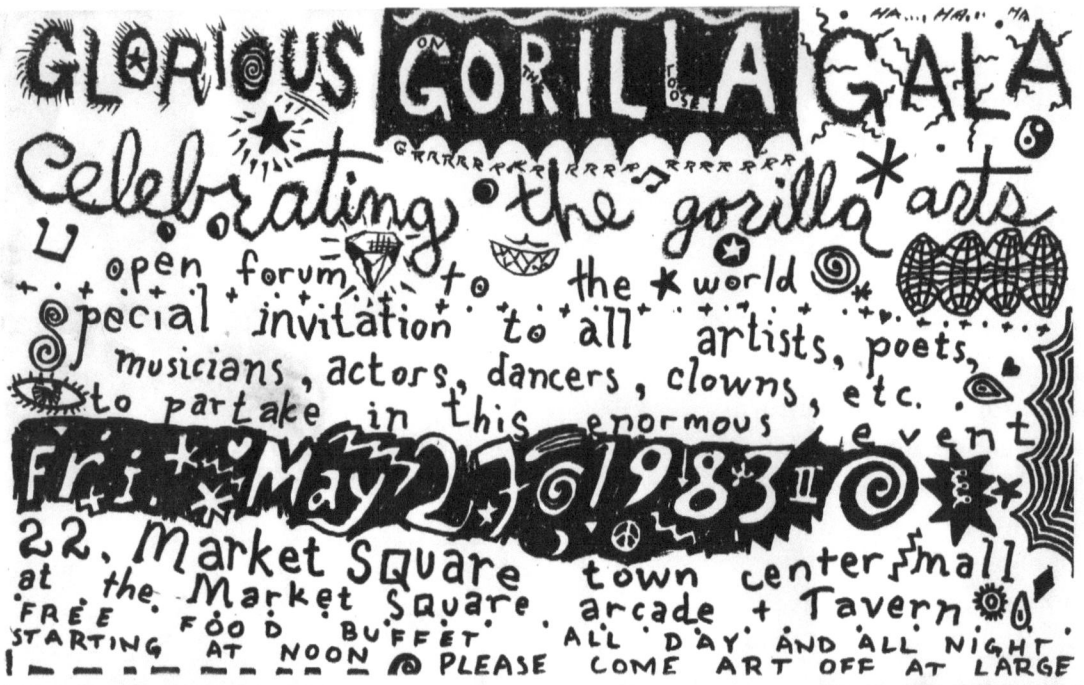

-Well, nobody knows, but by that spring it all kinda blossomed into the GLORIOUS GORILLA GALA bunch of'em put on up on Market Square. Horace done rallied with some them gypsy artists and they filled up a building there with art. I just remember it was on Horace's birthday cause he told me so up on the Square. And he was feeling good and having a big time and strong you know, and they all jumpin round like they in the circus or something. It was a very cool event, and wasn't much happenin on the Market Square them days. It was dead, just a few 'stablishments tryin get something goin. One of them musta let them have that show. And they done more them Galas you know in other places round town. They was a group of'em now see, could lay it down whenever they needs to, when they find a space or want to take a space. And Horace he was the gorilla if they got one. He define a lot just being there, if you know what I mean.

-I can see.

-Now that same month of May they was another big show, it was up at the Bijou Gallery and Horace was in that too. Some lady come into town from New England, I believe it was, who got all set up to host a series of readings at the Bijou in their big upstairs gallery. And she have different groups in there. One time it was Marilyn Kallet and UT professors and writers and another time be someone else. Well, the Hard Knoxville Review got signed up for one of those. And they come in there, Eric de Red and Arh Be and Horace and all kinda artists and writers, Roger Smith, Jack Rentfro, Marilee Hart, Dennis Hundt, Ken Britton, some of them. They had artwork all over the walls, which none them other groups had done. They make it a mix event with art and literature and music. I 'member they had bundles of HKR's that was stacked up to make a big podium that everbody stand around. They was a lot of artists involved, lotta them that was in the Hard Knox, and they was musicians too. Hector Qirko was directing the music man, you know him? He a blues guy come down from Chicago and stayed, right. Man he world class, and when they go off on a song or poem he know what to do man, he know what it needs and what it don't. You know what I'm saying? He don't have to be in no hurry for nothing. He like Lester Young backin Lady Day man, he just right there and no where else. And they laid down some songs and some spoken-word with music, all that shit. I 'member they give the first public reading from *Suttree* that night. Cormac McCarthy was only getting to be known them days. And that same night they read the whole first chapter of *A Death in the Family* too, James Agee's book. He a local writer won a Pulitzer Prize years before. But you know, I'd say most the Arts Council then couldn't a'told you who he was. See both them books set in Knoxville, one in Fort Sanders, and that's what they knew. They was tryin to remind people of Knoxville's literary heritage and connect it to the new thing, thing goin down right then see. And they was bringin it that night.

I 'member Don Fiene come to that show. He the Russian professor at UT, you know, and he the man who wrote the bibliography on R. Crumb. Yeah, and he was into it. He come to a number them events they put on, and he bought art too, I 'member that. He put his money where his mouth was, you know, HA. I just know he encouraged lotta those artists when they need it.

-I tell you though, what was really some kinda turning point was in June on the Solstice. Man they had a gathering of the tribes down there on Cumberland at The Place. I'm not even sure how that all come 'bout, but it was a happenin. The Place been happenin for a long time, always had music, you know, lotsa bands play there over the years. But it was pretty much closed then. I think it was in between being The Place and becoming Vic & Bill's Rock n Roll Deli, you know. If I'm not mistaken I don't think it was even open for bizness at the time. But somehow they opened it long enough to let a bunch of us go in there and have a big multi-media art show and throw down with bout four five bands. Which included Smokin Dave and the Premo Dopes, first time Horace and I ever seen them and we become fans for life man. Man oh man, the music was like a revelation for me, just to hear what it was they

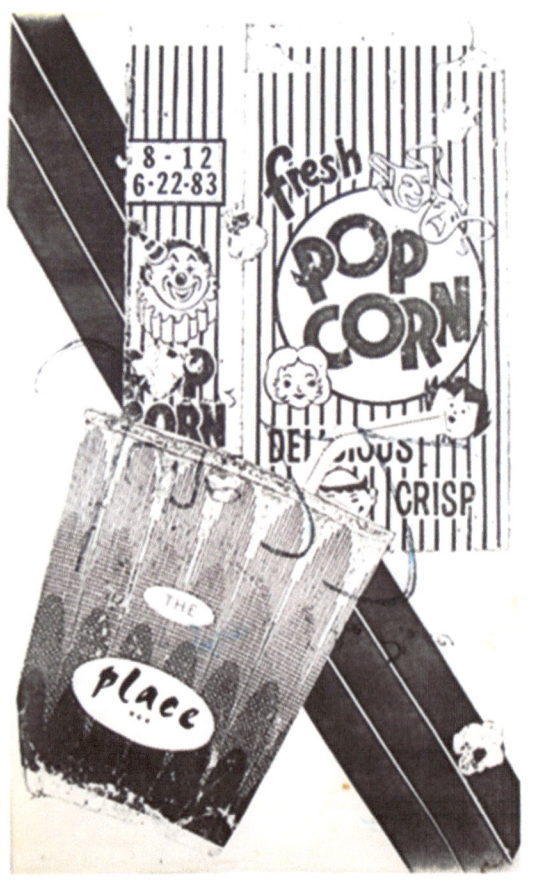

was doing with the sounds we all knew from before. You know what I'm saying? Like they be going off on Bird Bird Bird, Bird is the Word right, doing they shake on it all. And that was the first time I ever heard it like that see. But they was all kinda stuff go down that day. I just 'member Horace drummin up people to come in there. He outside on the street announcing it to everybody in that big VOICE you know. And he had rolls of paper he made art on and he rolled it down the sidewalk and into The Place right. Yeah, and everbody following him in. And they was all them bands and groups of people in there. And you know, they was not all friends. You know what I mean? I seen right away you had different factions different groups right, and some them was tauntin others. You know. And in some ways they was separated, but it's so crowded everbody have to be together too. They was mainly younger people, like you had you punkers, you skateboarders, had you hardcores and you new wavers you know and you rockers. And whatever group they all was. I could feel tension mongst'em but it was all cool and then it was all flying, you know. Them bands brought it together. And they was big art hung all over them tall walls in that club. Eric de Red and Marilee Hart and others hung bunch of art. I think Marilee and George musta had something to do with all that coming together, cause he worked the sound. And they was a big screen and Eric de Red had a slide show of photographs and images that Arh Be done some music to. That was mixed in with the bands. And the bands was cool, they was givin it up. Maybe it was just the solstice or something you know, summer kickin in, but everbody seem to be feelin it and it was good. And a lotta them folks just gettin up next to each other first time, and that was good. And then, then man, Kathi Freeman come drivin right up to the front of the building in a car that's all lit up with black lights right, and she had the inside of the car full of little sculptures she made that was painted with black light paint, and it was dark out and everthing all aglow right, That was crazy. Horace had welcomed everbody in rollin his art out on the sidewalk, and then when it bout over, suddenly Kathi pull up in front in this car with the music blastin and everbody gatherin round checkin out this black light show she got on wheels. It was a very special night, man. And it was a gathering of the tribes.

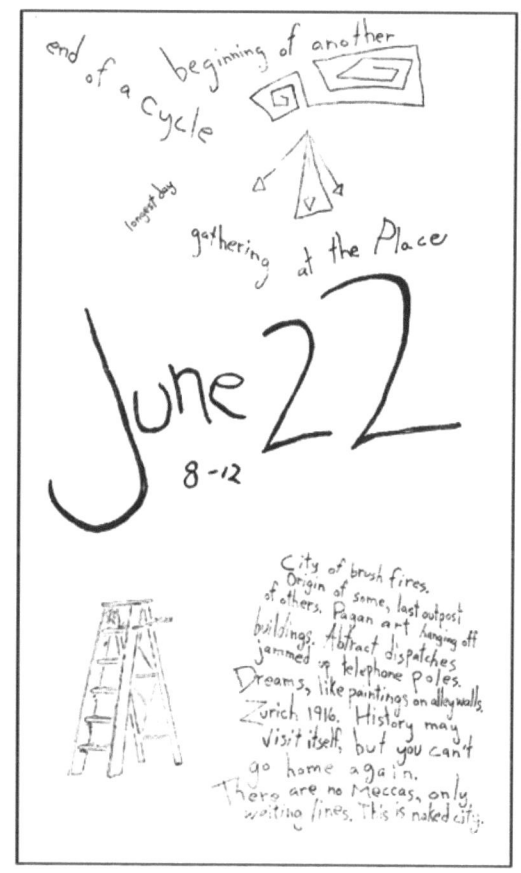

-Yeah, sounds like it.

-After that I think everbody just knew, you know. You could feel it. And more people comin round all the time. And all them little rivulets startin flow together, right. You could tell. And you know, it wasn't no time and Horace was in with all of 'em. Yeah, he was everwhere now.

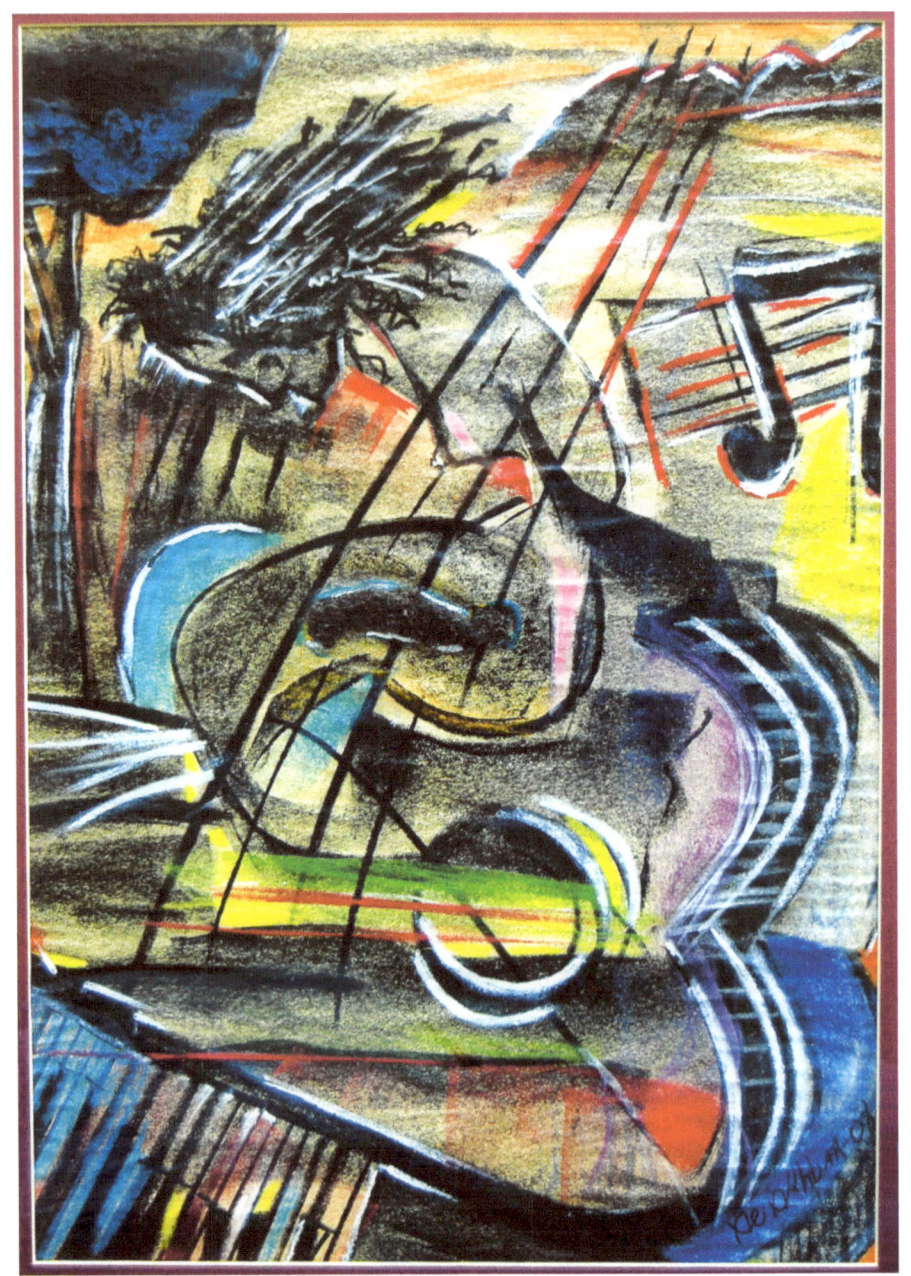

From then on, you know, you see him anytime you out, like he catchin everthing you catchin and he catchin everthing else too. Ever art event somebody having, ever poetry reading, all kinda gatherin's they start having. And he out to all of'em and all the music shows too. You know he love the music man. Ever week for a while they playin jazz down at that Italian place on Cumberland and he be down there. They play that modern jazz fusion on some nights, you know, and he be there gettin down with that. But on other nights they have Rocky Winder and Bill Scarlett, Rusty Holloway, you know, some them playing the cool sounds right, and man those guys can do it, they can get there. And Horace right there with'em, just lovin it.

-Yeah?

-Oh yeah. But you know he be down in the dives with the punkers and the thrashers too. Rus Harper, John Sewell, all them crazy bands. Yeah he love it and they love him man. You know they think he wild or something maybe, but they respect him too. They keep a eye on him. I mean they learn from him. They talk to him and get a bigger fix on things cause he older and they trust him tell'em what he think.

-But he fit right in.

-Yeah, he fit in anywhere he go. You know, if they don't throw you out at the door. If they let you in. Horace was curious man, curious a'people, all kinda people. You know he study'em, how they walk, talk, what they wear, and how they carry theyselves. And really how they think. And if he fascinated enough he roll right with it.

-Yeah.

-But it ain't like he just trendy, he just love it. 'Fact he always different. He dress or do something to identify, you know, but I mean he stick out in a crowd right. He not tryin to blend in. But he come join your crowd for a while if you got it goin, you know. And pump it up.

I rip off the days
Tear them from their weeks
Stripped bare of their names

Delete seconds out of time
And erase the entire line

Only the point remains
The dot over the i

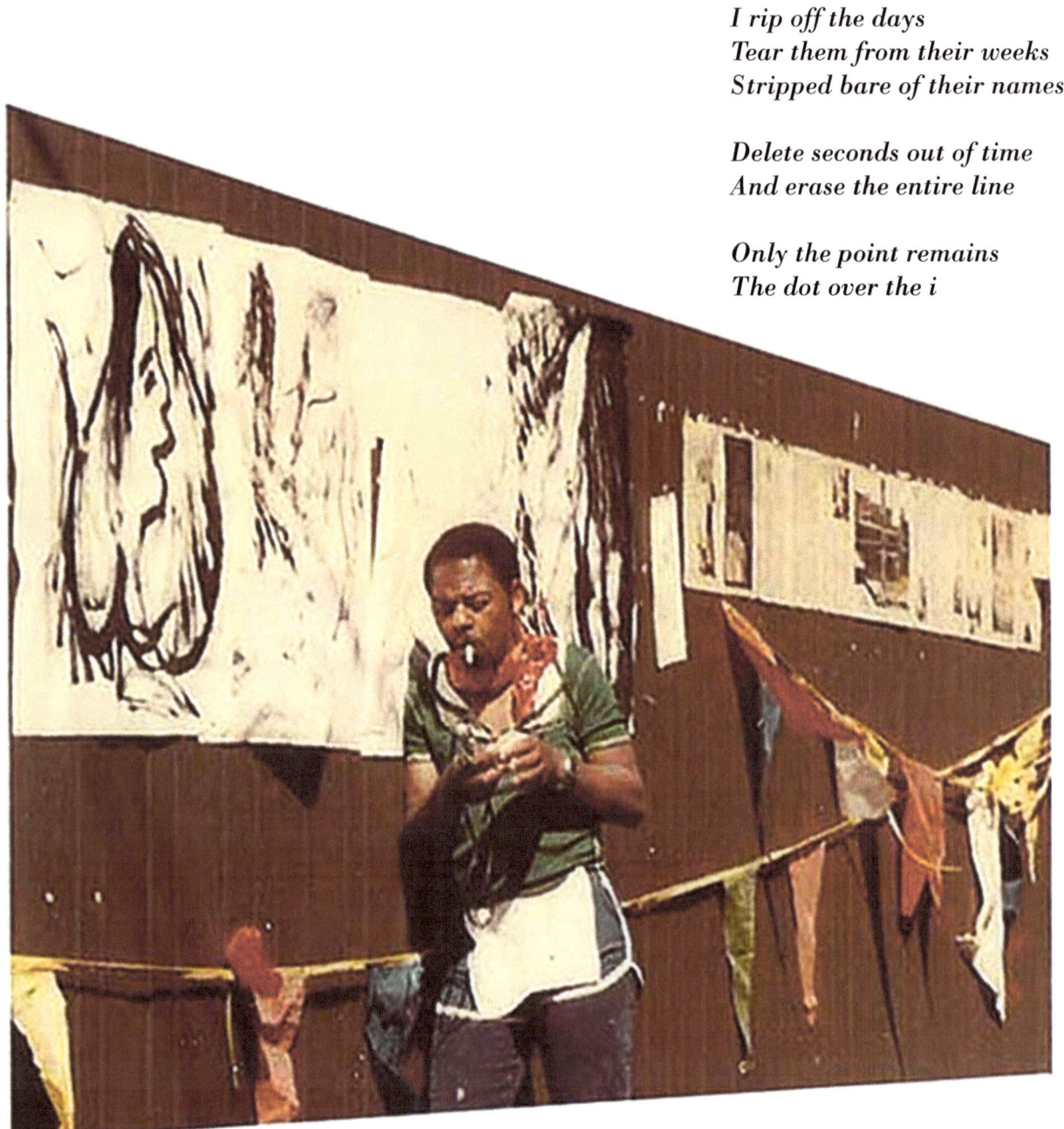

Between zero and one
The moon and the sun
Fish and the bottom of the sea
Birds and the blue sky

You and yourself
Life and death

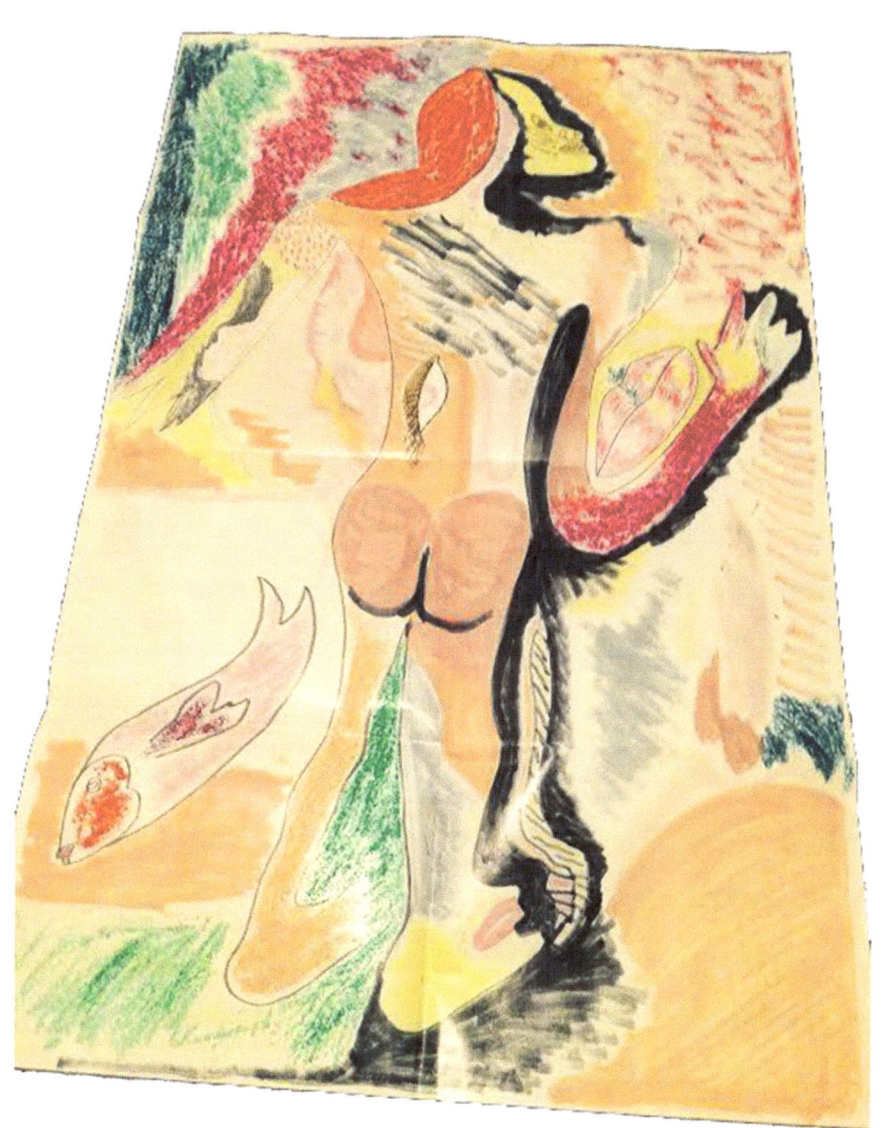

Somewhere in there he and Peter Artin got goin on some art. I don't know how they ever hook up, maybe through the Galas cause they was both doing that. But yeah, them two was a collaboration. Peter, his mother Birgitta, she Swedish and she a artist. And Peter he study art up at Cooper Union in New York right and come back to Knoxville. Just a beautiful young man you know, and got more talent in his little finger than most artists gots all over. And he know everthing, but Peter kinda quiet

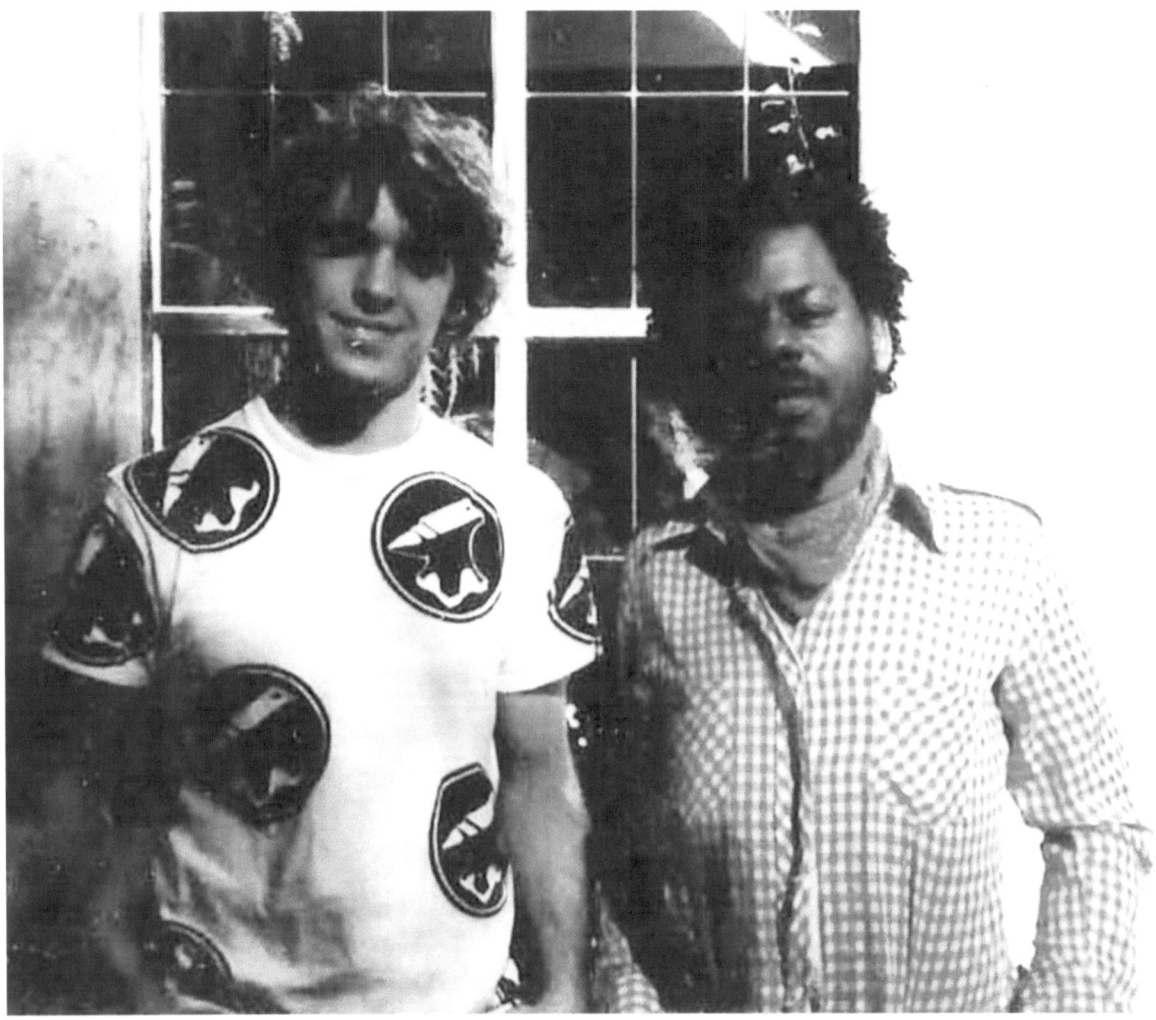

and considered you know. Just the opposite of Horace who want to come from the UNSCHOOL if you know what I mean. HA, he a natural, but he raw, and he loud too. He make a big noise. Yeah, them two was a pair, and there for a while they was swingin with that guerrilla. They posts art over signs and hang art over big showcase windows of

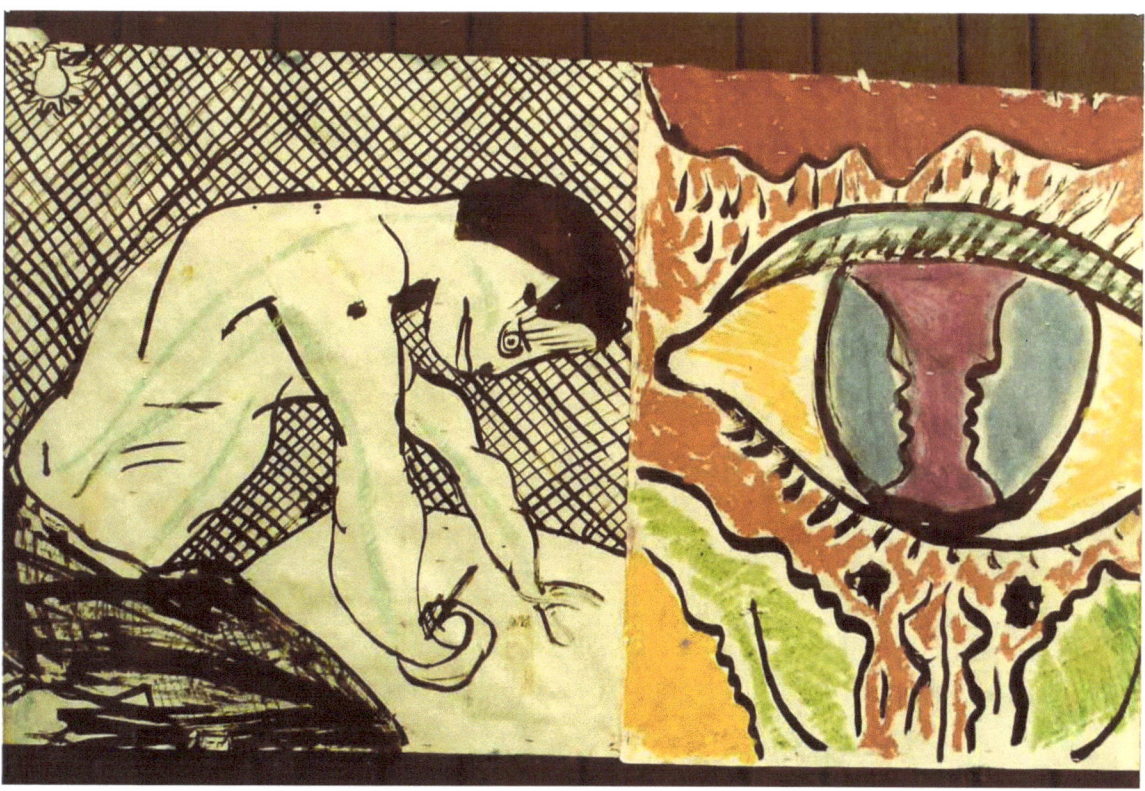

stores or wrap part of a building, just take a notion and go artin off anywhere. I mean people be coming to work next morning and WHOA! *What de hell is that*, you know. You had to catch it 'fore someone took it down. They had a lot of fun and they done a lotta art. People seen it that wouldn't never be lookin at no art, you know? I imagine Peter tell you a story or two 'bout all that.

-Thing was, it's like anything, you know, you get what you give. You got to give of youself to see how you really connect with something. And art no different. You got to get you hands in it and get you head and heart in it and gets lost in it in order to get found in it. You know what I'm saying? Well, Horace he got with it. He give himself over to it. Yeah. He dove off the cliff see if he could fly. And he could fly.

-I guess that's why we talking about him, not somebody else.

-I guess so. You talk to Eric de Red some them others and they tell you more bout all that.

-Okay, but.

-More 'bout Horace and how it was.

-Yeah okay.

-But, you know, Eric de Red told me one time, he said Horace took his art down to the river one day and he stood on the banks of the river and set some his art to float off in the water. Yeah. He crazy, but in his way, he was givin himself over to the muse, you know, to the muse of the river and the city and the arts, you know. It was like he was freein the muse to sail through the city, what he was doing. Yeah, he makin his sacrifice what he doing and givin hisself over. And there for a while he was a naked man walkin in the city, you know what I mean? I mean, he was always that really. He was a open soul. And you know, maybe the muse like that. Maybe the gods shine on a fully blossomed creature that give over to the mystery, you know what I mean?

-What did Horace think about God? I mean, what would he say about all that?

-God? Well, at that time, he probably say *God? She black*, you know, like Corso say. But see, it don't matter what you say, 'specially talkin bout God. It just matter what you do. Whether or not you *give over*. And that true in Art too.

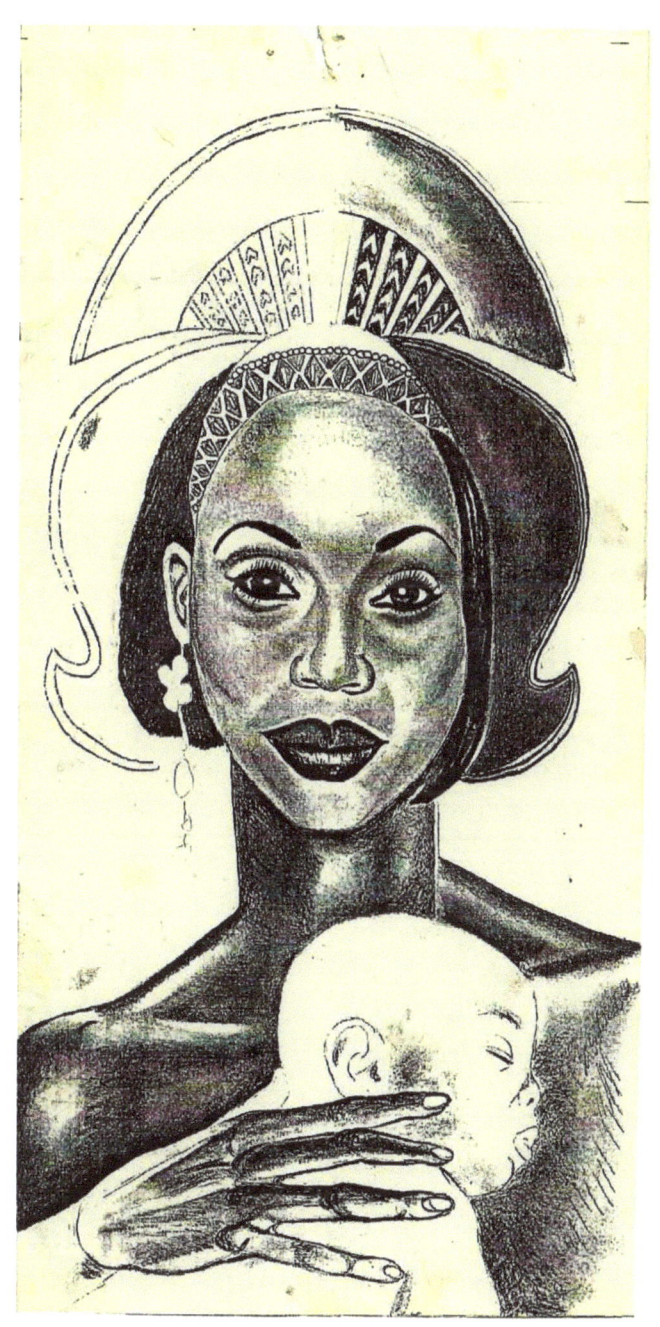

Neither are oceans divorced
   from their embracing shores

Nor lands parted
   from their lovely skies

How can love segregate?

This is how love lives

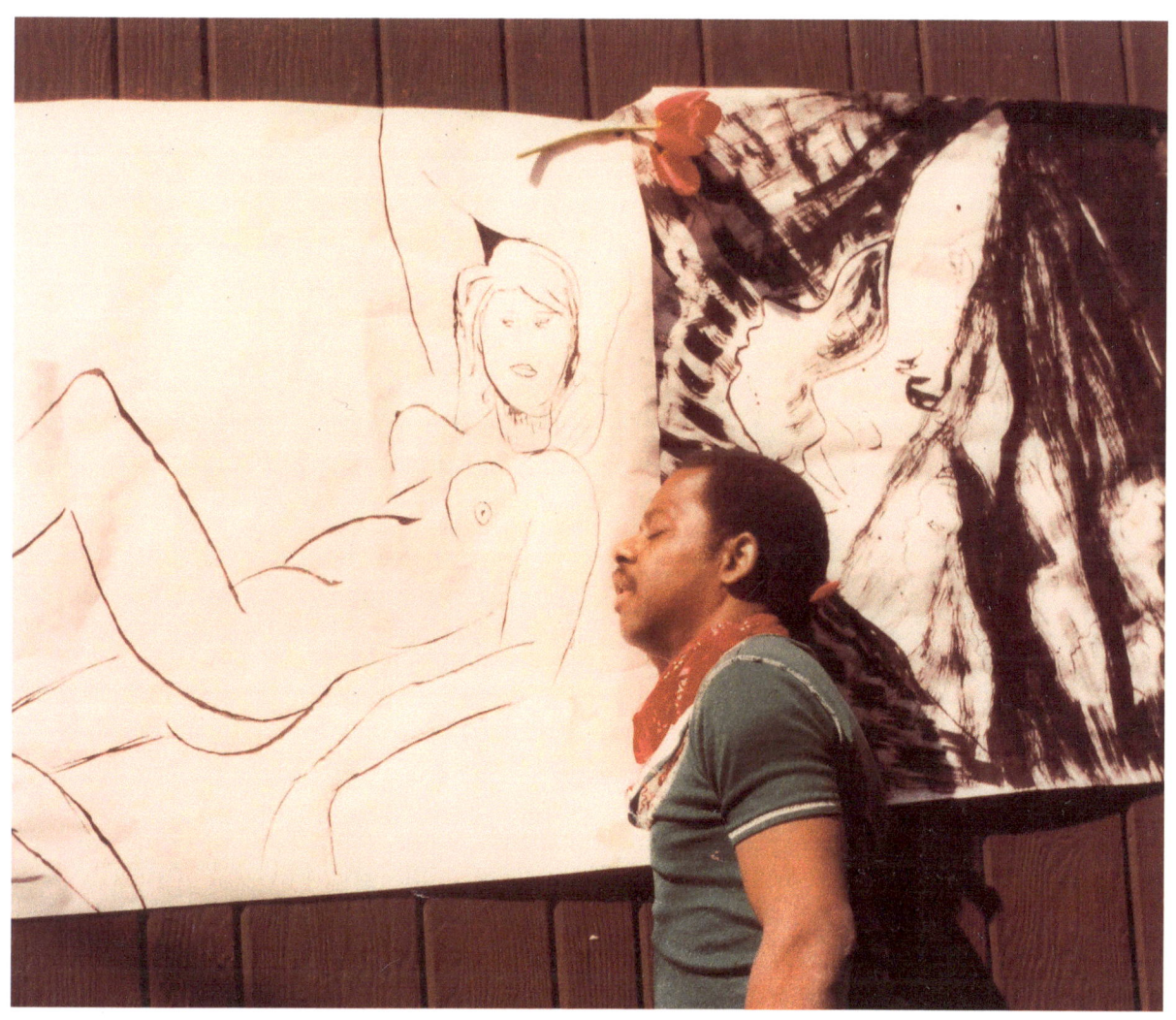

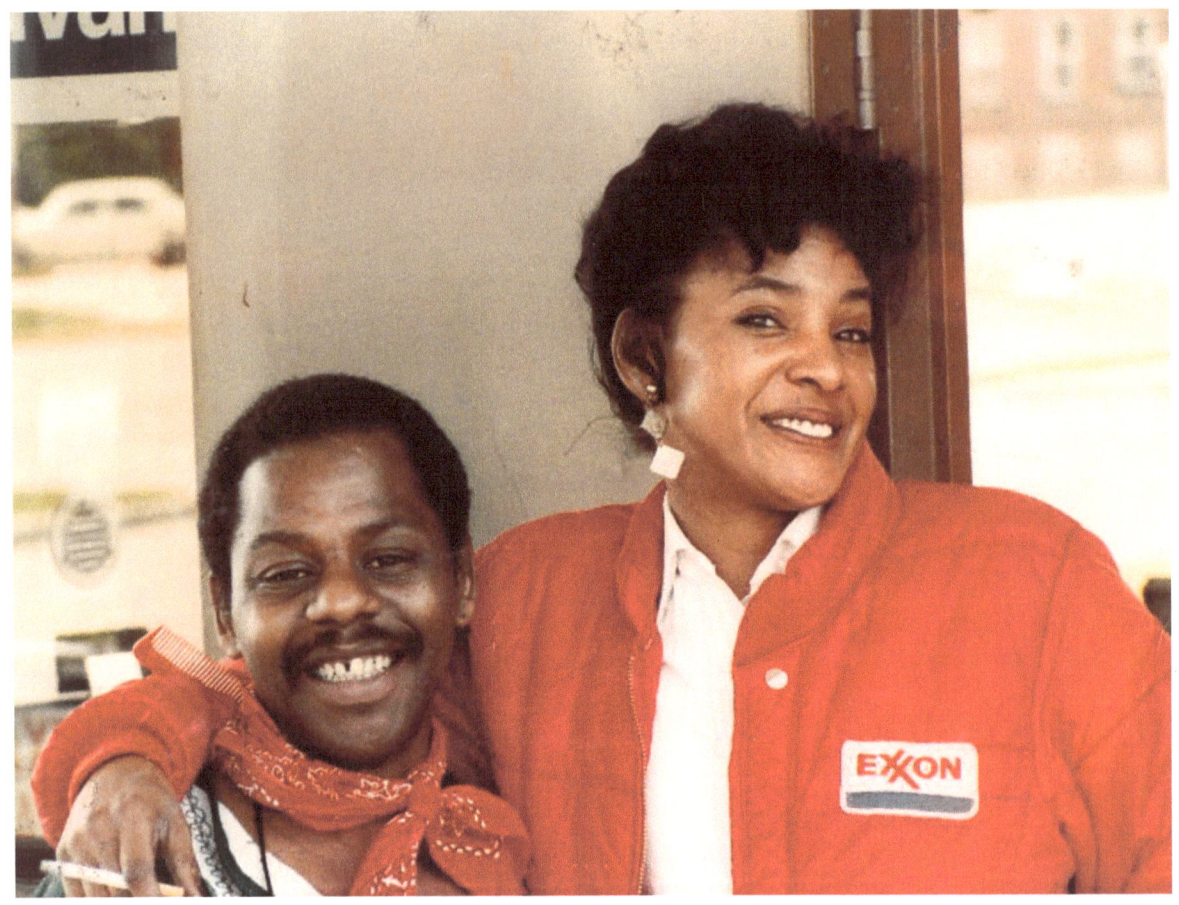

-You know by then the Old City was crankin. Annie Delisle open up a French restaurant down there. And music clubs and condos and all them buildings was comin alive. Old City was the happenin place now. Yeah wasn't but a few years they had music clubs ever corner and restaurants and coffee shops and new galleries too. And 200 East kept going, they had some great exhibitions, lotta fun shows, and different bunch a artists was running it. They moved up the street on Jackson and got a bigger space. And Eric de Red stayed with'em for a while there, til he moved into the Artists Colony.

-*The Artists Colony?*

-Yeah.

-*What's that?*

-That's them seven houses on 11th Street that was part of the world fair.

-*11th Street in Fort Sanders?*

-Yeah, on the edge of the Fort there up against the world fair site. See, what they done when the city have the world fair they take them seven houses on the downtown side of 11th Street and they fence them off and make'em part of the world fair site. You know, like one was the Budweiser Pavilion and I don't know what they all was during the fair. But after the fair see the whole 70 some'um acres just be fenced off right, keeping the public out and waiting on whatever they gonna do next. And see they don't know, the city don't know. They had no particular VISION for the future see. Nobody thought that a little town like Knoxville be able to host a world's fair exhibition, didn't think they could get it together to pull it off you know and make it happen. And if they did nobody thought nobody come. Well, they did. Spite all de naysayers peoples come to check it out, and it do good. They was peoples from all over the world here brother. But, typically, the city got no plan for what happen next. They not looking too far ahead see. So the site, the world fair site, just sit there for two years all fenced off waiting for someone figure out what it is. And it become a political football they throwin back and forth, right. Like what one think ought to be done with it and what another think ought to be done, and ain't none of'em know shit right? Well, first thing that did happen after two year was they decides to open back up just them seven houses that sits on that side of 11th Street. Open'em up for bids to be art galleries or something like that, right. And the city calls it the ARTISTS COLONY. They want artists to live upstairs and have galleries downstairs. Now see, they open up these houses to artists cause they done run outta options. They always hoping someone from somewhere just come in and buy the place and do whatever they wantsa do, right. But they weren't no takers see, nobody wants to touch it. Been so much trouble and controversy nobody want to invest in that insecurity.

And all the peoples saying what you gonna do with this property, you know, and all the leftover pavilions startin to rot away. Yeah. So after two years of that it come down to asking the artists do something and make it look like something happenin there, you know, til they can find something better.

-So how'd that go?

-Well, none the artists wants touch it either. I mean it was the city's baby, their beautiful scam to make'em selves rich. And now some of'em in jail and the rest off countin they money right. Well. Fix it youself, you know? They come in here drummin up some carny dream and drove all the locals crazy with get rich quick schemes and turned the city into a yardsale for a couple years, and kickin people outta houses, condemnin properties tryin to wheel and deal. Now they want the ones got left out come help they ass. Mosts the artists I know say suck on it til you choke, you know.

-Yeah.

-But what happen, surprisin thing to all us. Eric de Red's old man Carl Sublett, right? And he a renowned artist and tenured art professor at UT, much respected man. Well, he and his wife Helen decides to bid for one of the houses to open a gallery. They think it's a good thing to do. And the city glad to see that right, and so they gets the first house. It was the first bizness on the fair site after the world's fair, the Sublett Gallery. They s'pose to have a gallery downstairs and someone lives upstairs. So the Sublett's get Eric de Red live there and run the gallery, and Eric de Red gets Arh Be move in there too and help him run that gallery.

-Okay. So they move out of the studio?

-Yeah. They move down the street into the Artists Colony. And pretty soon they had all seven them houses rented out to artists who gots galleries and shops and theater or something in ever house. And behind the Sublett Gallery and the gallery next door to them a big porch that come off both houses and gots steps down to another level that has

a big Quonset hut on it
and this become a bar
they call THE PORCH.

*-The Porch? And it's a
bar?*

-Yeah, they licensed to
sell drinks there and have
live music too right. Well,
everthing bout to change
some more.

*-Sounds like it. I mean
this sounds like a step up
from street art. And
they're working with the
man now.*

-Yeah they be working
with the man now.

*-Well, how'd that go?
How's that work with
artistic freedom?*

-Well, you know, bout like
you 'spect, I guess. They
get in there gets it goin.
They was hittin on all
cylinders pretty quick.
All them houses havin
regular events, art shows

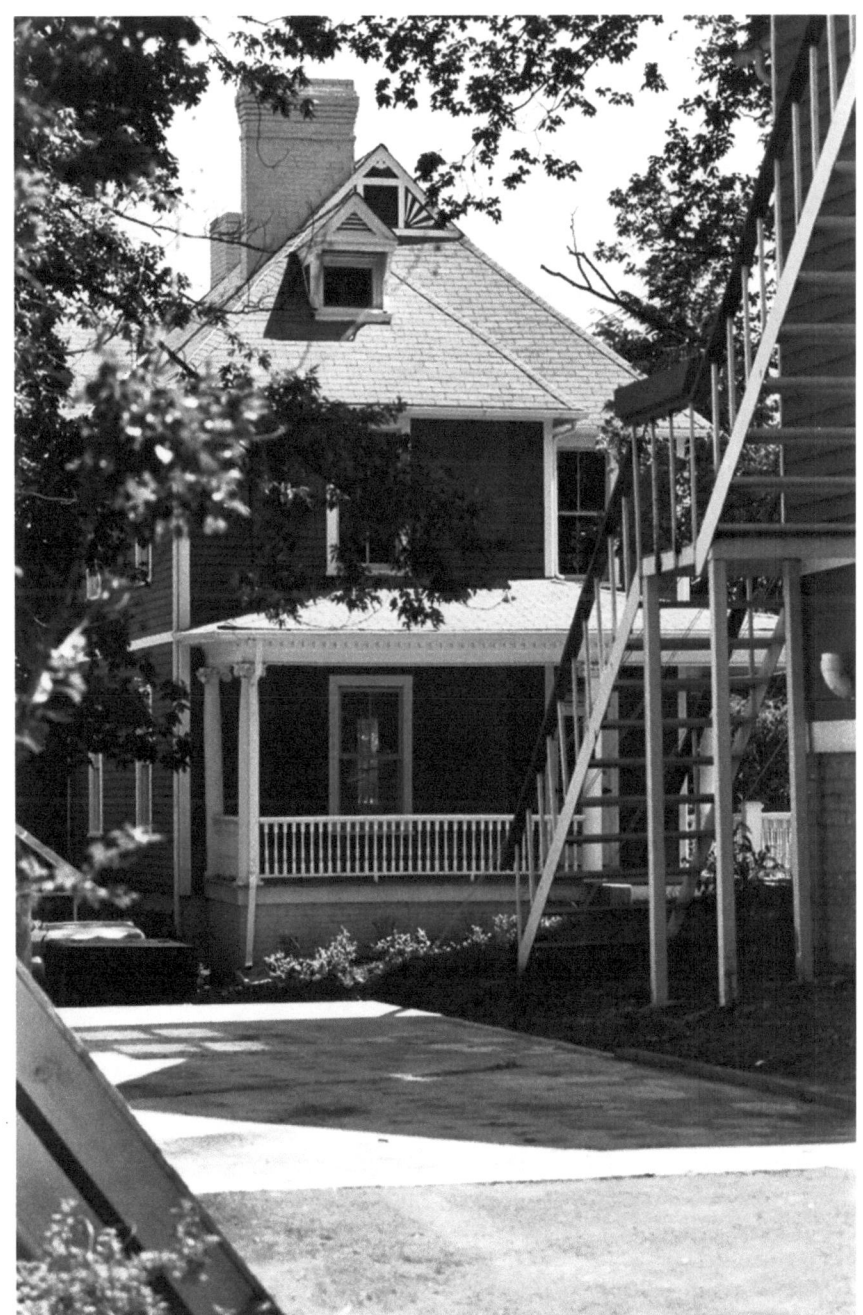

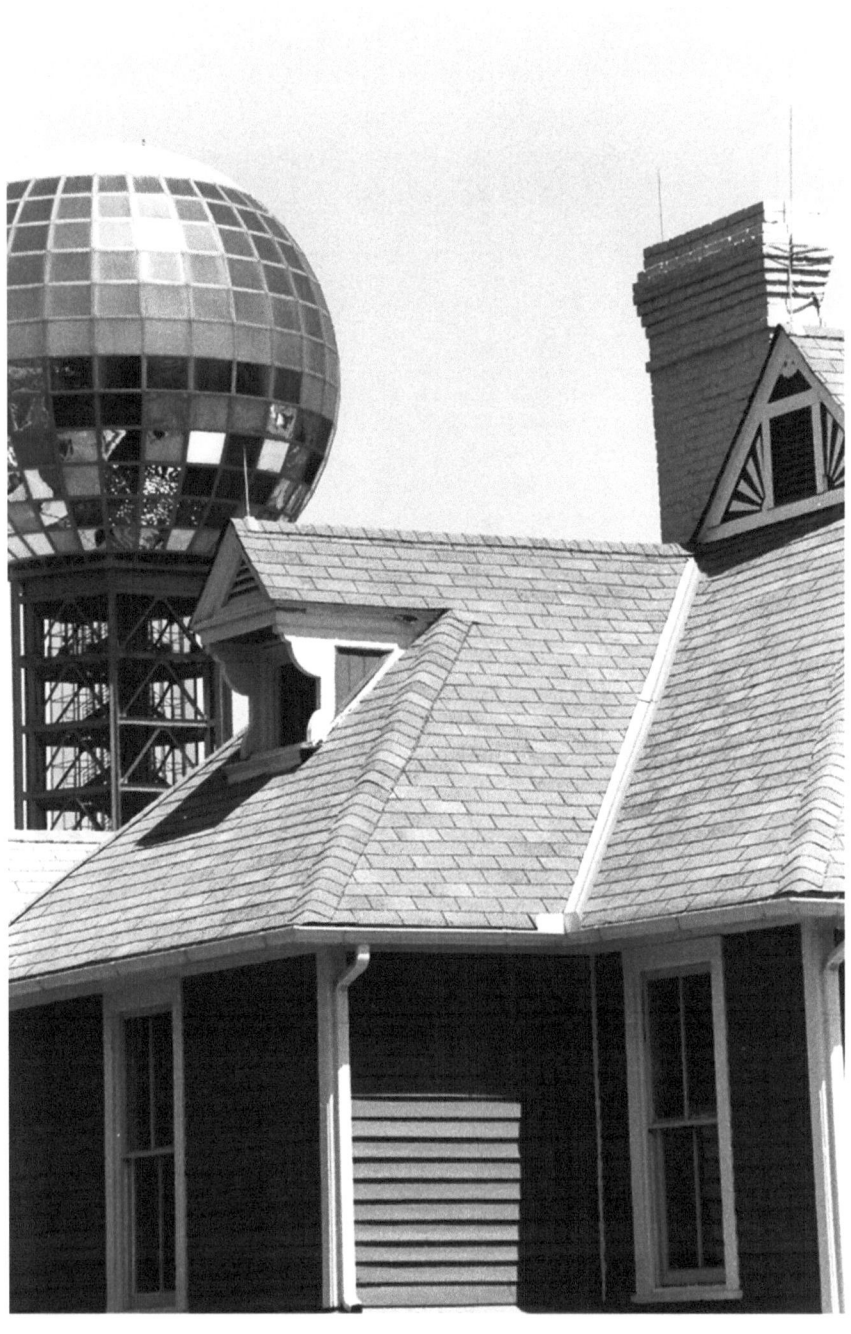

and plays and readin's and all kinda gatherin's. Lots a people comin check it all out. The papers was writing it up, you know, looking for something to write about. And The Porch was the main happenin thing. It was really a good bar and a favorite hang for lotsa folk, all through the warm months 'specially it was full a'people and they had bands playin regular, you know, at night and afternoon stuff too. Open for bizness. That was the good thing. The city got what they say they wanted, something happenin on the fair site. But like you might guess they got more than they bargained for. And they was always uneasy with it, you know, and pushin back. The music too loud, crowds making noise for people cross the street, or something. See, somebody complain bout noise during the world's fair they ax them go move some other city. Now though they say keep it down or don't go late or open you gallery earlier or whatever. I 'member hearin bout it all. So they had a bumpy road and in more ways than that. But it was happenin anyway. And you never seen so many artists comin round, seem like they just poured outta the woods and hills and streets and suburbs. I mean they was a lot going on and a lotta people involved. Somethin happenin ever day, but yeah shows, openings, events ever week. And they was outta town people coming in to do shows or see shows at these galleries. And that energy was happenin all over. It was down in the Old City and kickin up on Gay Street and the Market Square, and it was happenin at UT too. Just like the Sublett's takin that house and Don Fiene coming round to the art shows, a number of UT professors and students got involved with all what was goin on.

-*Sounds like all the dots are connecting up.*

-Well they was. Ways they never had before. It was a inspiration man. It was good to see all them people mixin it up with other people and doin shit, you know.

-*I guess Horace was pretty active in all this?*

-Oh man, yeah, well these was mostly his friends, you know, most them houses. And over four five years lots of different artists moved through them houses. A little later Kathi Freeman and Steven Pogue move into one of'em with the USEE'EM MUSEUM, right. They had wild shows, all kinda fun gatherin's and group shows. And Horace was in on a lot a'that. He was involved in everthing from the art shows and performance art to things happenin on The Porch. Everbody knew Horace. He was a presence.

-*Yeah.*

-It was a time of Art man, and he was a artist at large.

-*Yeah, sounds like he's at the heart of most everything.*

-Yeah he at the heart. Yeah. And you know one of the troubles them artists have with the city was the big fence that stay up there on the sidewalk right in front the houses. Them houses don't have no front yard or nothing, just the sidewalk right there with a big twelve foot fence in the sidewalk that was put there to keep the public out during the fair. They want them galleries be open to the public and do bizness with the public, but a person walkin by cross the street think them houses still off limits the way that fence shuts'em out. People have to walk on the other side the street all the way down to the end to cross over and come in a little gate there, if the gate at Laurel ain't open. They try and try to get them take that fence down, at least the part in front the houses. But for two years after they open they kept that fence up.

-Seems counter productive on the city's part if they're trying to get the public involved?

-'Course it was. But hey, they not really concerned about the public being so involved, they gettin all the public they want, you know. They just want to keep that ribbon round they little package. And they did for over two years. But one morning they come to work and they was two and half blocks of fence wrapped with art. All down past them seven houses and The Porch all the way to Clinch Avenue. Now that was a sight. And somebody gonna have to clean up this mess. But then, it wasn't long after that 'fore the city got out there and took that damned old fence down. And you know, when they did, in a way them houses come back into the Fort after that.

-And I guess you know who performed this act of urban art?

-Well I'd say they was 30 or more artists done it, at least for a day or two startin out, and maybe eight or ten on into that night finishin it out and hangin it. Some them guerrillas stayed til they got it done. They had a floor in one them old buildings up on Gay Street where they could roll out that paper bout 100 feet at a time and go to work on it. And they's all slappin the paint to it.

-Well, it seems like a lot of work, you know, just to have it trashed afterwards. I guess it helped getting the city to take the fence down.

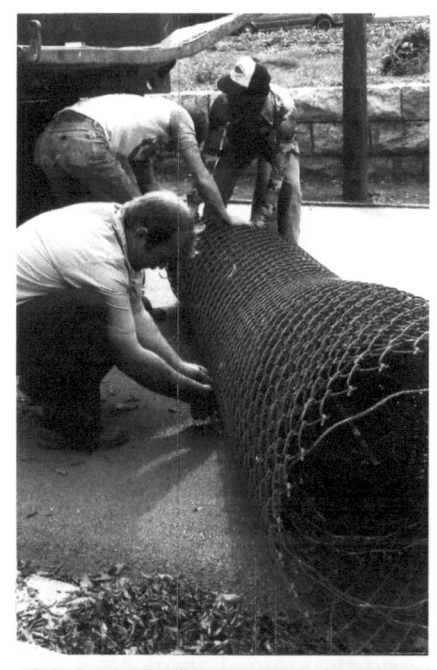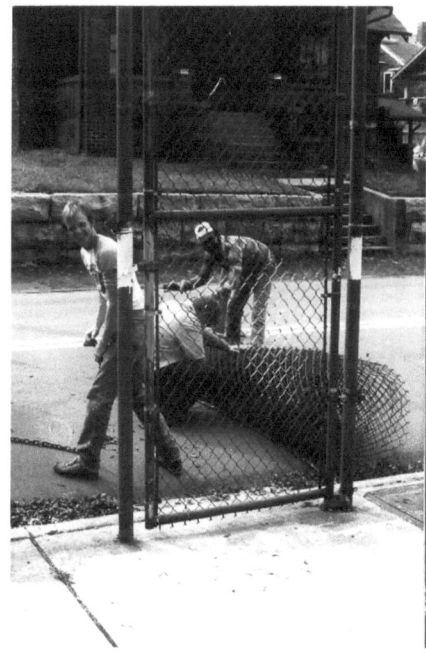

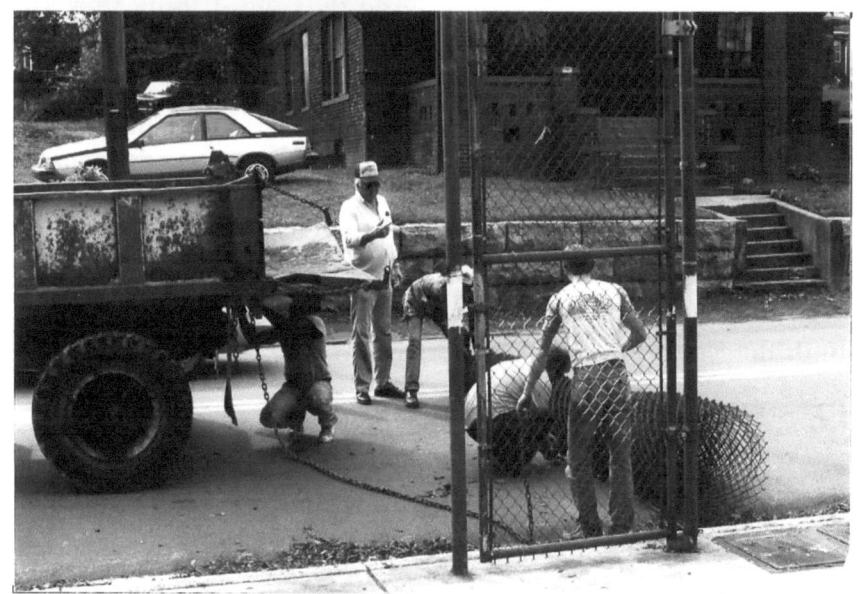

-Hey, you Cristo or something you wrap a island, okay. You gots money and media and whatever you need and a art scene followin you round and document you ass and blow it up all over the world, sure, then you a artist. But you got shit 'cept what you wanta say and do, and wrap two and a half block of art all of a night, and have to jive off the cops who stop to question you, not wantin no one document you ass too close, well, you done some art too. Now who say different? Let me hear'em say it.

-No, I agree with you. Totally.

-That shit have an impact, you know, on anyone who see it.

-Absolutely, I would imagine. And sounds like the only recourse to effect change, I mean, that they left you.

-Well, the whole thing was all an experiment anyway, working with the city and all. I know lot of them went into it knowin they was no future as a business there and they was gettin used by the city. But hey, they was using the city too, figurin they could gain more in a compromised situation than the city would. And they did. I think they all did. City got what they needed. But the artists have they impact upon everthing see. Just cause they up'd the energy level so much, and they created so many exhibitions and events and brought so many artists and peoples together. Over four five years or more they had lotsa different artists living in them different houses and doing different things. And after they gots the Artist Colony goin the city opens up the Candy Factory just down the hill, right. It was a happenin place during the world fair, had restaurants and shops and shit all through bout six floors right. Well they gots opened up with even more galleries and bizness. UT put a gallery in there too. And then a couple years more the money come forth and they built the Knoxville Musuem of Art right next to them.

-Big changes for any city. And really, sounds like the city was supporting the Arts.

-They was. Yeah, you look at it from this distance, it look pretty good. The Arts was growin and the city was makin a place for'em. But really, after they had the art museum there they was ready to get rid the artists and do something else with them houses, maybe just tear'em down, you know. So the city start movin the artists out, working on that. They changin policies and reworkin things to move that along. Just like in the Old City, the artists come in early when nothing happenin and got it goin, you know, marines hit the beach first. Once it's happenin and some money get interested, time for the artists to pack up if they not owners. But that's just the way it is. Same way everwhere I guess. But it work good, and Knoxville come a long way through there.

-Yeah.

Thing was though, the artists couldn't just let'em tear down those houses, which the city had already tried to do before. That was the plan. So, they put up some resistance to the

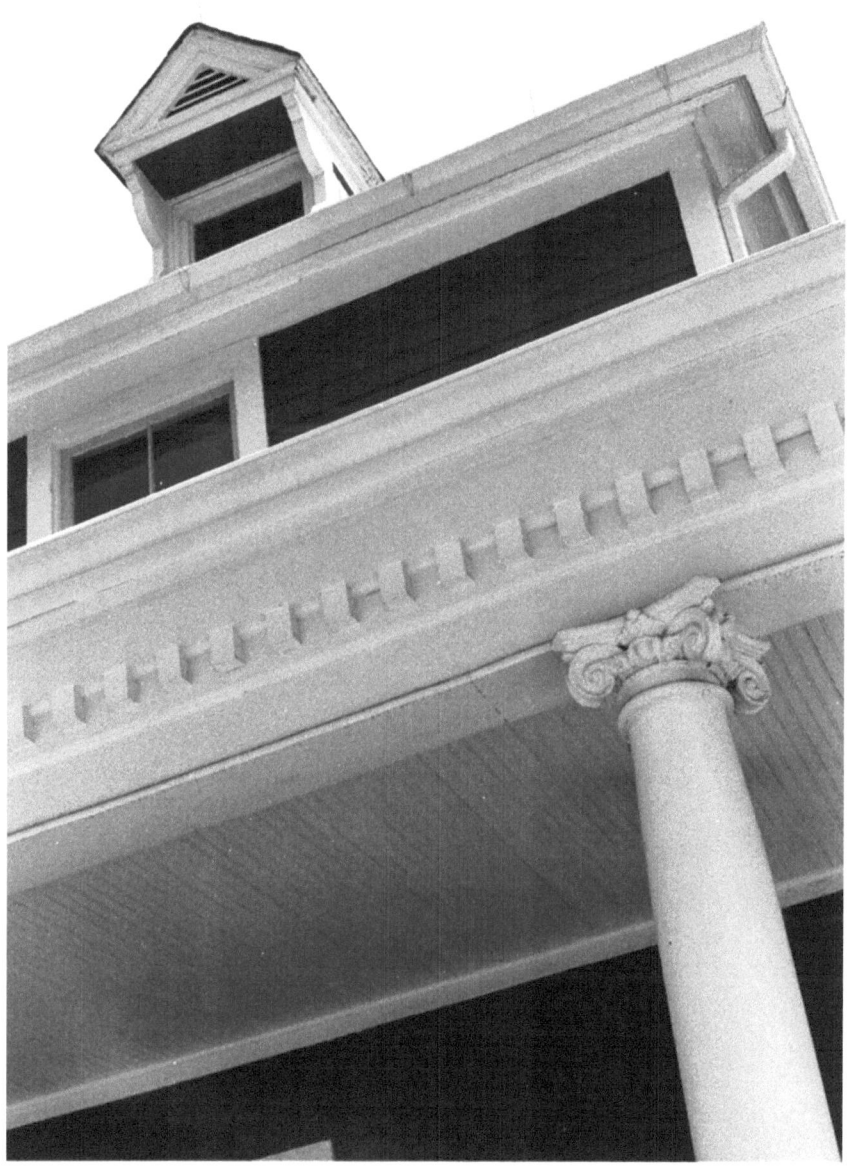

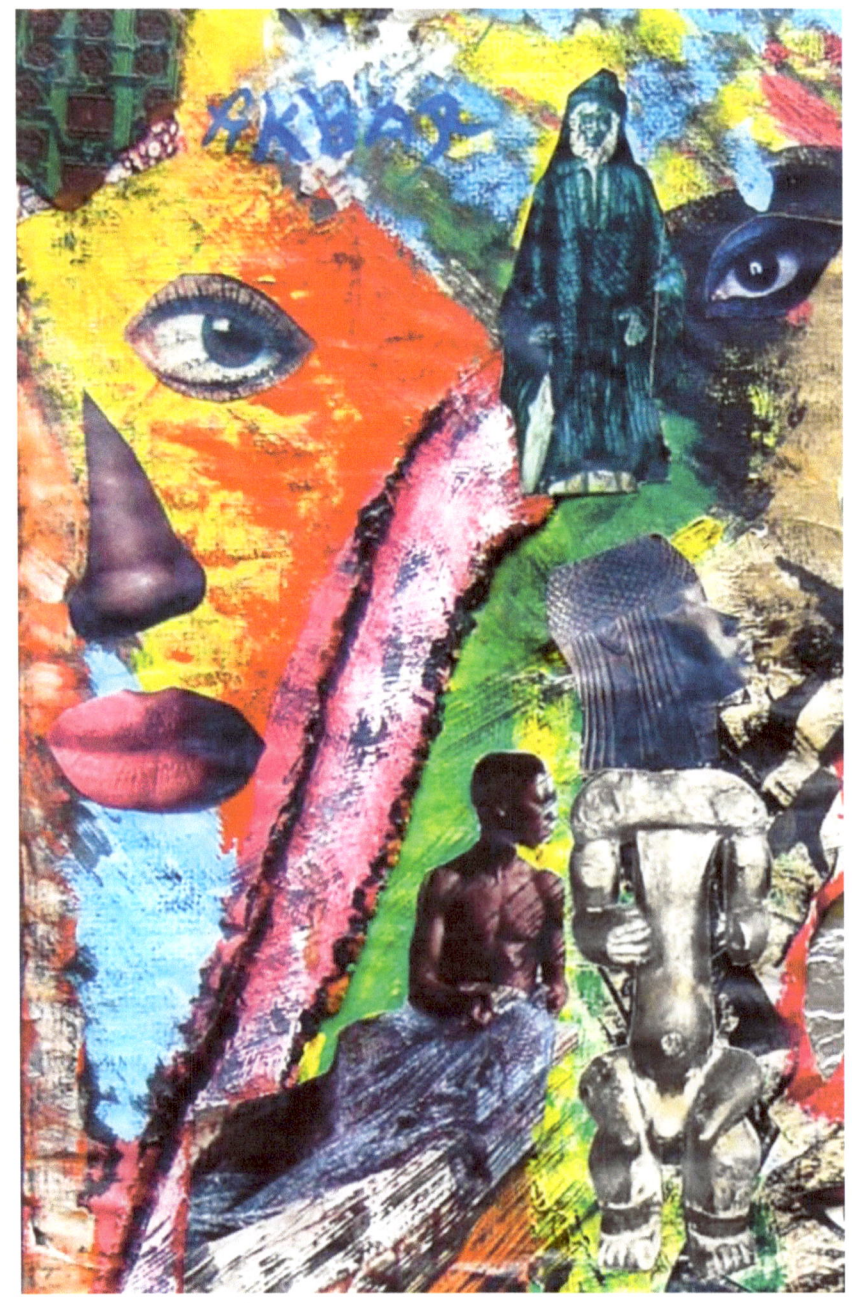

new deal. The writing was on the wall far as the Artist Colony goes, but they had to draw some attention to what was goin down in order to get some help saving the houses. They started doing special events and plays and stuff to raise awareness of the situation, and gots other entities involved, you know, some lawyers and politicians. And the artists formed a non-profit group called CHROMA just to be organized enough to get a seat at the table, you know. William Rawson, the painter, he was involved with all that. They took meetings with the city, with the museum's board a'directors and spoke at city council meetings, you know, and they was articles in the papers and all. You just have to check out some'a that. Talk to some them people involved with all that. But they did, they saved them houses. The city back off on tearin'em down.

-*Is that right?*

-Yeah, Chroma done that, and they was the biggest group of artists yet. Most organized too. They moved out the Artists Colony and started doing exhibitions at the Bijou Gallery on Gay Street, same place the Hard Knox show was back when. And they was rockin the art there for a few years to come, and now it was ever month something new. And those shows was the coolest man, they always bring a mix of poetry and art and music and dance now too. They might have forty artists in a show, always a few dozen, you know. They fills that place up with art and bring a lotta people in.

-*You involved with that group?*

-Some, but I kinda got out of touch there somewhere. I went to a few meetings and seen how they put some them shows together. But you'd need to talk to the artists, they know more bout all that.

-*Hey, you're an artist.*

-Well thank you man. I have been known to art off, but I wouldn't call myself that. Horace he a artist, and them he run with, they was truly artists if they ever was any. But I was a friend, you know, and I was around. I helped out.

-Well, okay. Perhaps you're just being modest?

-Well, I bear witness. And you know when you around them they make you a artist too. Something bout that energy, you know, and what they putting off come into you too, and fore you know it you slingin paint and drawin out shit you never 'spected be doing.

-Yeah.

-But to carry that with you, you know, when you ain't round energy like that, that's a different thing. To keep that fire goin all the time you have to spend by youself to do a lotta art, that'a whole 'nother deal, ain't it? I mean them peoples wake up to it, you know, they dreamin 'bout it when they sleepin. And hey, they still awake doing it when we sleepin.

-I will talk to them.

-'Bout the biggest thing I 'member they did at the Bijou was that KNOXRAGEUS show, some time round '92. That one they did in the main theater, and it was an extravaganza man, all day affair, you know, and into the night. They had all kinda bands playing on the Bijou stage, and comedy acts and what all, and the local writer and actor Greg Congleton was hosting it. And what they do, they have that big stage that's like two three big curtains deep right, and in the very back they all painting on a big movie screen back there. So like a dozen or more artists workin all the time back there on scaffolds and shit and painting this giant screen through the day and evening. They be behind the curtain when some band playing in front of'em. And then they close that part off too when they setting up for another band and be entertainin out in front of that big curtain. Then ever once in a while they open all the curtains up and you see where they got now with the big group mural. And, you know, they have Terry Hill up in one those little soap box balconies, right. He up there with his guitar and rig man layin down all these ambient sounds floatin 'cross the theater while they paintin and the peoples listenin and watchin them paint. Terry Hill, he like from outer space, you know what I mean, that music he playin.

94

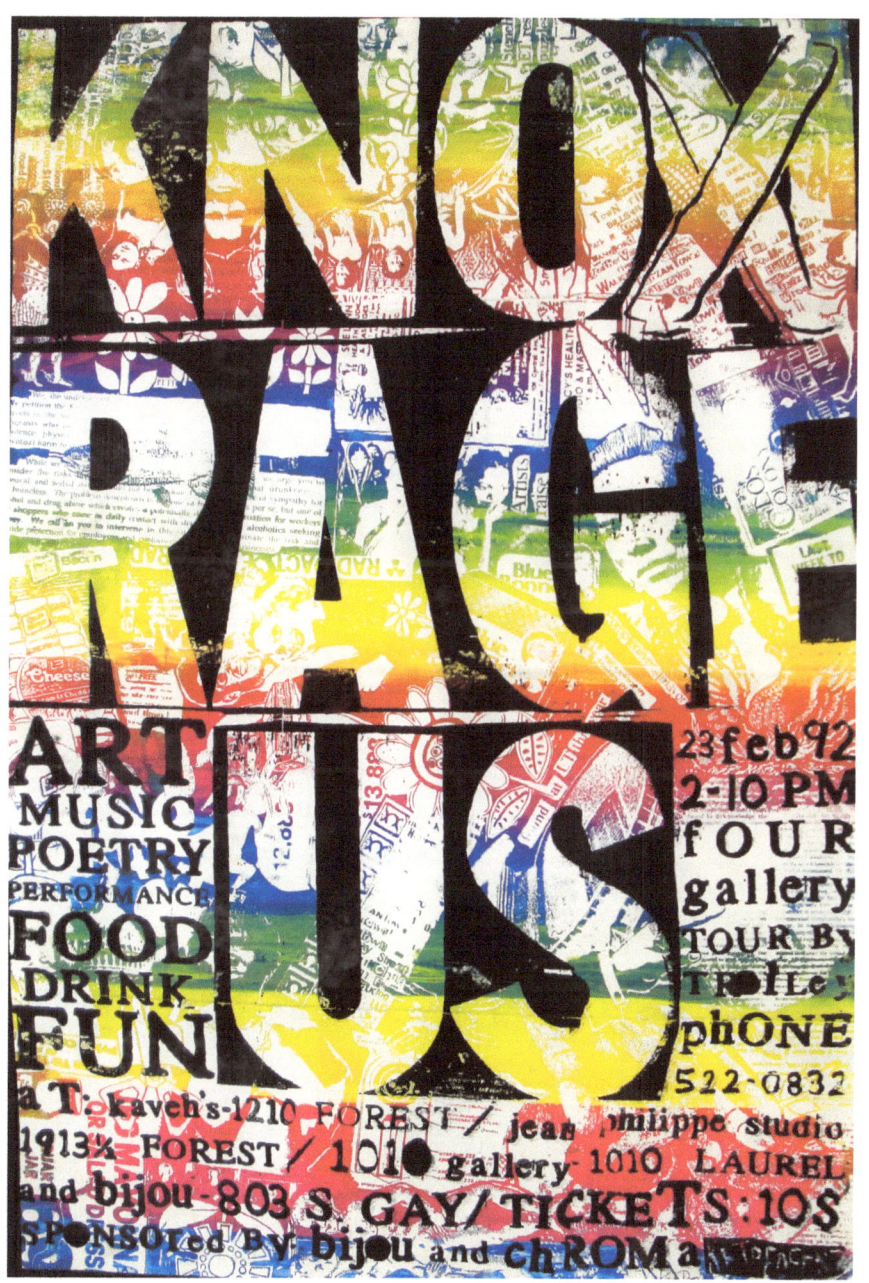

95

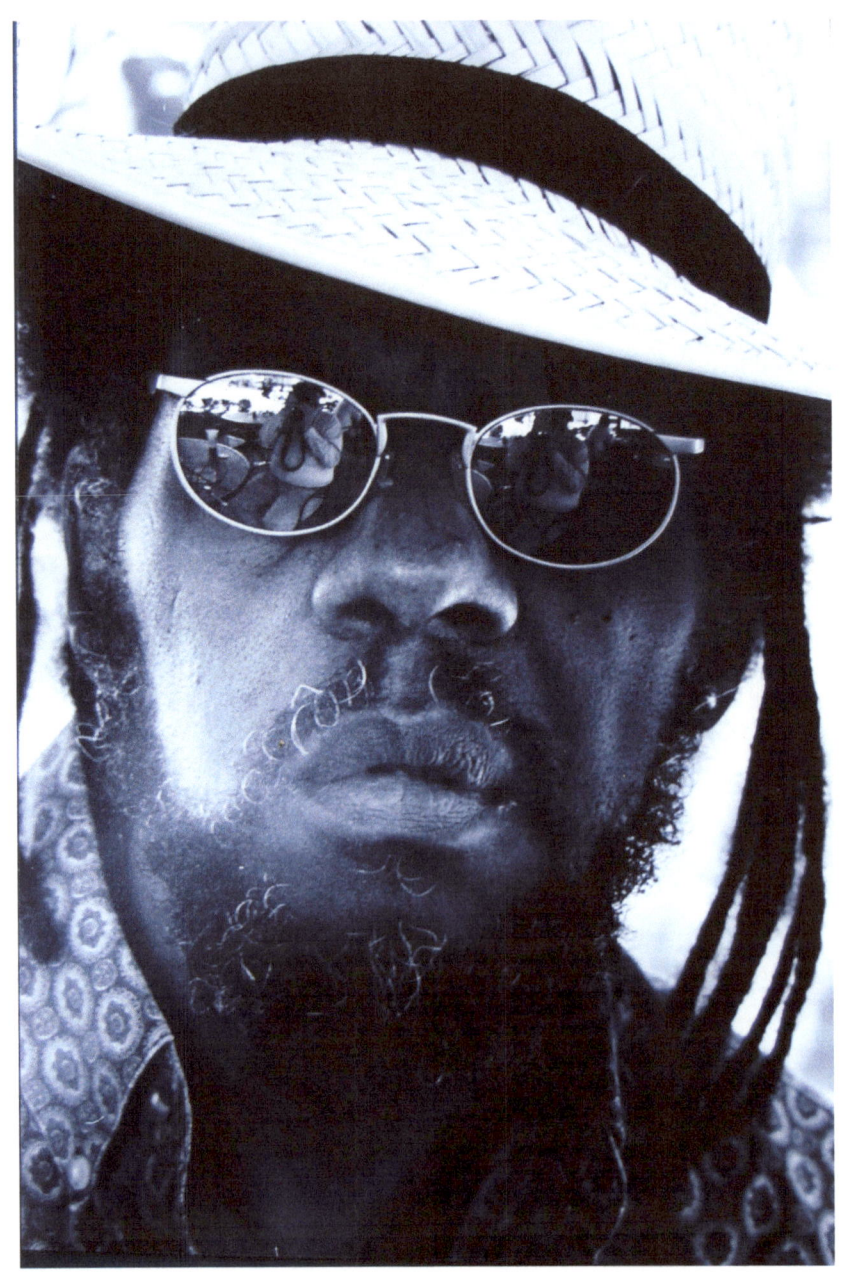

-This sounds like a major production.

-Yeah it was, but they also got like three four other galleries participatin too, you know, one or two in the Candy Factory and a couple in Fort Sanders, and they have shuttles takin people back and forth from the Bijou out to these other gallery shows. And Horace and ever other artist you can think of involved some way or 'nother. And you know, they didn't have no money, no grants to do none a'that.

-This is a big group of artists.

-Yeah, well the nucleus of it was that same bunch, you know, Horace and them. But they was a lot of'em now and it kept changing far as who all was in it. That Knoxrageus was like a decade long crescendo, far as shows and exhibitions go. Not to say it was the most important thing they done, cause it was all like one thing in a way, but it was the biggest single event in ten years or more of artin off. As they say, it was a moveable feast. Not just here and there and everwhere, but a lotta different people 'long the way. And everbody got a different take on it all.

-Right.

-And you talk to other people they all tell you things I can't remember, you know, someone that was hangin more regular with Horace after that. Cause like he belong to everbody after a while, you know? We was friends from first on, and it was the same whenever we hook up, but we go different ways now and then and don't see each other for a while. But he always seeing somebody, you know. Like I say, Horace belong to everbody.

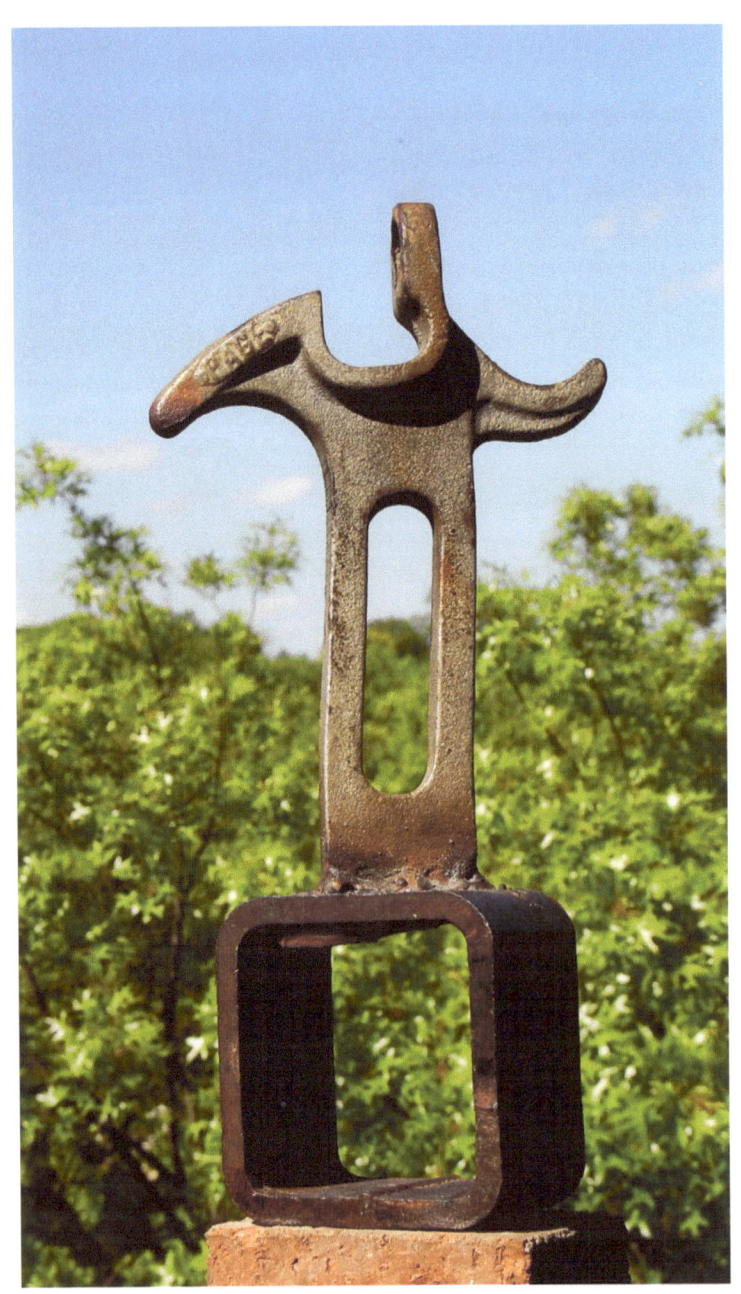

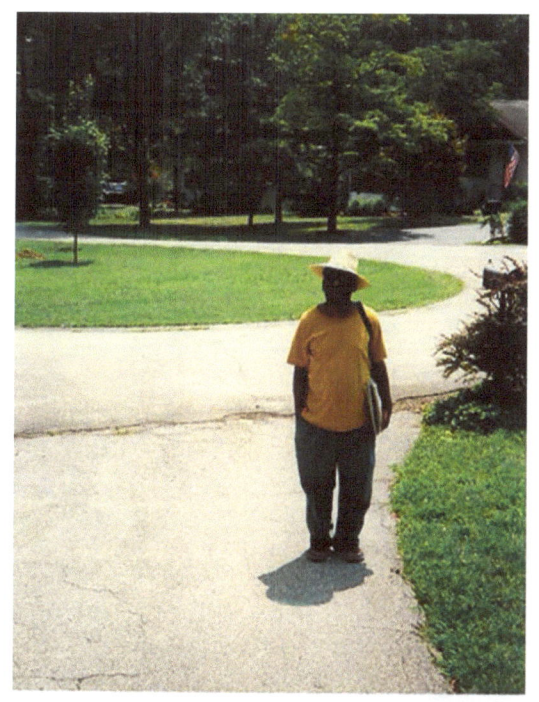 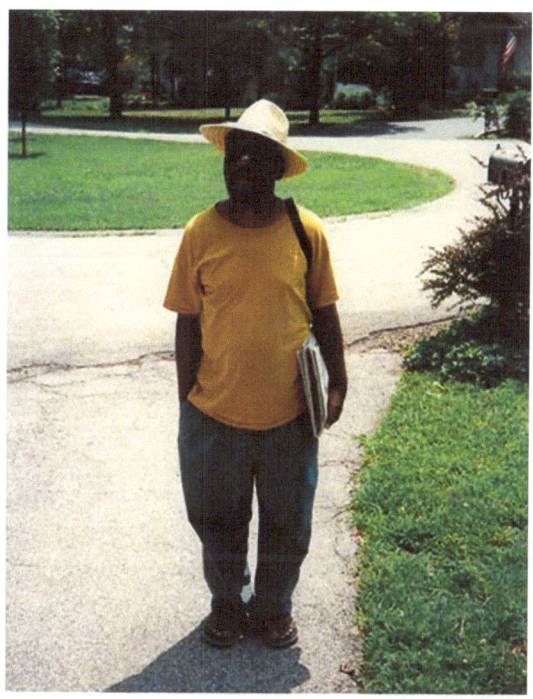

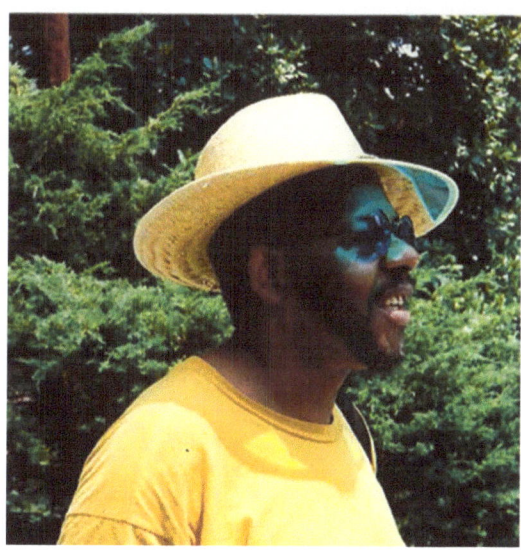 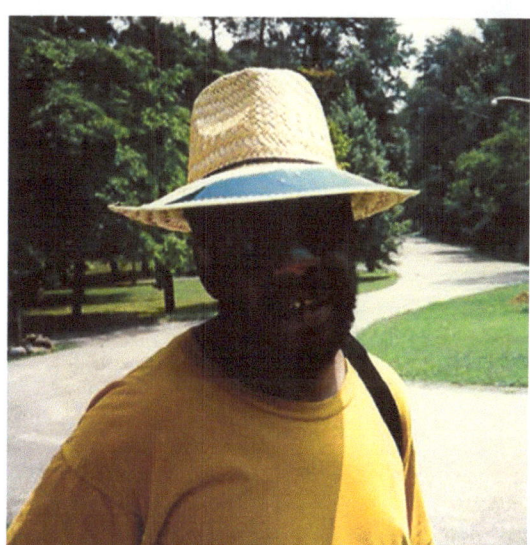

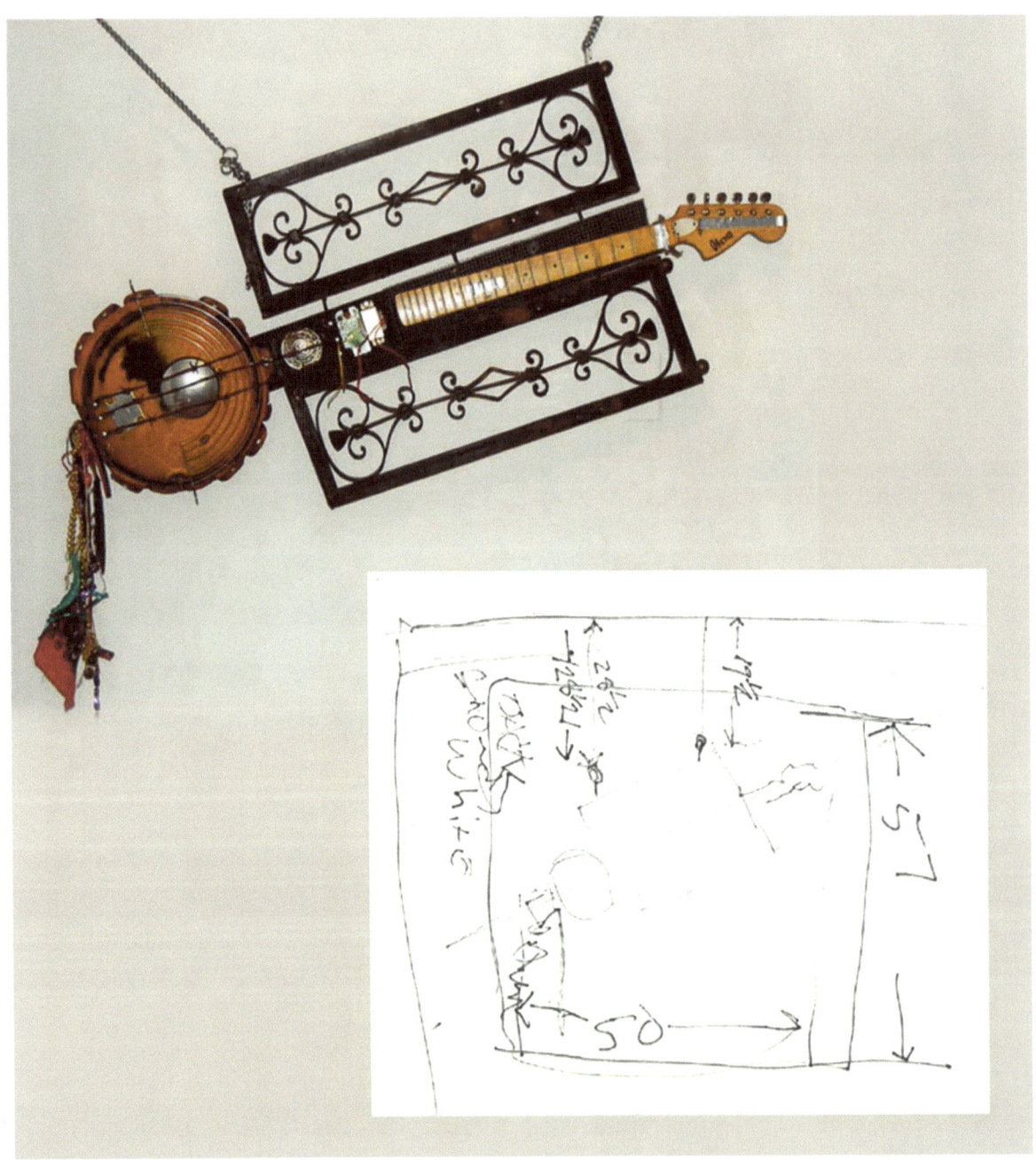

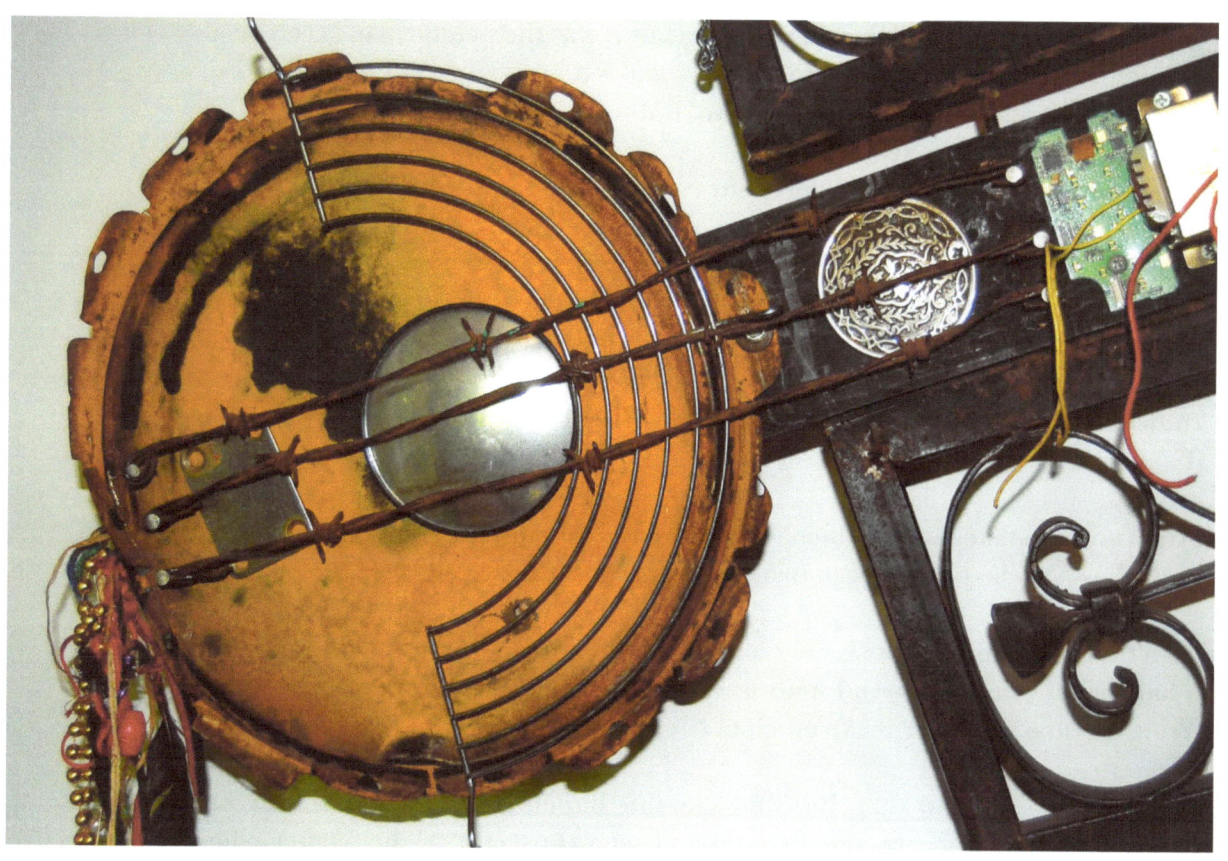

-So I been hearing about Horace, or I should say Ali, and the city and some of those years after the world's fair.

-The city have what you call a renaissance man, you know what I'm saying?
-Yeah a renaissance.
-That's about right.
-Yeah.

-Okay.

-It weren't just no worlds fair man (no), or the City or the University or no Arts

Council. They all there somewhere (yeah) but it was the people man (yeah)(right). They was ripe ripe ripe on the vine dude. They make it happen. You know what I'm saying?

-You right (yeah). Knoxville on fire man, it done caught fire.

-The city was havin to deal with it.

-And you had artists and entrepreneurs and everbody pushin for it.

-Yeah after the world fair maybe more of'em have more confidence, you know?

-May be. But same time they been havin to watch from the sidelines too while the city decide to join the 20th Century (yeah). You know what I'm saying?

-What you had see, you had all these young artists round man, and they comin into they own, you know, ready to blow they stacks (HA)(yeah)(yeah), ready to unload. And they know the deal is you have to go somewheres else make it happen, right?

-That right.

-Always.

-Ain't no big stakes in you hometown (right). You gots a go to New York City or LA (yeah Los Angeles) or Chicago bro (yeah), or Nashville or somewhere, right.

-That's right.

-Can't make it happen no big way hangin round here.

-That's what I'm saying. And it always been that way.

-Yeah, anyone who ever make much of his art have gone off to somewhere to do it.

-Have to.

-And everybody know that. But now see, this bunch they young and they been out in the world already and traveled round and seen shit right (right)(right). They been to all the meccas (yeah). But they back, they home, and they don't wanta wait no more.

-That's right.

-They say right here right now.

-Yeah, right here right now.

-That's right.

-And they start artin off with a high degree of visibility see and energy, and they pushin it. All a sudden everthing start to open up, and then everbody gettin on board, the entrepreneurs, and the club owners and shop peoples, and professors and deejays, and journalists. You name it. And first they revive one part of town and then another.

-*How do you mean?*

-I mean all over the center of town they's like a new geographical continuum man, from the music clubs on Cumberland and the students at UT up through Fort Sanders (its occupied neighborhood) that slam up against the Arts Colony and the world's fair site right into downtown and the Market Square (and Gay Street) sliding down into the Old City. See. It's all one big moving piece of connectivity now.

-I see.

-Yeah, the activity level done jumped all over.
-Some point, Ashley Capps open up Ella Gurus down there on the corner of Jackson and Central (right), and man in no time it was a world class music venue, you know what I'm saying? Everbody from Dr. John to Sun Ra play there. They have all kinda good shows man, JJ Cale, the Neville Brothers, John Prine, you name it.
-Yeah the city was crankin' like it ain't never before.

-How much were y'all aware of that then? I mean, did you have that as a goal, or what were you working towards?

-We all about it.
-Yeah all about it.
-Talked about it everday.
-I mean, it's not like we got some game plan with a designated goal like you say. But we talkin bout it all the time see (yeah). And we aware of the city and where it's at.
-Yeah, we love the city. But the city reckless man, and let's just say a-historical (yeah), you know? They was just prone to go backwards (yeah) you leave it up to the 'ministrations and lotta the bizness peoples.
-Yeah, what they care bout? Making money in they pocket. Keeping they cronies in the jack, and keeping the flow goin (yeah). They tear down some historic building and grease some developer's palm goin give them a campaign contribution, then everthing fine, right. That's a good system for them, and they say good for the city (yeah)(exactly). But it not good for the city.
-No.
-City got to get past that shit.

-*What about the world's fair? That seems like a visionary idea.*

-Could be.
-Should be.

-*And would certainly take some sharp business people and developers and community
leaders to pull off, right?*

-Yeah they done it. And some of them have a big idea.
-And they found the money to back'em.
-But cause they doing it for the wrong reasons they hurt a lotta people putting it together.
It was like an assault on the neighborhoods coming up to it.
-Yeah how they done all that was written up in the national papers. And when I was
travelin back to Knoxville then people from other places askin me why they doing that to
the peoples livin there, kickin out homes and shit. You know?
-And that's why they didn't have no plan for what happens afterwards neither, cause they
was doing it all for the wrong reasons. They wasn't thinkin bout the city at heart.
-And that why some of'em end up in jail too.
-But look, I don't care bout that shit. That shit always go down. I'm glad they have the fair,
glad they got it together and glad they done it. People enjoy it, and it was good for the city.
It open up peoples eyes. But the thing is, things being what they was, you had to react, you
know, you had to step up and try to get a hand on that energy and help push it in some
good direction.
-Yeah, that's right.
-You know, whole thing s'pose to be an energy exposition right?
-The Energy Expo.
-Yeah, damn right.
 -That was its theme. And the U.S. Pavilion was the energy pavilion (yeah). And it the
biggest one, sitting right there in the middle of the fairgrounds. And after the fair it just sit
there neglected til they tore it down.
-Yeah.
-And it had an IMAX theater in it too, which they tore down. We still ain't got no Imax
theater in this town.

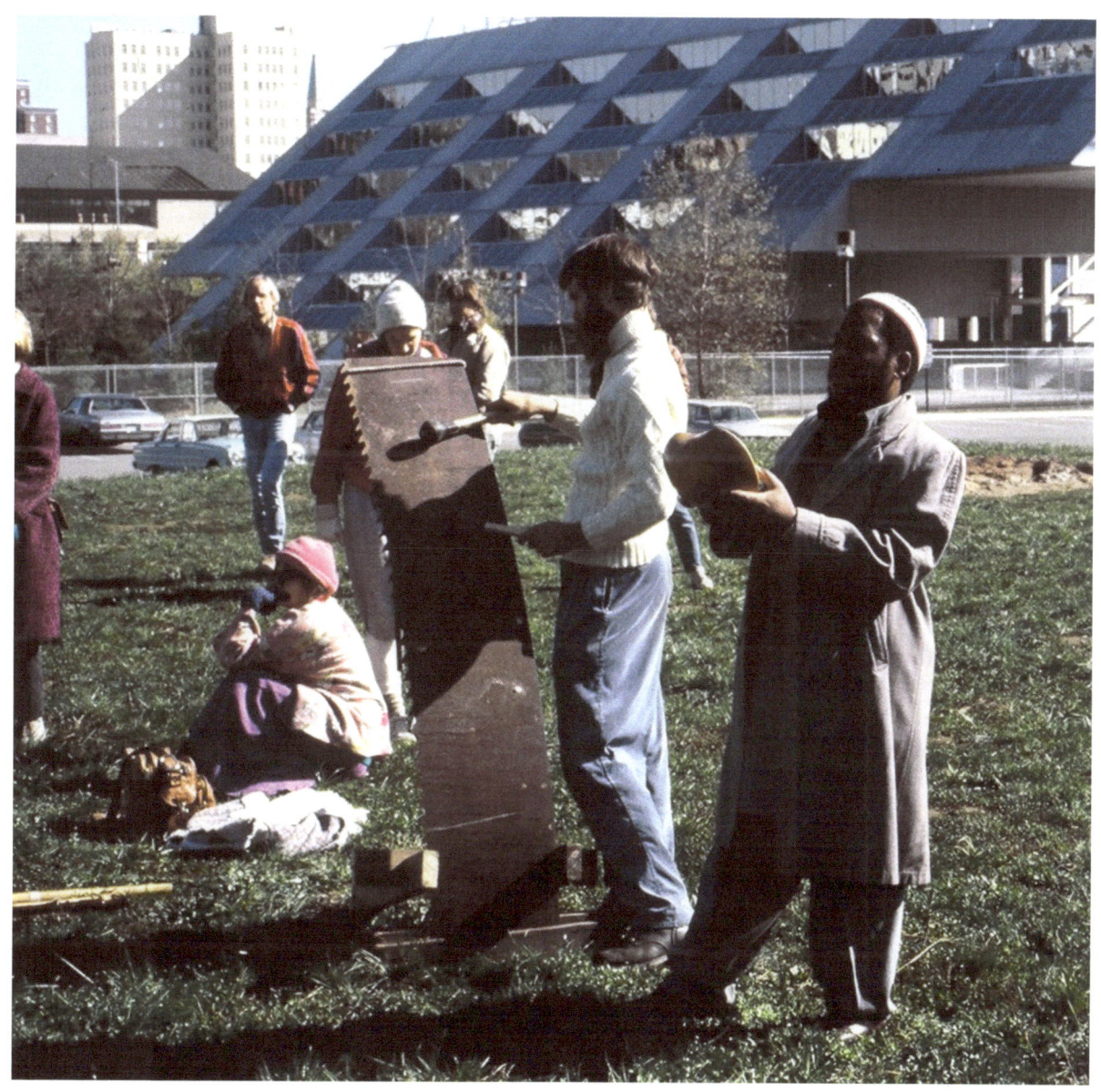

-And see, they coulda took that energy theme and built on it. Kept those facilities in place and made Knoxville the new energy capitol of the U.S. of A. (that right)(yeah). They was set to go. They coulda been rakin in billions by now. But see, wasn't any of them city fathers or bizness peeps ever thinkin bout anything like that, when that was their premise to begin with (yeah) (yeah). I mean, that what you workin with uptown. Are these your best and brightest?

-These were definitely heady times for Knoxville. Like you say, welcome to the 20th Century.

-Yeah, well I don't mean to go off, but just to give you some context.

-No, I'm interested to hear any that.

-Well, I know we was tryin talk bout art, you know, and say hey we artists, but we was tryin to talk about the city too, its history n'shit. This before you had you Jack Neelys filling everbody in on what they don't know bout they little burg, right. Back then they don't know nothing but it got founded sometime, had a civil war battle, and now we had a worlds fair.
-Yeah, and we been playing football all along.
-Right. That be you civic pride and understanding man.
-Yeah, that bout covers it.
-We all loved the city, loved the streets, you know, loved its history man. Loved the hills it built upon. Loved the river. You know, the invisible river down there. We all tryin get some kinda reckonin with the city, you know? Tryin do right by it (yeah), give it what it need.
-You said it there man, we all tryin to get some kinda reckonin with the city.
-I think that's why more artists was comin forth. And more artists comin back to town.
-Yeah.
-Like the old Apache thing'a going where the fight is good.
-Yeah, some of us just come back to town.
-Right, like Peter Artin. Pogue, Arh Be.
-Dennis Hundt, he come in from Ohio ain't he?
-Yeah he just come in, and I guess Ken Britton too.
-Kathi Freeman been up in New York City.

-Yeah they wrote some article bout her and wearable art or something in Time magazine or Newsweek or one them.

-Some like William Rawson and Walt Fieldsa and them living out in the country and other counties, you know, and come in. You think about what all they done.

-Yeah.

-Yeah, first time I met Walt I was in the Sublett Gallery.

-And artists who never been here before, like Ali. Certain people was drawn to here. Some was tourists, you know, got money to spend and come see the latest roadside attraction. But I tend to think some was just called.

-What about Horace, or Ali, I guess I should say?

-What about him?

-They only one Ali.

-Yeah, only one Ali.

-I miss him man (yeah), I just tell you that much.

-Oh yeah, me too. You can't replace him man.

-No way. Ali was the man.

-Yeah, Ali the man.

-Yeah.

-He was a force man.

-I know it.

-He had big spirit man (yeah)(yeah). You just think about it. You couldn't hold him down.

-You couldn't really discourage him.

-No, he was like indefatigable.

-Right (yeah). Whatever that mean.

-You know, and he live without nothing. He get by fine. He figure it out and be okay. I 'member one time I told him, I say Ali I don't have to worry bout you bro. And Ali say, yeah man I tryin to quit worry bout you too. HA! (HA)(yeah). He funny man.

-Well when did he get to town?

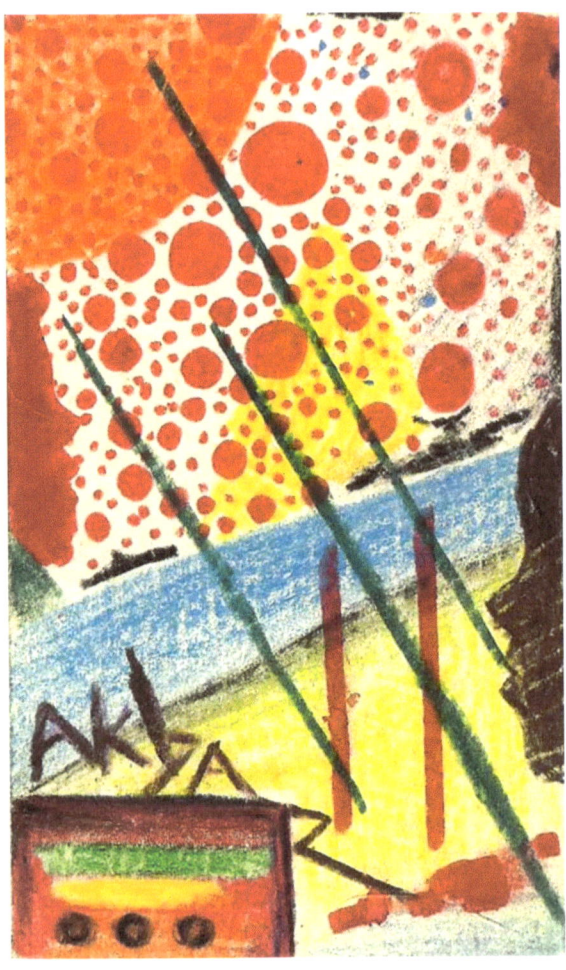

-I don't know. First time I seen him sometime round the end of the world fair.
-Yeah sometime there.
-Well he was at them first 200 East shows.
-Well that was the end of the fair.
-Yeah he went off at that big poetry reading thing they done.
-That was the first time for me, first time I seen him.
-He was down there at the gallery when we was fixin up for the show.
-I don't know.
-Well he come in there one afternoon when I first seen him.
-Yeah, I 'member that now.
-You know what I member? He signed his name on the register there.
-Oh yeah?
-They had the book there. So mighta already had the first show.
-I just remember he signed his name HORACE PITTMAN in a long smooth script you know. And I seen it while he was signin, I was standin there, and I said something like that's a mighty fine signature you got. And he say, yeah I want to be ready 'case I get famous, you know, he said something like that (right) (yeah). And he was kidding but he was serious too.
-Yeah.
-That sound about right. I don't think I know anyone who knew him or seen him much before then.
-Didn't they say he have a aunt who live here?
-I heard that, but I don't know.
-Yeah, I heard that, but I don't know.
-I never knew.

-*Where did Ali live?*

-Back then I don't know.
-Tell you the truth I always thought he lived on the street. I mean back then.
-I wasn't too sure at first cause he always just appeared. For a while there I know he stayed downtown some them old hotels other side of State Street down there. But some point 'course he move out off Sutherland to that apartment complex.
-Right.
-Yeah, room 606.
-I take him out there many a'time.
-Yeah me too.
-I been up to his room a few times, but usually I just drop him off or pick him up in the back there.
-Right, me too.
-And he live there for years.
-That become his place from then on, he stay there for years.
-That's where he died.

-*How exactly did he die?*

-Don't know. They found him up there.
-Some repairmen or someone (yeah), just come in there to check on something.
-He had a lot of physical ailments.
-Yeah.
-Mighta been a stroke. You know he had a stroke when he was in the army (yeah) after he was wounded.
-Someone said they thought it mighta been diabetes.
-Oh yeah? He have diabetes?
-Yeah, he had a lotta things wrong, I know that.

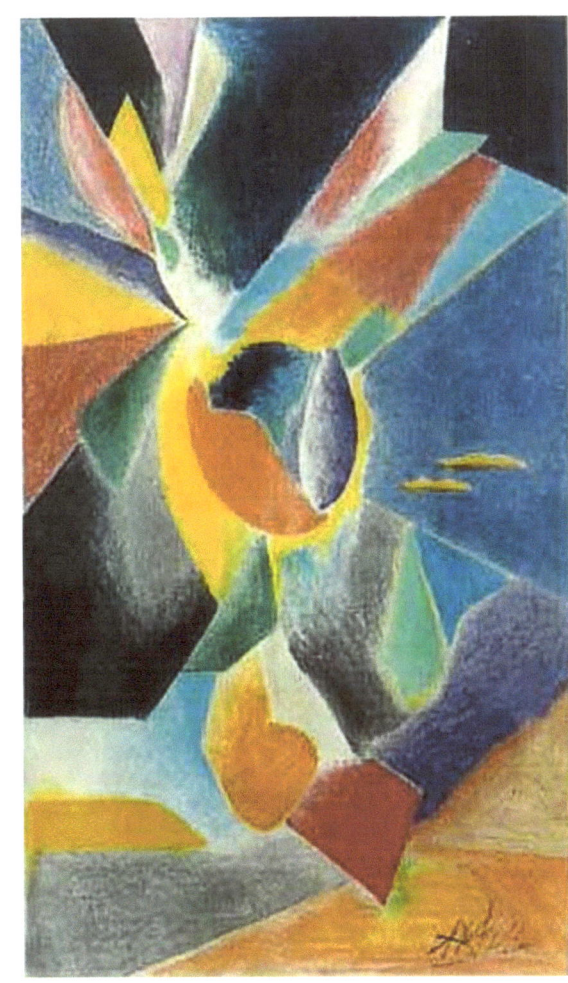

-Yeah he had slowed down. One the last times I seen him I took him up to Jefferson City to the VA up there for him to see a doctor, and get some of his papers and shit straight.
-Yeah?
-Yeah he was havin health problems alright.
-I know when he come by to see me there in the Fort got to where he holler up from the ground, you know, see if I'm there cause he don't wanta climb them outside stairs two floors if ain't no one home.
-That voice's still workin huh?
-Ha, yeah you know I hear him.

-I keep hearing about his voice. It must be some feature? Was he just loud or what was the deal?

-He could be loud alright.
-Yeah he had the power.
-But it wasn't like he loud all the time or nothing.
-No.
-Just at times.
-Yeah.
-Well, you know, he was a black adult male who would talk loud in a public place, like all a sudden make a proclamation like IF NOW IS THE HOUR THIS MUST BE THE PLACE! (yeah), and that's unusual enough for a lotta folks.
-Or at music shows sometimes he say GODT BLESS DE MUSICIANS! (yeah right) GODT BLESS DE MUSICIANS!
-I heard that.
-Yeah.
-Or in the middle of some art opening, you know, people be looking at the art and talking one 'nother and suddenly he go off THAT THAT IS IS THAT THAT IS, THAT THAT IS NOT IS NOT THAT THAT IS, THIS IS THAT THAT IS!
-Hah, yeah.
-Yeah, and you know the immediate impact of his voice is a physical thing man (yeah), you know, more than, you know, intellectual or communicative. Just the power and

abruptness of it hits you man (yeah) interruptin everthing else occurrin at the moment (right)(right), and with no cue and no prompt, right. It ain't somebody on a stage see, they no prior attention of it. So it's a physical thing you know (yeah right). It's a shock, the surprise and volume of it. If you close you might recoil like some bomb done gone off in the street (hah right). You know, at first. But then, you know, you find yourself considerin what it was the man just said (right). And is this guy touched? Or is this performance art? Or what the fuck, you know. And who is that man?
-Yeah it was a feature. He was a feature, like a walkin talkin poetry bomb.
-That's right.
-Yeah.

-Tell me more about his features. I mean, just the way he was and how it was with y'all at the time?

-Ah, Ali just fun man (yeah). He had more energy than most. He just childlike and fun, and physically he was very capable.
-He move like a cat man, Ali move like a cat, you know. He kinda short legged and he crouch and move his legs fast like that. He could get around.
-Yeah he had some physical prowess now (yeah man). 'Specially early on.
-I seen him drop down n'break dance with some kid there on The Porch one day.
-Oh yeah?
-I mean he put the moves on. It kinda surprised me (yeah). He had some juice.
-Oh yeah.
-He like jumpin in when someone gots something goin.
-He like stickin out now, he preferred it. He was okay with being the center of attention.
-Oh yeah.
-He could be the village idiot on purpose or anyway (yeah), you know what I mean? He enjoyed being a bit of the fool, (right), just like he like being the wise man sometime (yeah). He was both, and both was natural for him.
-Yeah, you know, Ali was a little older than most of us right (yeah). He been to war man (yeah). And though you never thought much too much, you know, he had that.
-Yeah.
-Part of his experience.

-Man, I always think of Ali like Bob Kaufman the poet, you know, only on these streets. You know what I'm saying? He like the one who's been everwhere and done everthing right, and done great work, but the cat who's a little crazy, or you don't know, right (right). You not sure what he knows (yeah). But you watch close (yeah), you keep an eye on him, right (right). He might speak in riddles and rhymes, you know. But you listen cause you be wonderin what's this riddle all about (right). You know?
-Kee zee op a jee zee oint?
-Yeah!
-HAH! Right.
-HAAA!
-Oh yeah man, he talk that carny talk.
-Right.
-Sure if somebody around he don't know.
-Yeah, he just say it in the flow you know.
-Yeah just see how it sound.
-Or he say it loud like it some song or some crazy thing you know (yeah), knowing the people won't know what he sayin but they just let it go, you know, like it must be something somebody understand right, hah and just let it go.
-Yeah.
-Right.
-Right.

-*What is it you're saying?*

-Oh he just carryin'on.
-He talkin that carny talk.

-*Carny talk?*

-Yeah, they just talkin like Ali useta talk sometime when he slide by and they people there he don't know, you know, don't know if it cool to talk around.

-*Yeah, but what'd he say?*

112

-He say, kee zee op a jee zee oint.

-*Kee zee op a jeez eeoint?*

-Sure man, I got a bone right here.

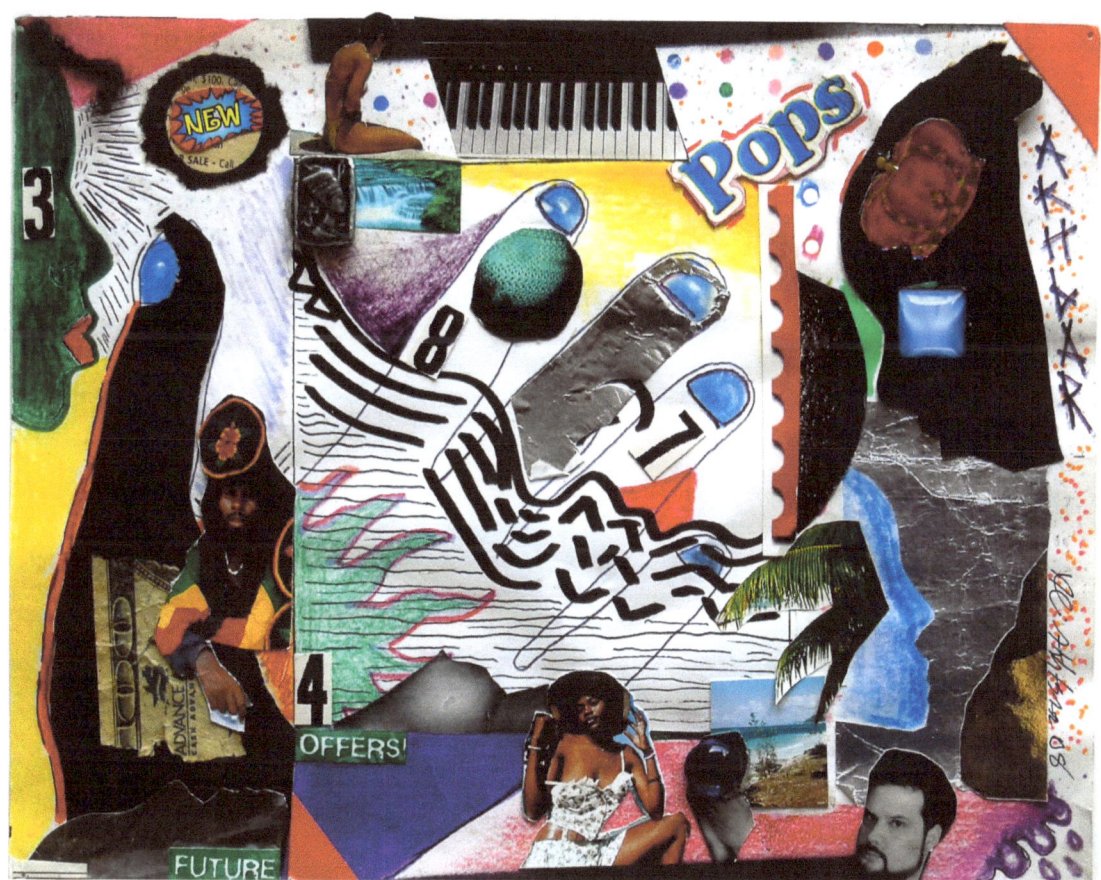

-Thing about Ali, he was unafraid you know (yeah), he would talk to toughs and
pimps, bouncers, cops, whoever he had to (yeah). He could be very disarming.
-Yeah, one night we was puttin up flyers for some show. You know, making the
rounds down through the Fort hitting all the usual spots and was down on

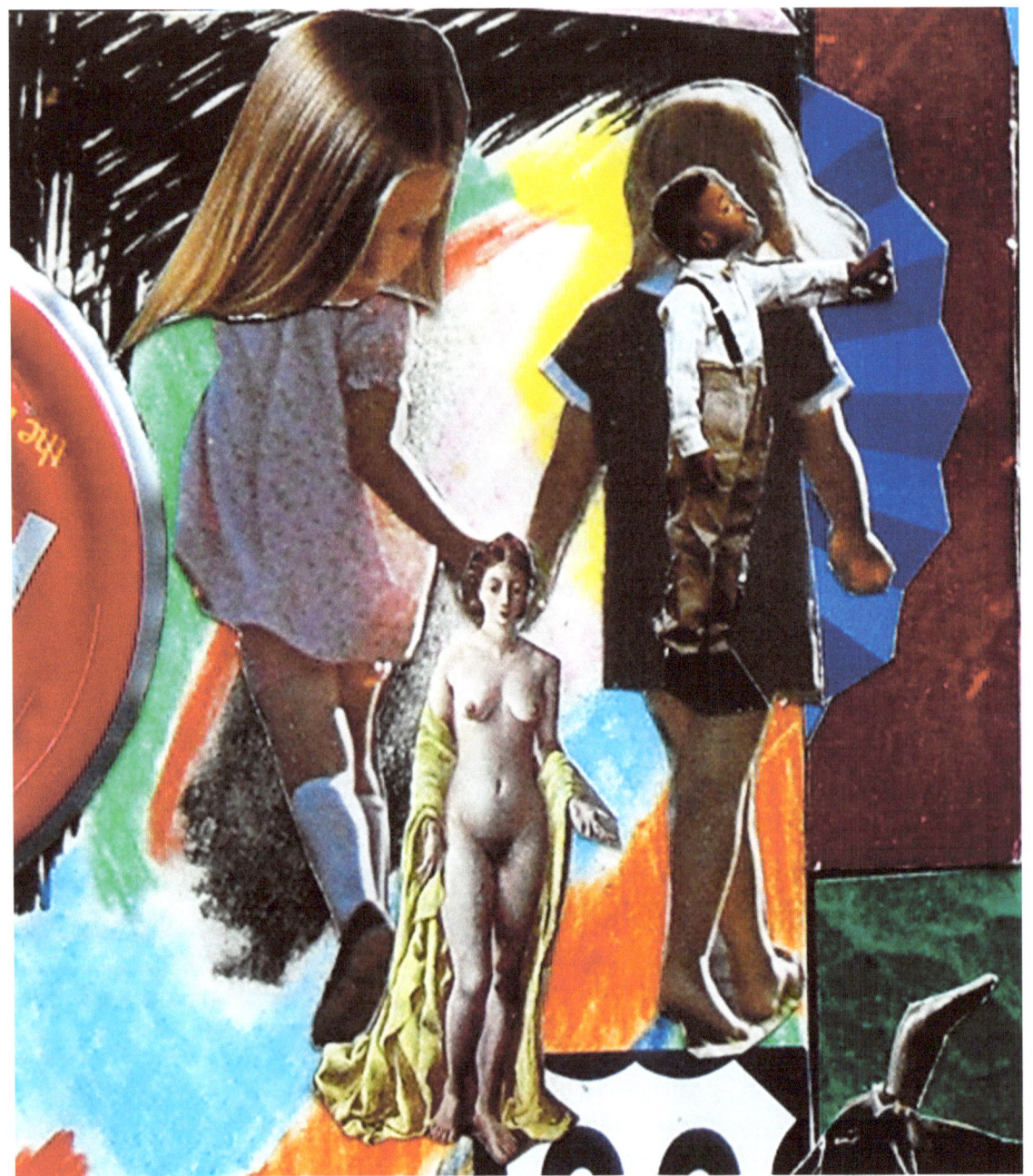

Cumberland, right. And was at that parking lot there in front the Krystal I believe it was, and while he hit a couple of poles there I lean back on some car, some bright red new model car just to rest a minute right. Well all a sudden two big black dudes was standin over my young ass with some serious intent in they faces. And they say YOU ON MY CAR ASSHOLE. Upon which I was quick to remove myself, only they left little room for me to be anywhere but on the car. Man I was amenable. But like a flash man Ali was over there talkin at them and they turned to hear him and he just engage them in such a way, you know, it was like they was hypnotized or something, and we just walk away.
-I know what you mean.
-Yeah man.
-Strictly amazing man how he do that.

-*Well, sound like there was a lot of street art. I heard about the Alley des Refuses and some of the art exhibits in houses and studios. This all starts to feel like some sort of art movement, 'least on a local level.*

-Well the whole world was local at that time.
-Yeah, the world had come to us, hah.
-Right. So it was like whatever you had goin artistically you could cast it in a worldly way, if you know what I mean. And you could cast the city in a worldly context. I mean, it always is, but you could feel it then.
-Yeah, we was speakin local but we was talkin to the world. Or speakin to the world and talkin local.
-Yeah, local man, he universal.
-It was a magical time in that way.
-And we was all bout carryin that forward on after the fair see, that newfound perspective, and not let that go.
-And street art, that just startin at the bottom and workin you way up. And that's what had to be done.
-Yeah.
-And you right, there was a common feeling and idea, you know, that have to do with art and the city. They was some history involved, a bit of civics if you think about it, but

we didn't call it no art movement.

-Yeah, but you artists, and you was moving.

-Oh yeah man, it was good. But like Eric de Red say one time, you give it a name and that's the beginning of the end.

-What's he mean by that?

-Hey, he just mean what he say.

-Okay.

-He mean soon as you give something a beginning it has an end too.

-Okay.

-Which is not to say it ain't worth doing. But it could mean harder you try to hold something the more it slip away too.

-But they gave a name right, after Horace's painting?

-Well, for a minute, you know, and that's only natural too. You see it happenin and some name come to you. Just depend on how you want to declare it. You know, like Glimpse of a Manifesto, right, *nameless but names appear*. They knew all that shit man.

-Okay. But it was a group of some kind? I mean, all these people working together right?

-Yeah some people working together, but no, weren't no group per say. Nobody joined nothing. Nobody paying no dues or nothing. Nobody telling nobody what to do.
-And everbody got they own take on all that, anyway.
-Yeah, but we felt like we was Dadaists right, like modern day do it youself artists (yeah)

116

CITY OF BRUSH FIRES. Origin of some, last outpost of others. Bermuda Triangle of the Appalachians. Caves beneath the river. Pagan art hanging off buildings. Abstract dispatches jamming up telephone poles. Dreams, like paintings on alley walls. Zurich 1916. The wailing of the primordial intellio modern. History may visit, but you can't go home again. There are no Meccas, only waiting lines. This is naked city.

AND THE SUN comes up, and the Spectre reappears like a barnacle on the hull of the thing. Some of the fires keep burning. I imagine writing a letter.

GLIMPSE OF A MANIFESTO. Notion of affirmation. Declaration of undoing. Idea of form. Nameless, but names appear. Like a glass bead game, ultimatum/infinitum. Wisdom of chance. Negative space focus. X factor deviled up through Finnegan. History being mother and lover to the artist, both having moved away. Ob-la-di Ob-la-dada. A new game of go with silly no rules.

(right). Hey, you a baseball player you know who Hank Aaron is, Mickey Mantle, Babe Ruth. If that the field you work in, you gonna know what happened before, you know, and how you fit in. That only natural. That the way you learn you art man.

-Yeah, you know, we was tryin to connect with the city and the artists come before us too, in our own way (yeah), not just say we breakin away.

-Which we was breakin away too.

-Ever bit a'that.

-Eric de Red directly connected through his dad to the KNOXVILLE SEVEN right, and them the ones who built the Art Department at UT, Buck Ewing them guys that got the A&A Building over there on campus. I mean those guys blaze a trail right. Early on they work outta little houses over there and drove all round the South having shows and introducing peoples to art. They got it going, and Eric de Red just a boy riding along with'em and checkin out ever show, and he seen it try to grow in Knoxville. And he know all them old guys and he know the artists between them generations too that come just before him, that a little older than him, you know. Maybe his dad teach some of them and he get to know them that way, but Eric de Red he always been there see. He born into it and he took it up.

-Yeah.

-Yeah, that right.

-We was trying to keep it coming, you know.

-Yeah, keep it coming.

-I mean in the big picture we was all way underground. Like Roger Smith say in that song, it's *a small town situation overlooking underground*. We was off the map right, but we was tryin to make a map. And 'cause a all that a lot of art was made by a lot of people. A lot a consciousness raised, you know what I mean, just by the creative community (yeah). People was havin to give of themselves, a lot a collaboration.

-But also people havin to drag they work out of they backroom and show it to the world, you know? That make a artist finish more work, you know, sign that name to it, and put it out in front of people.

-That's right.

-And then they move on to something new see, and quit tweakin on that other thing. See that just a natural part of the flow, you know, you got to SHOW.

-Yeah, it like breathing in and breathing out man, you gots to do both to be breathing.

-*Seems like an endless amount of exhibitions among all these artists. All these galleries popping up and group shows. Was there common characteristics of the art that held you together?*

-Not really. I mean, we was all in it together, and a lot of it was street art at first, but stylistically people was all over the place, you know, wherever they coming from.
-Yeah, see wasn't no one style like some art movement might have, we all cubists or abstract or pop art or whatever. Everbody just coming from where they coming.

-*What about Ali's art, who would you say was his influences?*

-Raushenberg.
-Robert Raushenberg.
-I say Romare Bearden. They much alike.
-Yeah, 'specially late, you know, when Ali working in collage more.
-But he was influenced by everbody and everthing, you know.
-Picasso, Matisse.
-Yeah.

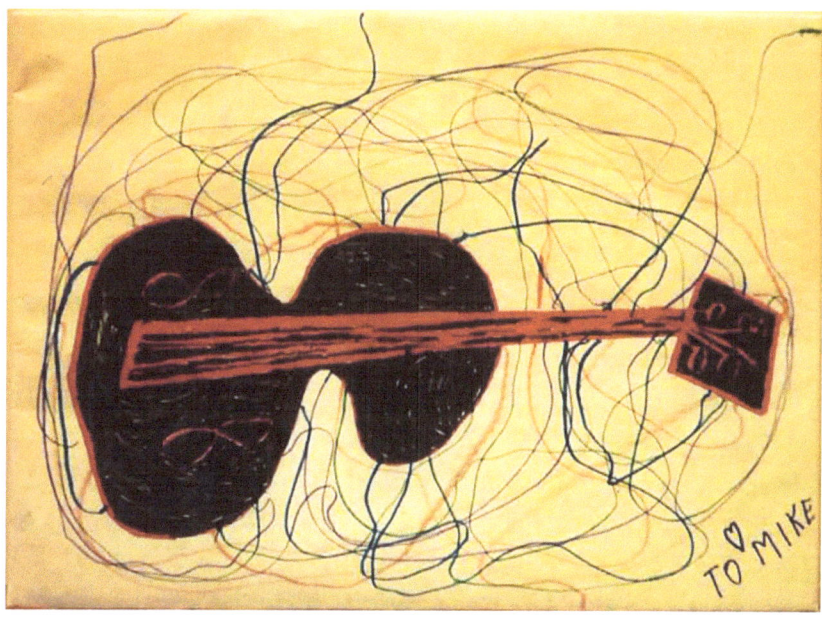

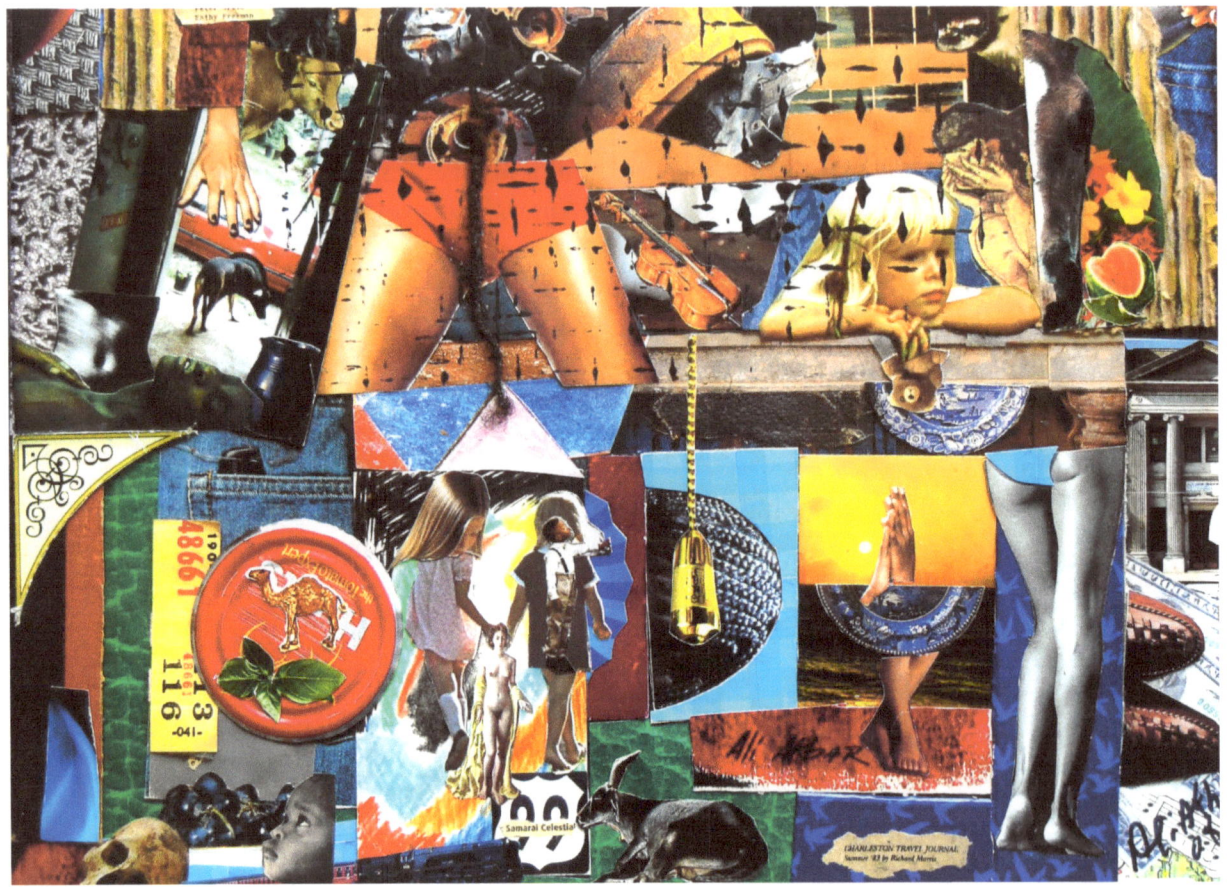

-Ali was always fascinated with the human figure, you know. Humanity and Love, those was his themes.

-Yeah and that true through all his changes.

-Yeah the human figure. The face, the head, the body.

-He sorta had a evolution of those themes, you know, through the years.

-Yeah, but he a poet too.

-Right.

-And those was his themes in poetry too.

-He wrote poetry down, but his big power was to SPEAK it.

-That's right. And that's the voice you askin bout before. See, the voice, that's the poet.

And what he say has the power of the word and the power of the sound go with it. And it's not always same thing. I mean, when the poet speaks that's when the crow caws, right, that's when the wind blows.

-That's when the volcano blows!

-That's the poetry. And if you can't hear it here, you prob'ly miss it there too.

-Yeah, you know Ali funny the way, I mean, sometime he speak it, and he say it so slow that the sound of the words just be a RRRROOOO of a sound and you let go whatever the word s'pose to be, you know, and just feel that sound (yeah), and then the spaces he take between the words where you waitin, he waitin, he pro'bly waitin on the next thing to come to him, and your mind have this extra time to sail off on it all, you know what I'm saying?

-Yeah.

-Yeah, the poet speaks.

-Thing bout Ali, you know, and his influences in art and living, he changin changin changin all the time.

-Yeah.

-That right.

-I mean, he the same man most ways (right), but he move through influences and trends and styles (yeah) or whatever you wanta call it (right) at a high velocity sometime.

-It's true, Ali on the move.

-I mean, when he in Rome he most definitely be doin some Romans (right about that) (yeah). You know what I mean?

-But hey, if he feel it, he good to go, good to flow.

-Yeah that the way Ali roll. I mean, he roll with the people, you know.

-Yeah.

-You know how you say something and he repeat it? Like you say something like *and that's why it is the way it is*. Then he say *Yeah, that's why it is the way it is*. You know what I'm saying? (yeah) He repeat what you say (yeah), and he be affirmin what you say, but he want to try it on for size coming outta his mouth too, right.

-Yeah.

-Right, I know what you mean.

-But he absorb everthing, He the man who go through the changes. He change and change some more.

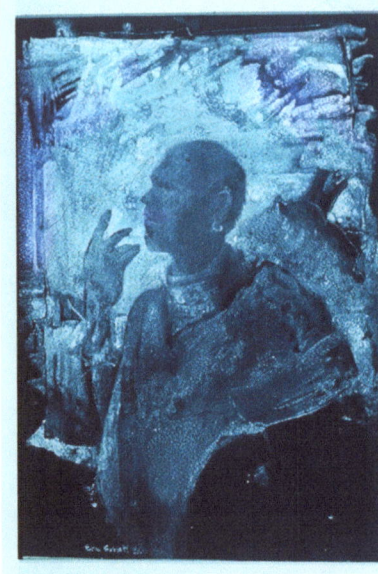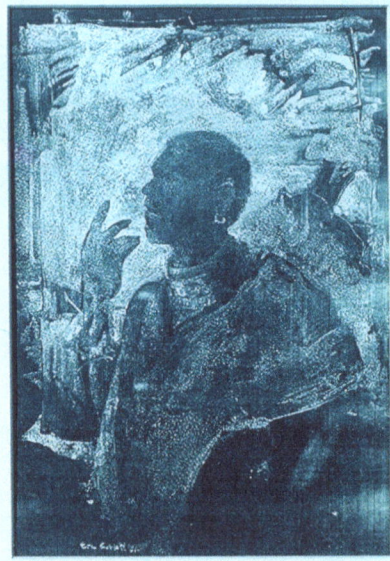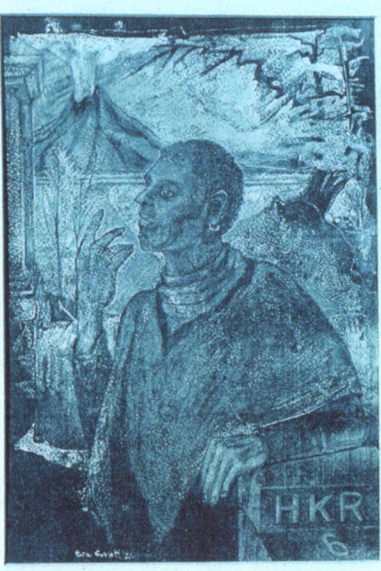

-You know, to tell the truth, Ali changin so much he make the rest of us look like we standin still, you know what I mean?
-Yeah, that's about the truth.
-He EVOLVE man while he livin here and you could see it day to day and year to year.
-That right.
-It's like the evolution of Ali.

-Where was that evolution going? I mean, he got religion right, he become Muslim and change his name. What can you say about that?

-Can't say nothing bout that. I mean, that's a personal thing to him man.
-Yeah. What can you say?
-That right, the Tao that can be spoken not the true Tao anyway.
-I heard that.
-It's a personal thing. And only person that can speak to it is that person, and they can't speak to it either.
-True enough.
-Yeah.

-But did it change him?

-Yeah it change him. He took on the dress and demeanor of a Muslim brother.
-Yeah, but that in itself wasn't no big jump for Ali. His appearance always changin (yeah), and something to check out.
-Right.
-He could be a quick change artist.
-Right.
-But he change his personal habits, you know, a more disciplined lifestyle, least for a while.
-Yeah, he quit drinking.
-And he studied and prayed, and took on a way of life.

i garbage my silly ego
trash my foolish pride

like cellophane
i am clean

-Physically I think he looked different, you know, not just the dress but I think maybe he lost certain anxieties and just the weight of living.
-Yeah, I say so.
-He found some joy, you know. And he was a man of joy, always, but he seemed to be lifted there for a while.

-Did it cause some falling out with any of you?

-Not me.
-Never have no fallin out.
-What can you say. My brother he a Muslim, and now my other brother is too. If he say he changin his name, that's okay with me. I mean, it gotta be don't it?

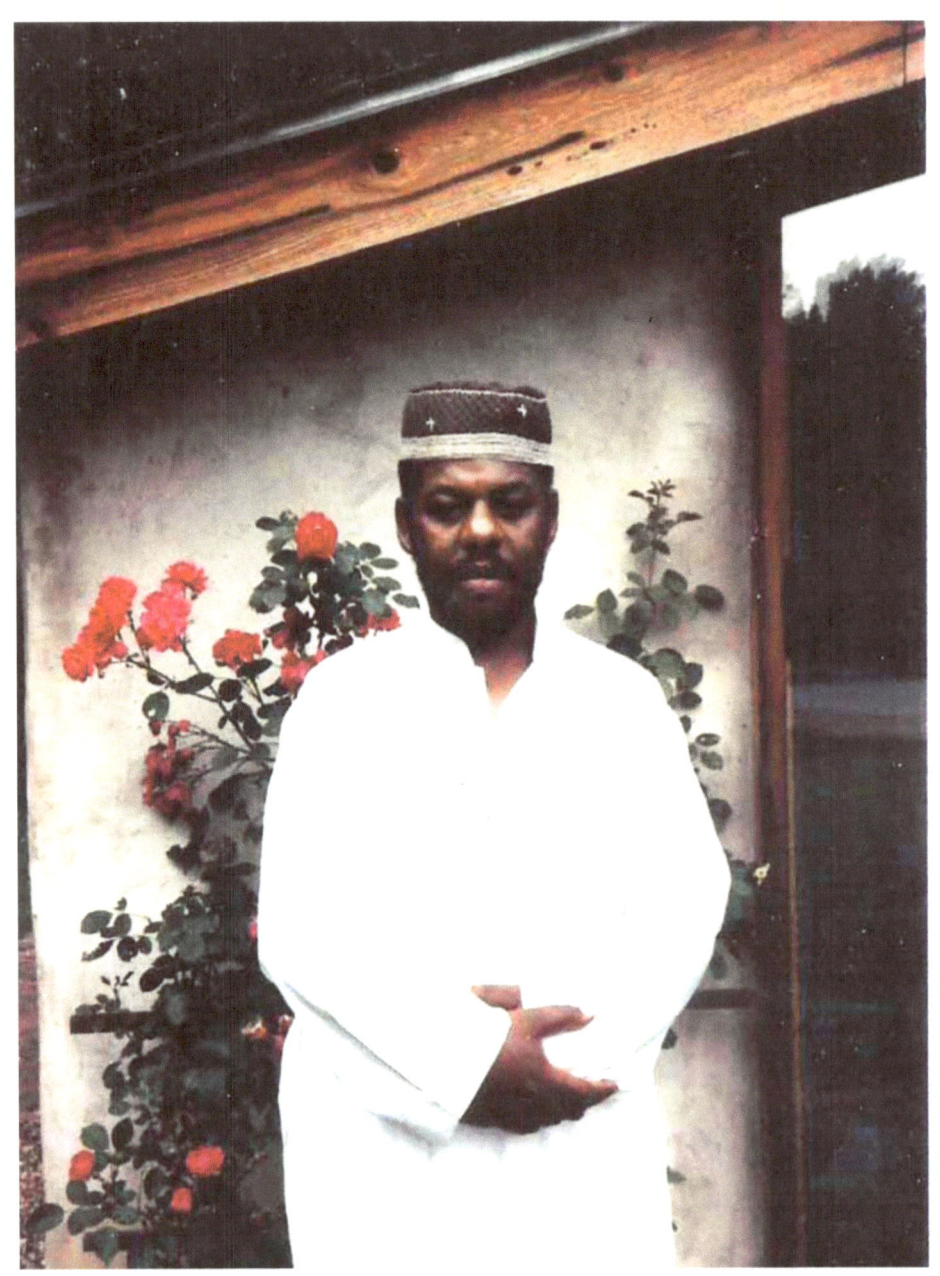

No longer
Am I swindled
By evasive sunrises

No more
Am I cheated
With fraudulent sunsets

And the moon
Deceives me no more
With the illusion of night

His jewel smile at dawn
Birds sing his praise
The sun appears
He laughs over the horizon

-I guess so.

-Well, it does. What you gonna do, say no way man I can't stand you be changin right in front of me, believin one thing or 'nother and changin your name. If you love somebody, if you a friend to somebody, you try to understand 'em, s'all I know.
-Ali was always in love with the world man, you know, and him getting religion just him fallin more in love. You can look at it like that.
-Yeah, he just gettin closer to the light right, to the mystery, to God, whatever you wanta call it, Allah.

Through Islam I've become
An excellent Christian
A perfect Jew
A pure Buddhist
And a pious Hindu
Though I am
An ignorant Muslim

-Okay. But what did he say?

- I don't know a thing he say. I mean, he say Praise be to Allah.
-Yeah, Praise be to Allah.
-He wasn't preachy if that what you mean.
-He was happy, I say that. He just open up even more, you know.
-Yeah, it's like he got his mind in the wonderment even more than usual, you know, he just there.
-Well, he talked about it to me. Told me some of what he learned from some them shakes and all. I couldn't speak to any of it, you know, what he said, or how it was connectin up for him, but it was. I mean, it just a way for him to worship right?

126

-Well I don't know. Or I don't know what it was for him?

-Well, I don't either, but then we can't can we? Religion like a language man. Them words have to fill with light, then you get some insight. Then you can SEE. And if they don't it just a dead language, mean nothing. It had meaning for Ali.
-Yeah.

The worst sin I committed in life
was to expect someone to understand me.

-I 'member one time I's going off about some little thing, you know, I think some leather bracelet this girl give me, you know, she put it on my wrist. And I say something to Ali like hey man put some good mojo on this thing so it don't come haunt me, you know. I was only half serious half jokin, but I was showin it to him and said that. And Ali he say, hey I don't do that no more, you know, just simple like that. But I know like he saying I don't play with the fates in some casual way or whatever. Or maybe he sayin more like I ain't some holy man who cast out yo demons, you know what I'm saying? He wasn't tryin leave no big impression, you know, and he only say it once, like hey I don't do that no more. But I realize it was cause of him being a Muslim. I mean, he wasn't makin a thing outta it, but it just showed me that he wasn't so casual bout things like that no more. And I 'member that.
-I always thought Ali musta come from good people, cause he was a good man. I mean, he had some mischief bout him, he could be a trickster. But he was not mean hearted (no). And he could be mysterious but he wouldn't lie you (that's right). I say he was goodhearted (yeah) and far as he ever was to me, very generous.
-Yeah, you gotta say that's true.
-But what I'm sayin, his family pro'bly give him some religion when he was young, you know, probably sweet Jesus and God, right. So he had the language already, even if Islam a different language. He had the language. See, it just have to speak to you, but you give it the meaning.

-I 'member when his momma died.

-Oh yeah?

-Yeah, he told me. I seen him downtown when he just got back from her funeral in South Carolina.

-Yeah? I don't remember.

-No I didn't know.

-It was a few years back there. Said he rode the bus over after he got word (oh man). Told me on the way that he got lost or something, you know, didn't know where he was.

-Really?

-Yeah, what about that? Man who know more bout the street and gettin round than anybody you ever meet, and got lost somewhere.

-Lost?

-Yeah, he said he was lost. Don't know if he lost his ticket, his bus went on or what happen. But he said he kinda broke down and was lost, said he cried in the street.

-Yeah?

-Yeah, said people helped him, different people helped him, and he got on over there.

-Ah man.

-Yeah, he cried on my shoulder when he tellin me.

-No, I hadn't heard that.

-It's like surrender man. And that's what religion is. It's like you fightin against something all you life tryin to stay on top a'that. And somehow it come to you that you can beat it better by surrenderin'. Somehow you can get on the other side of it that way, you know what I'm saying? I don't know, but it's like you got to surrender something you didn't never want to give up 'fore you can free youself enough to change (yeah). You know what I mean? That why they say *surrender*.

-Yeah.

-Well, that sound like a nice transaction, but usually my guess it a little more desperate than all that. Which I don't know bout Ali and how it was.

-Yeah, you right there. But hey, you can't live like he was living and not have some trouble with the authorities sometime.

-Yeah that right.

-He was like a free soul, you know, just layin it out there and givin it up everwhere he go. Lotta ways that was really his art, you know.

-Yeah I know, and he was spending some nights in the lock up for it.
-I know.
-They had his number.
-That for sure.
-He was spinning out here and there.
-That's right. That's true.
-I never seen it all get the best of him.
-Well, me neither, but had to wear him down some.
-Who was it with him that night in that hotel downtown they come in there and arrest him?
-I don't know, was that Brian?
-No, Brian was in the tank too when they brought him in. Who was it told us bout that? But somebody (yeah)? They come in there say, Are you Horace Pittman? Right? And he say, I am INCREDIBLE.
-HAA, yeah.
-Yeah I 'member that.
-They took him downtown, you know. And they was more nights of that than we know bout, you know?
-Was that the night he met Ron Williams?
-Oh man, mighta been. I don't know.

-*Who is Ron Williams?*

-Ron Williams a painter man, a landscape painter.
-Yeah, he a character been around a long time, right. And he crazy, or sometime he crazy.
-Oh man, Ron Williams he like one of the best painters you ever seen, right. Am I right?
-Oh yeah, he something else.
-He can paint man. He has a very special talent.
-That right.
-But he and Ali meetin in jail. Can you dig that? I mean just think bout that a minute.
-Talk about two of the wildest artists and wildest characters ever and there they are (yeah), meetin in Knoxville jail one night.

Love: this compulsive serial killer
Astray in my heart
Decapitated bodies clutter my life
Every idea of myself slaughtered

All the nowheres I've been in
The nothings I've been
The many anythings I was
For no reason why
Just to get by

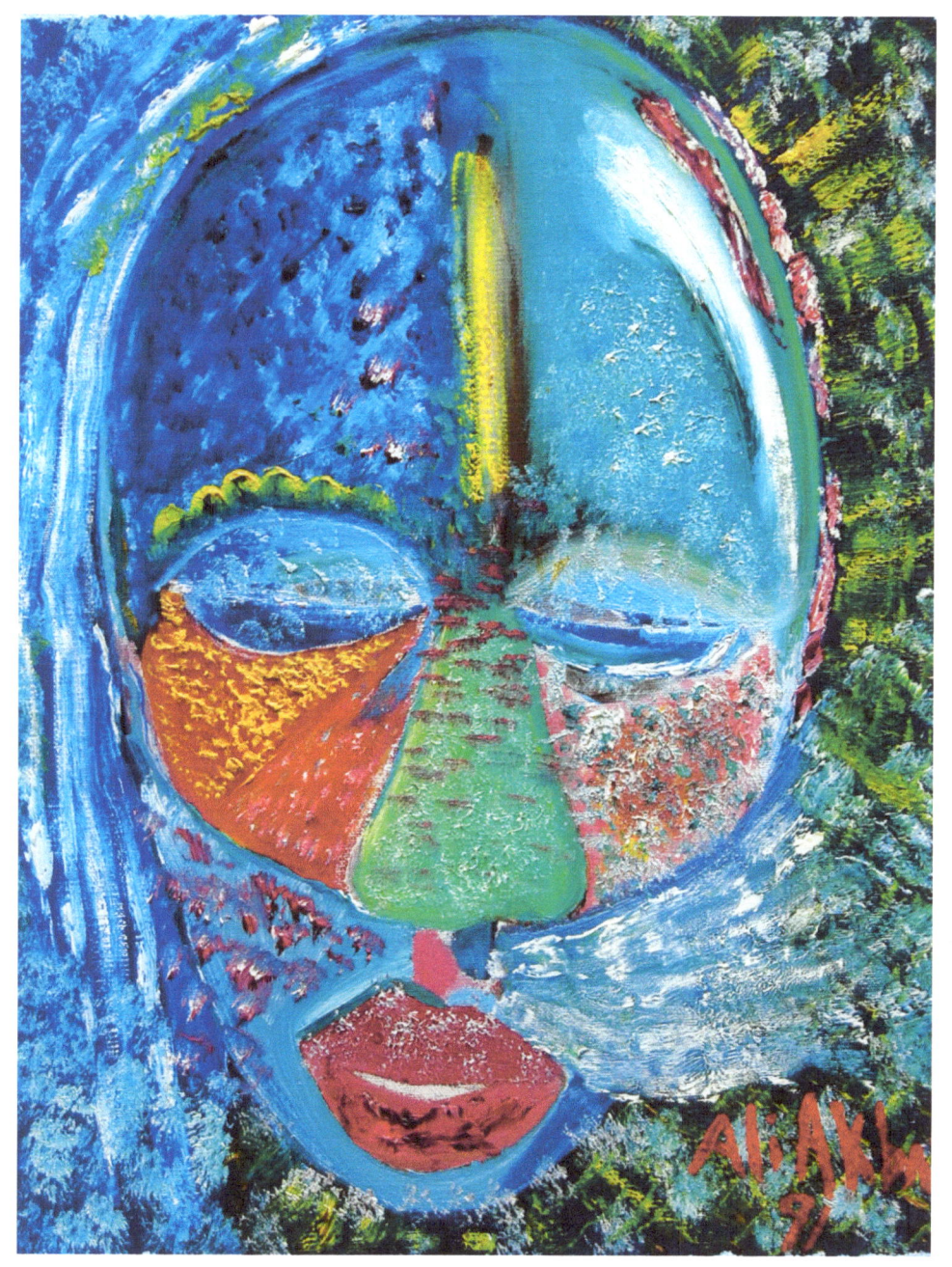

131

-Yeah.

-Well, if you think about it, Ali done been round the block as many time as you could count, right. And he done bumped up against ever wall they got. You know what I'm saying?

-Yeah, I know what you sayin. He could probably feel a change coming.

-There you go. I don't doubt it.

-Well, I don't either. I don't really know what was goin on with him. But I do know he had stretched himself out there far as he could. And then where you goin take it?

-Yeah where you goin take it?

-He probably come to a point. I mean, he stronger than us in that way, you know, it like he could go on forever, go up against whatever. I mean he did.

-Yeah he did.

-He musta found what was there for him to find. I'm just sayin.

-I hear you.

I felt this horrible feeling in my gut
Nauseated I wanted to throw up

-Man I'll just tell you, I don't care bout none them religions, you know. You can keep ever one of'em (yeah?). Wrap'em all up in a book and put'em in a special little library just for them, and then burn it down. Them religions just an excuse for somebody do something they shouldn't. Like I go knock on some stranger door and start botherin at him, or I go tell somebody how to act or dress, or I go over to your country and kill bunch of you cause you got some other religion than mine. Man, they ain't nothing but trouble.

-Yeah, you right, but they more to it than that. For lot a'people it's a way of life, you know, give'em some connection to the mystery and glory of life.

-Yeah, some people.

-I mean my gran'ma she had religion, and she was like the best person in my life. She talk about it if you want to, but she don't push it on no one else. And for her it was goodness and treatin people like she wantsa be treated.

132

-I hear you, and my grandmomma just like that too and so was my aunt Jo, but when the country go persecutin somebody or bombin somebody that call the almighty some other name, they don't speak out against it. They don't act like it's the devil's work we up to then.

-Well, I don't wanta talk bout no religion neither, always lead to nowhere and bad feelings. But I say this bout Ali. He was my brother, you know what I'm saying? I ain't just blowin smoke at choo cause you ax me to. He was my friend for 25 year or mo, you know, and we seen some shit together, hard time and good. And he never lied me once. He never cheated me a nothing see. How many peoples you say that about? And he on the down and out all the time. He have a code for the road. He was a man see, and he have a code for the road. So you ax me, I say that was his religion, cause that the way he do.

-Yeah.

-That right.

-And the rest you can talk bout til the cows come home or go to war whatever you think.

-That right.

-How did religion effect his art? Was it a productive time?

-That's a good question. It's not like something you can just add up, but for a while there he was tryin find his way with it, I think.

-Yeah, he had a thing there.

-I think he always creatin something, you know, even if he just takin notes.

-Yeah.

-But he had a thing with the graven image, I know that, to

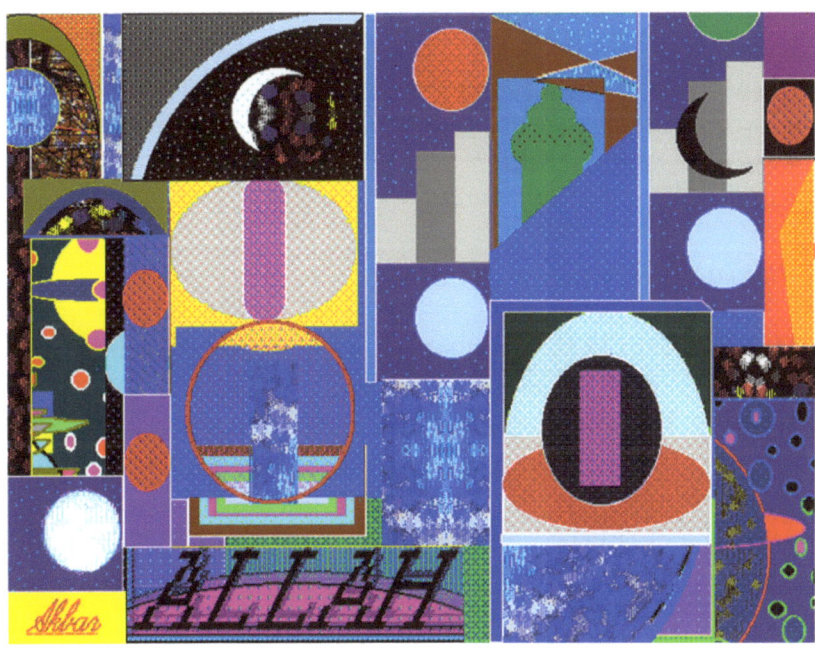

not create any images that was an insult to the scacred.

-Yeah. For a while there you look at what he workin on and they no images of people in it, you know.

-And that was a big change, cause Ali always paints the people, the human figure. And then he didn't there. He was tryin to find his way with the Islam.

-And for a while when he was at Pellissippi studyin computer graphics he not using certain images.

-Pellissippi?

-Pellissippi State, he studied there.

-Yeah, he graduated there some time the mid 90's.

-Studied computer draftin and design.

-He had a big exhibition there featured his paintings and poetry.

-Yeah, I remember, they made it part of Black History Month, which was interesting cause Ali never wanted to be considered a black artist as such, you know?

-Right.

-It wasn't no big deal to him (yeah), but he didn't want to be thrown in a group like that, you know, separating people cause a'ethnicity 'n' shit.

-Right.

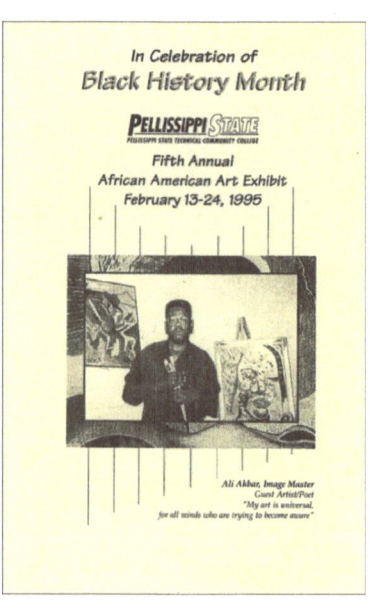

-Oh yeah?

-Yeah. Ali went back to school, wasn't no big deal for him. And I would say he become quite prolific. Some of his most notable work was around that time.

-Yeah, the Blues Man, the Sphinx.

-And that other one we always call the female Hendrix HAH!

-Yeah that one.

-And all that collage work was later I guess. But he was way back into the human figure by then.

In heaven
there's no race
In heaven
there's no gender
In heaven
there's no religion
as it is on earth

Rise unto

Leap
into the shoreless oceans
drowned in Eternity

From the void
within
comes the voice
of existence

All that exists
is Love

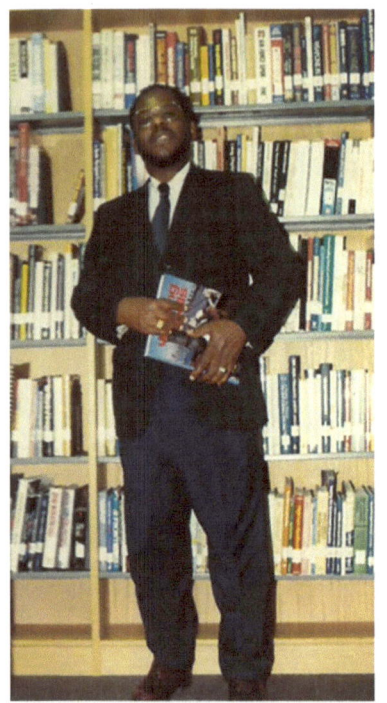
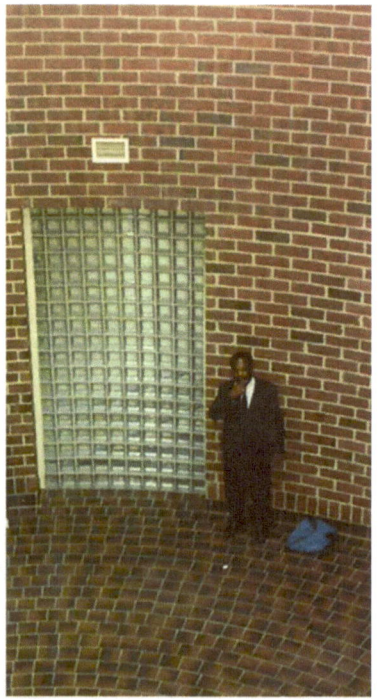
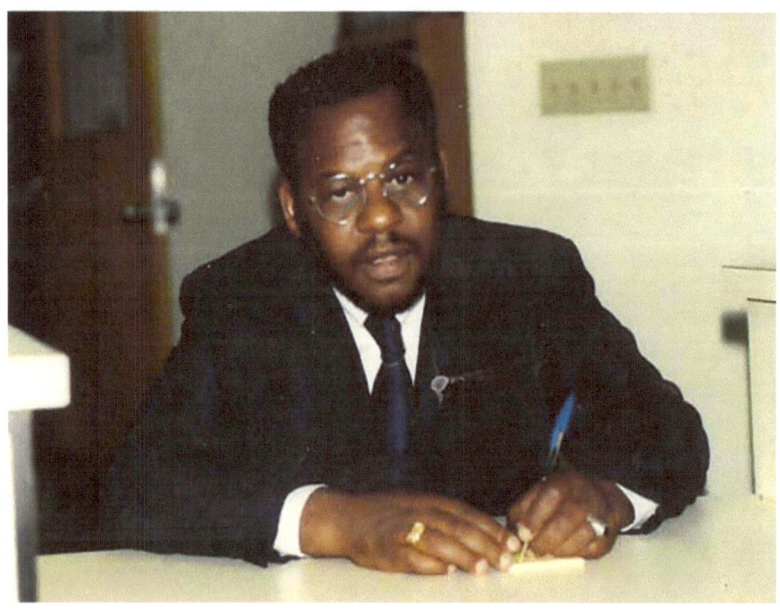

*Color has its own unique language, it's universal
and exists in the tradition of every culture.*

*Basically I paint color. Primarily for the sole
purpose of forging imagery beyond its usual
properties to create dialogue.*

*I love you in every color
with a love that paints
my world.*

My art is universal, for all minds who are trying to become aware.

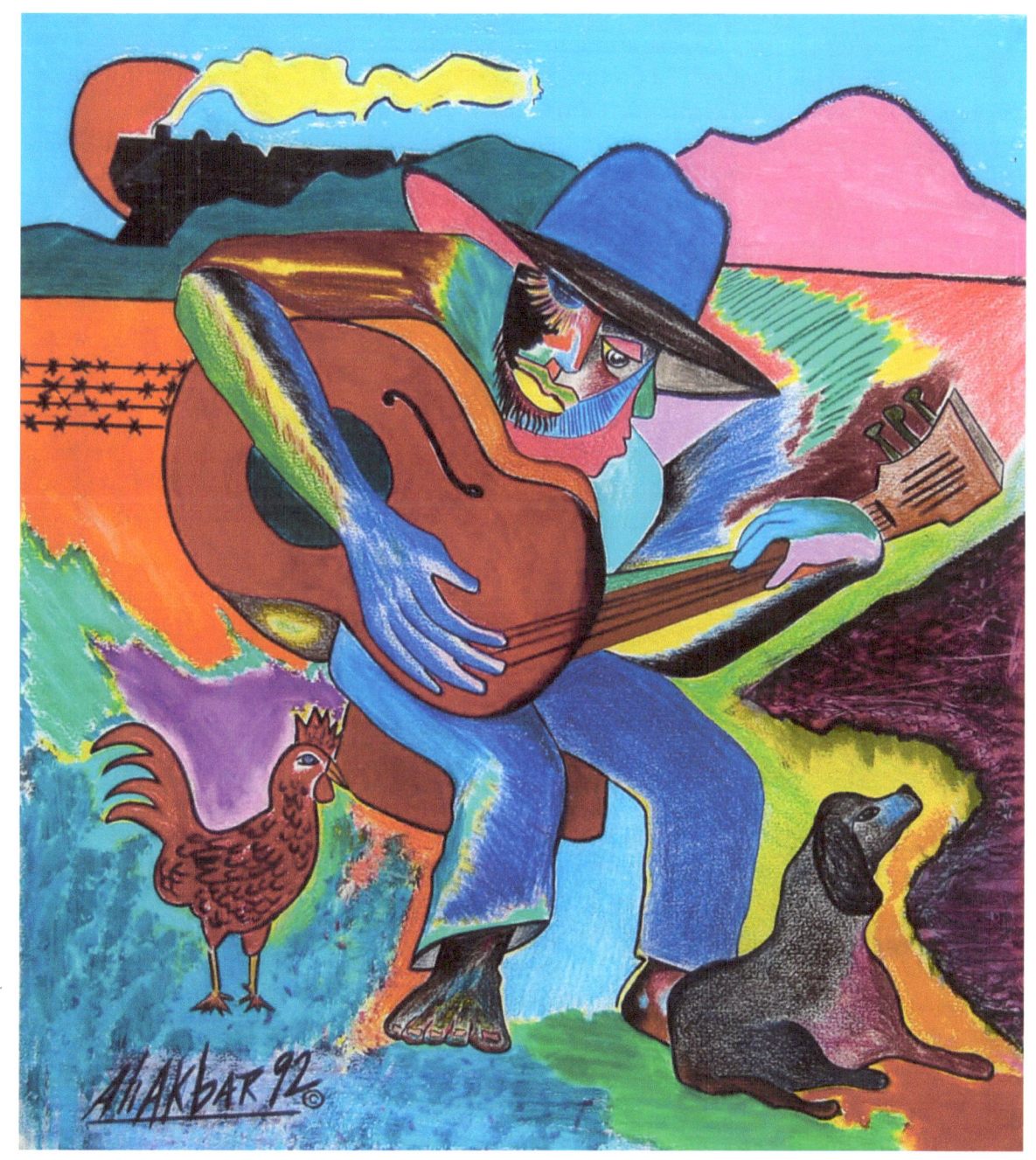

139

-Yeah see, that's where he made some kinda break with Islam some way.

-Well, he didn't break, he just moved on into Sufism.

-Right, but somewhere there he come back around in some ways.

-Well you ax me he was still evolvin (yeah), cause he kept studyin and he kept prayin but he returned to some of the joy of living. He was already past some of that anyway see. He just found what was his path, far as all that go.

-Yeah, he come back and joined the world a little bit. But that just make him able to give more love, you know.

-Yeah see, them Sufis they dance and go on, they whirling dervishes and shit.

-That right. And they poets too.

-Yeah like Rumi.

-They get to God by that path see. They ecstatic man.

The bartender serves the wine that existed before the grape

-And they cultures all over the world do that (right). Ali really a master of that (yeah), just to say it.

-Ha, I'd say.

-So he became a Sufi?

-If that the way you want to say it.

-Would he call it that?

-I don't know, he might.

-Yeah he might.

-I just know at some point there he found his place with it all.

-Yeah I think he got right with it in a better way.

140

-Hey and then you find him down with the music again (yeah), down to the jazz clubs and music clubs (yeah). He mighta been more reserved in public in many ways.
-Yeah he was more reserved.
-But when he get with the music, man, he still a gone daddy.
-Oh yeah.

In our mind we are not

Nor a mind we claim to possess

Senselessly we become delightfully

Mad in the Divine

-Ah man, he all bout the music. He go out ever night to rev up the bands man. And when he there you know it goin t'be a goodt night.
-Yeah, can't be no regular band in front of Ali man, cause he aint no regular audience.
-Yeah, you a band you better rise to the occasion. Or else he be the occasion.
-That's right. He love that sound. And he was there for it.
-He knew it was like a portal man, you know, a way to get through cause that was where he want to go. I say that.
-He wanted to get there. It was a ritual for him. You know what I'm saying?
-Yeah man, it was his ritual.
-And when he heard it.
-He heard it.
-Yeah.
-And he could get there, you know, break on through to the other side.
-He there man.
-He waitin on you baby.

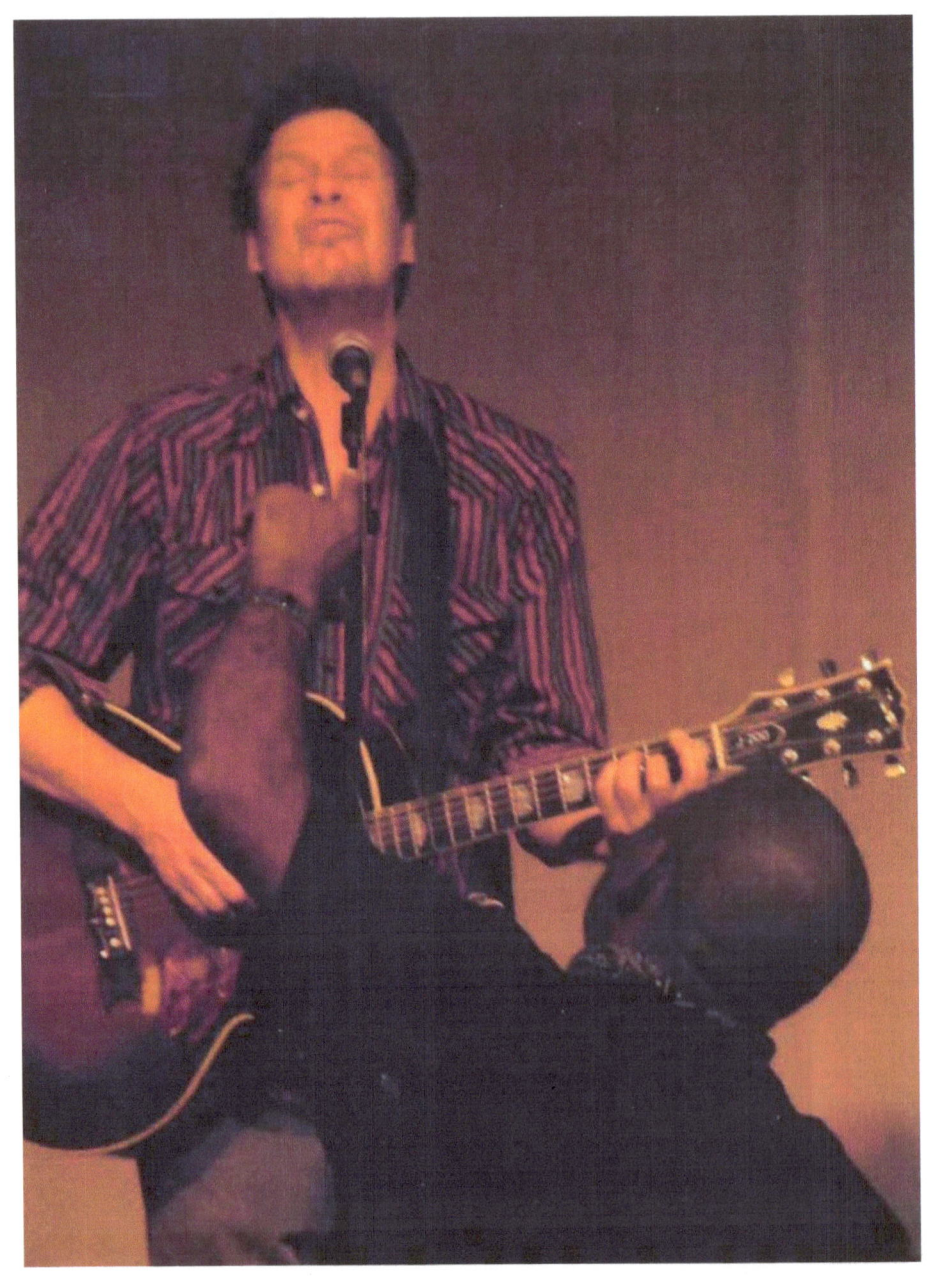

There's this music
This music that soaks into the bone
Penetrates the heart
And descends into the very
Depths of the soul
This music
It rises up in the spirit
With a rhythm that vibrates
Throughout the universe
In harmony with the orbit of galaxies
This music

-Who was that little boy, little white kid, that looked up to Ali so well and was hangin with him for a minute? And Ali took him down to the 4620 jazz club.

-Oh yeah, I 'member that.

-And the little boy underage and not s'pose to be in there less he with a parent (right). And the bouncer say he too young to go in, and Ali say he with me, I'll watch after him. Dude say, he have to be with a parent. And Ali said, he's my son. And dude look at him and say, Man how can he be yo son? And Ali say, Man how can God be God? Dude just look at Ali, and say go on in.

-Hah, how can God be God!

-Yeah.

-I just tell you man, there'a buzzin in my head, don't never go away, you know. It's always there even when I forget about it, like when things is loud and happenin. But when it get quiet, man that buzz get loud. It's always there. And I think for sure some them nights I hang out with Ali and listnin' them bands and dancin and gettin our joyful noise on, that pro'bly where I got that buzz (yeah). Just sayin.

-Yeah you got you buzz alright.

-Well, we sure did.

-I have to say, Ali was doing more work than what I knew.

-Yeah, I been seeing these pieces I didn't know he done. And then he wrote stuff I never seen.

-Thing was most his work just went, you know, out into the world. People buy stuff, trade stuff, but lotta his art he give away too.

-Or hang on a building somewhere.

-That was what his art was (yeah), it was for here and now.

-That true man, that where most of his creative energy go, just to makin it happen today (yeah). They's paintings and pieces of work people got, and I know they collected some more, but most I say long gone.

-Yeah, they like currency you know. And Peter Artin, you 'member he was making currency, making art money like dollar bills that they let him use at that corner market there in 4th & Gill. I 'member that.

-Yeah art just a way of life man, if you live by it (that's right). Most folk move on to more sensible shoes, if you know what I mean. But the way Ali live it, art is

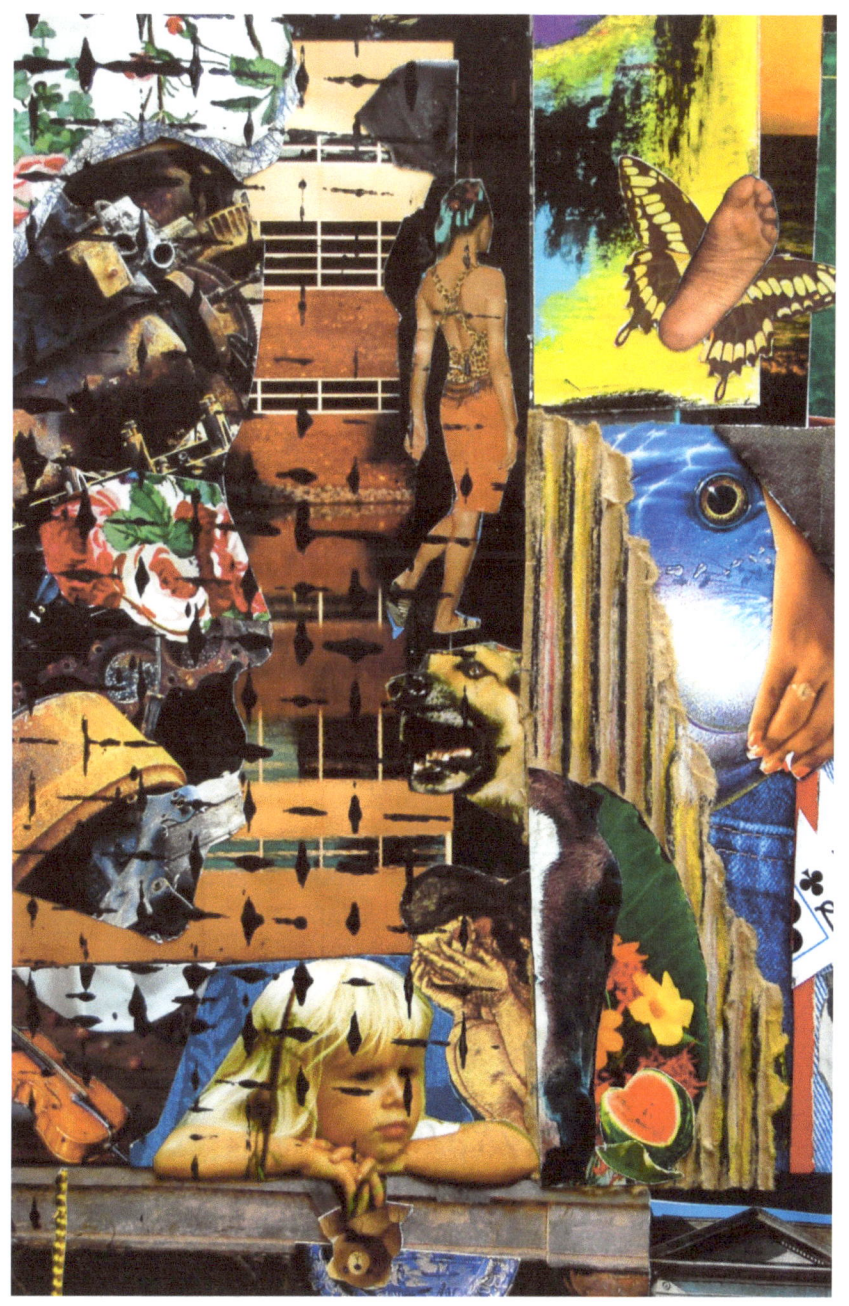

everthing. It's you bread and butter (yeah), you live and die by the brush, HA. And ever other medium and everthing else come into play (yeah) when it's a way of life, and that how Ali lived.

-It doesn't leave a lot behind to go at it that way. And there are some references but mainly just those who knew him.

-You have to be talkin to people cause that's the way it's done. Ain't no reference. So yeah, he belong to everbody and everbody tell you what you need to know.
-Yeah, you know how they say art is long, right, cause it outlive the artist. And that's right. But art for right now too.
-Yeah, in fact it is for now.
-That's what I'm saying, even if some of it lasts long, it's for now first. And you got to bring it now.
-Right. And that's what Ali did. He was here and now. His energy come into everthing no matter what he did.
-Far as that goes, that was his art, in the end, just him being here. You know what I mean?
-Oh Yeah.
-I mean, he always doing the work, works of art, but he was the art (yeah). And he always was that, but really he grew into it more and more.
-Yeah, that's right.
-You think about it, it true (yeah). He like a walkin talkin piece'a art, you know. He a little bit disturbin and you don't know what to think about it, but still you can't take you eyes off it. And he might question you and make you think bout things you ain't had to think bout.
-Yeah, all that.
-His life was always art.

-But why is he remembered.

-He not. He might be remembered for a minute, most folk are, but then we all be forgot in a minute too. That just the way it is.

-Not if you remembered longer.

-No man, it's all gone, all forgot. Ain't nothing longer than a minute. Somebody write something down maybe but it don't matter. Everthing forgot at some point, and that just what it is.

-He's not special?

-Oh yeah he special! But everbody special to someone, you know.

-Yeah, but he shines. And everybody knows him.

-He shines yes he do, but everbody shine or everbody got that shine in'em somewhere. Some folks just show it a little more, you know, to more people. But they just pointin up the fact that it in us all.
-But see, you come to see, it just matter what you doin here and now, you know, what you bringin to the mix now. Cause really, that's it.
-That's it.
-Just another soul that come and go. That's what we all are. Special as some people are, ain't none of us different that way.

-Well, then what would you say is special about Ali Akbar? Horace Pittman?

-His good spirit to live and love and relate, you know, have fun and be creative. He was a spark for all that. He was ready. And he was a good friend to the people he know. And really to people he don't know too.
-Yeah, what more can you be?
-You waiting on big awards man there ain't none. No honors, best of's, no fame and fortune. No golden rings daddyo. Just a lifetime lived man, no life story.
-Just one person's story s'all.
-That's right.

-Hey man, how many peoples in the world now, 8 billion give or take a few hundred million? Can you dig that? I mean can you wrap you little head round that. Who gonna manage all them peoples? Wait. Don't answer that. Just think for a minute bout all them peoples. Just think. That who we are (yeah). That who we are man. And what is it we doing?

-What you saying?

-Well, everbody walk around like they just themselves, you know, like they separate from everone else. But they ain't see. They are, but they ain't. We all just one person too.

-How you mean?

-I mean we all just one fungus spread over the rock, what I mean. We all like one person, one body.

-Okay.

-But see, as individuals we got to grow in the right direction so the whole body can be healthy.

-You too far out.

-No. I'm just saying everbody, and 'specially the artist, got to push it in the right direction whether the rest of the body know it or not.

-Yeah, the artist s'pose to help keep it in check.

-That's right, just like white blood cells or something, you know. In the bigger body they parts that got functions too. And if the individual cells don't know that, don't know what they s'pose to do, then the body in trouble.

-All the artist can do, or anyone else for that matter, is keep his own bad self in check and goin in a good direction.

-That right.

-But that help the whole see. Even if it just a small part of the whole, it help keep it healthy. And we forget, everbody forget, or don't think it worth it no more, you know, after it get hard and they don't make you no super star, right?

-Okay, that's what art do.

-Yeah, that what Ali did, all a'time, what I'm saying.

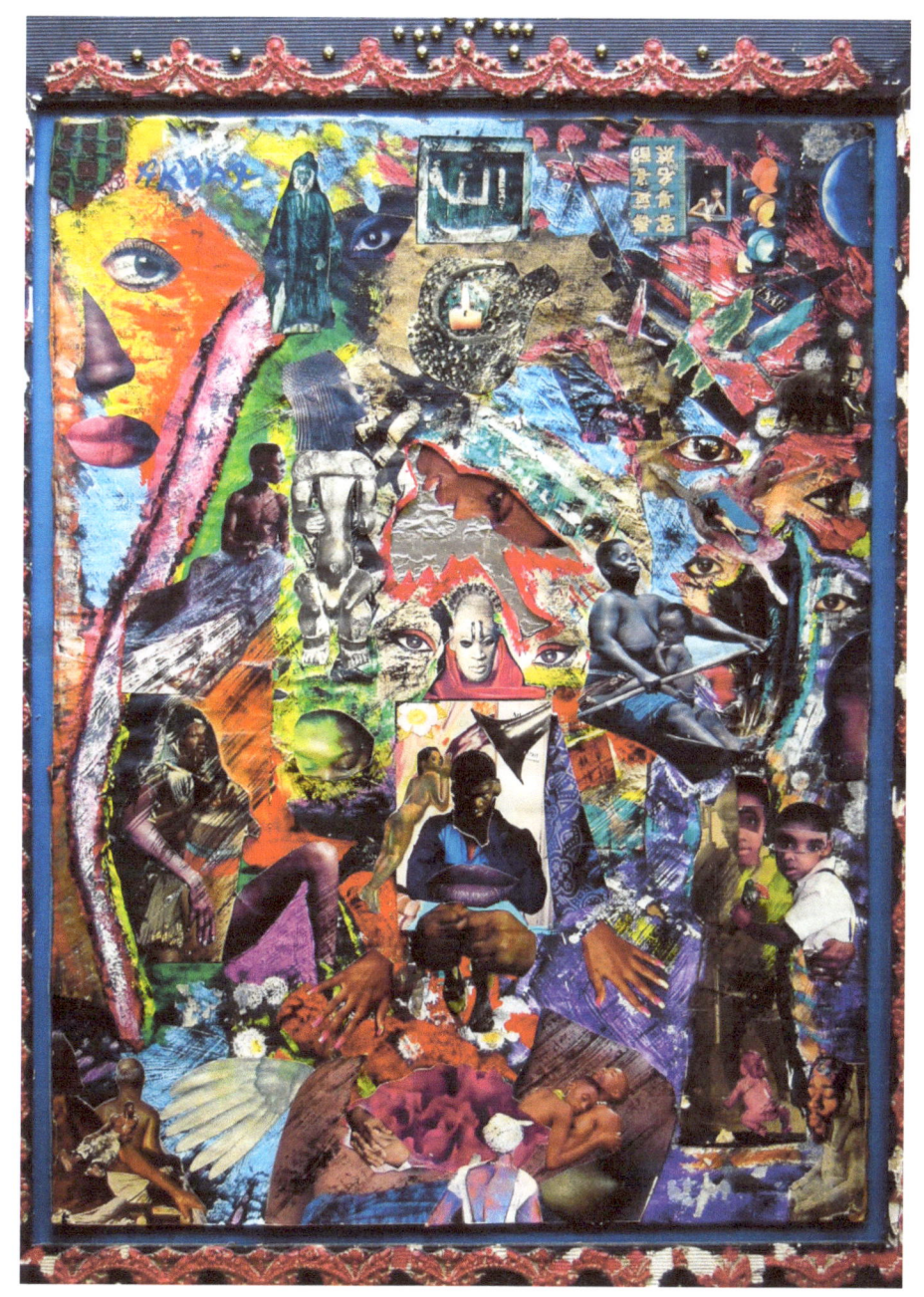

-What he live, 64-65 year? You do a lot in that time.

-Some people do.

-Yeah, he do a lot.

-Yeah.

-He touch a lot a people man, crossed many a path.

-You right about that.

-Absolutely.

-Everbody know Ali.

-Yeah, you know sometimes I think I see him. You know what I mean? HAA!

-Yeah man, I know 'xactly what you mean. I thought I saw him the other day.

-I see him out on the street like when I'm driving by, you know? I see someone who look just like him, least at first, you know. I think, there's Ali! Hot damn man. And then I know it can't be him. But for a moment there, you know what I'm saying?

-Yeah I do, I swear I had that happen too.

-Yeah man, you know, and sometimes I hear him talking.

-Yeah!

-You know?

-Yeah.

-I mean, his voice be talkin to me. He say, *hey man*. And I hear him tellin me stories like he toldt me way back some time.

-Yeah, I hear you.

-You know. And I remember shit when we was together, you know, doin something and he be tellin me something.

-Oh yeah man, I can hear him now.

-Yeah, we be hangin out all night right, and Ali and all us be talkin bout shit. I 'member he tellin us bout California and Vietnam and all kinda shit.

-Yeah. I must say, I 'member lotta stuff he toldt me one time or another when we was talkin.

-He was a smart man.

-Oh yeah.

-I mean, he knew some shit.

-Yeah.

-And he been a lotta places. And you know, he come from some good people.

150

-Yeah, I say so.

-'Cause he had love in him, you know, for people.

-Yeah.

-He might be confrontational.

-Oh yeah yeah, he could be.

-I mean, he was always callin people on shit.

-Right.

-And he might tell someone to leave him alone. Or get off the wrong foot with someone.

-But mainly he just want to have a good time. And he want other peoples to have a good time too.

-Yeah.

-That's right.

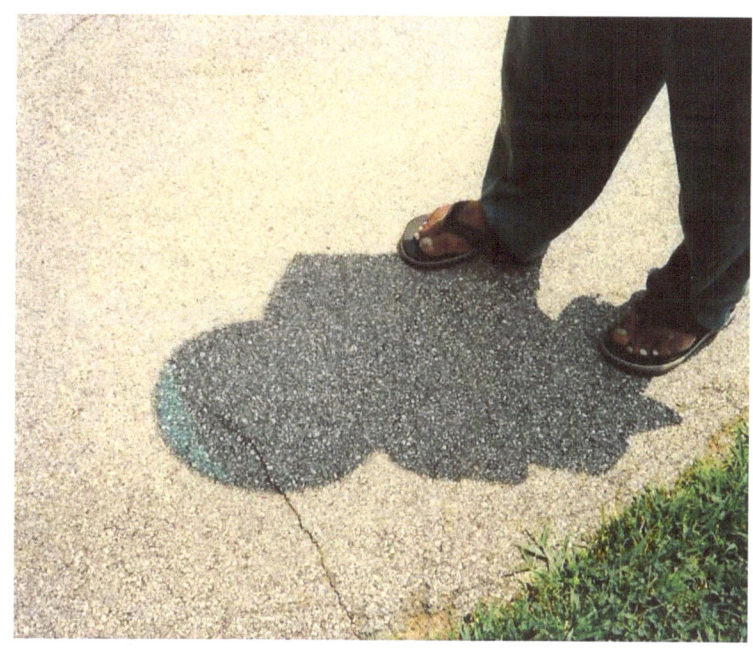

-But yeah he could be a contrarian, and he would not suffer fools. Older he got, you know, he didn't want the hassle. He like a old dog say get on wid you, leave me alone. Cause, you know, people wanta piece a'Ali (yeah), they wanta talk, they wanta jive, they wanta carry on, you know, talk to the man. And he would, but he could generally see where it was all comin from 'fore they even start.

-Right.

-Yeah.

-If he thought you was wastin his time or one'a his friend's time he would not let you do it, you know.

-Yeah.

-He would jump ahead, you know, and befuddle the speaker one way or nother.

-Lord, he crack me up sometime when he do that.

-Oh I know.

-Yeah, he was a man who worked on the intuitive (amen), I mean he had a sense'a what be happenin at any moment.

-That right.

-Ali would put his body in front them, you know, and talk at them and push them away. I mean, when he thought somebody was messin with a friend for no good reason, I mean, just jive ass'in and wasted they time, with his body and his voice he would put a stop to it.

-Oh man, you killin me.

-Yeah man, I can just see it.

-It like he can see the future there, you know, he can watch the film 'fore it happen and know what somebody up to (yeah) and he just intervene.

-Oh man, you killin me.

-Hah, I have seen that go down.

-Yeah, even when he slowed down he was up for that. He was up for a lively conversation.

-Yeah, we had a lotta good talks just hangin at the bar.

-You know one of the last times I saw him at the Branch he was upstairs singing with a little band had Tim Lee and Phil Pollard and some others playin (yeah?). And man I'd never heard him sing like that. You know, it was laid back and kinda bluesy. I mean, he was crooning. I believe he was makin it up, but that little thrown together band was groovin with him.

-Somenody was tellin me 'bout that. Yeah, and that was near the end.

-So how does this play out?

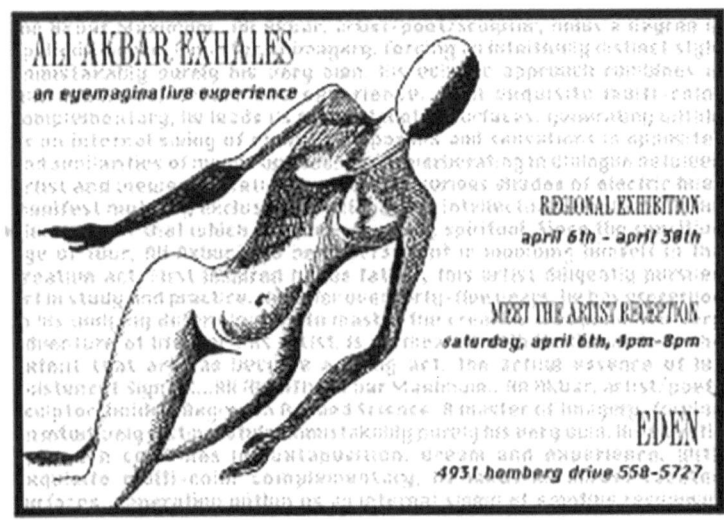

-What you mean?

-What were the last years, the last days, did he keep doing shows?

-He did a few shows I was aware of, like the solo show at Eden Gallery. And they was a big group show they done, that Good Ole Boys. And turns out he was workin on more art than we knew. All them collages was new to me, you know. He was

152

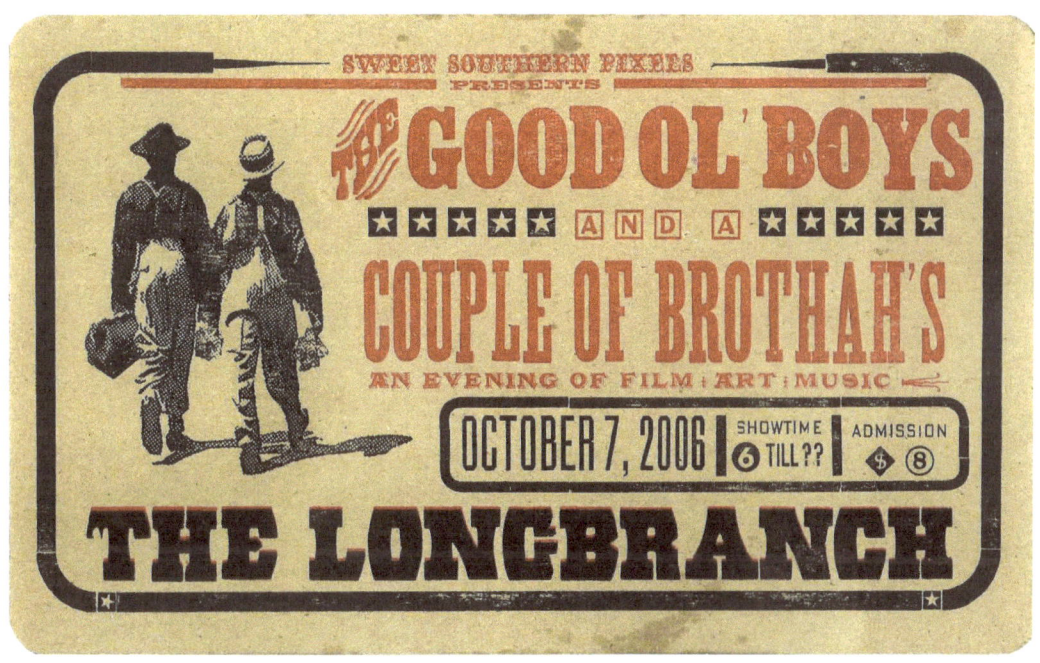

mixin his painting with that and gettin into some new stuff.

-Yeah. And he was always promotin certain bands and artists just by bein at shows.

-Yeah.

-That's where you see him last couple years.

-It was his spirit man, his spirit (yeah). He always bringin it, and that was his fine art.

-Yeah, the spirit love him and he love the spirit.

-Well, them last days, he knew he was goin, better than we did.

-Yeah.

-He never said nothing bout it.

-No.

-Not to me.

-I mean, I know he slowed down. But hey, we all slowin down. I didn't think, you know.

-Nah man, a surprise to me.

-Ah man, I hated to hear it.

-Yeah.

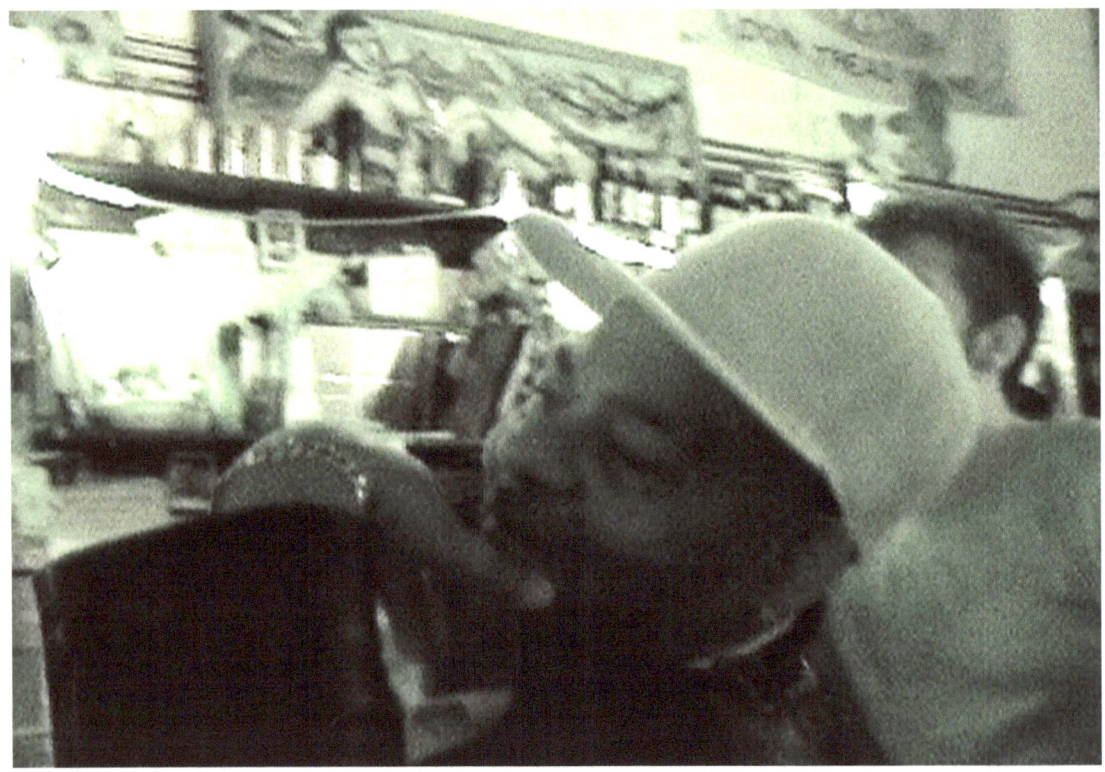

-Last place I seen him was at that Mexico City Blues thing they done.
-Was he there?
-Yeah at the Pilot Light.
-I didn't see him I don't think.
-Well, he was just at the bar there, he wasn't up none, wasn't dancing or nothing.
-They was a picture of that, I seen it.
-Yeah?
-Yeah, he was there. Them things was always crazy, you know, they done'em three four times.
-Right.
-They got readers and players and they go off on all them sounds, you know.
-Yeah, he want to check that out.
-Yeah that the last time I seen old Ali, if I ain't mistaken.

-I guess last time I seen him was down at the Branch.

-Yeah me too, pro'bly.

-He come in regular.

-Well he catch that last bus there cross the street.

-Yeah, he hang out have a few beers til that bus come and take him on out to Sutherland. That where I always see him in the last days, you know.

-Yeah me too.

-You know he walk in the Branch and let out that big whoop.

-Yeah big open mouth AHHOOOOOOOOOOOOOO!!

-Yeah, and everbody join in on that. HA, then everthing go back to normal and we all hang out and talk.

-Man, I love hangin out with him. It was always good, it felt like home man.

-I love that juke box they had down there.

-Yeah man, they gots cool tunes there. We always have a good time.

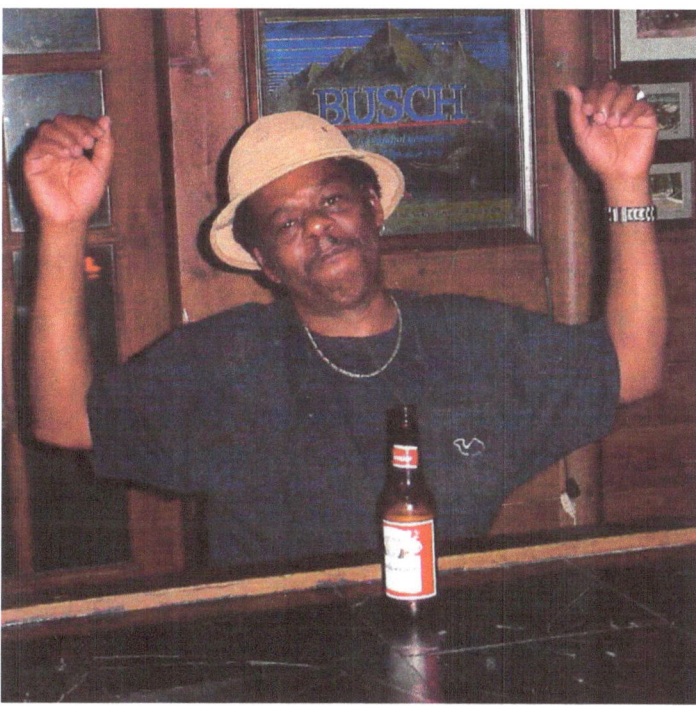

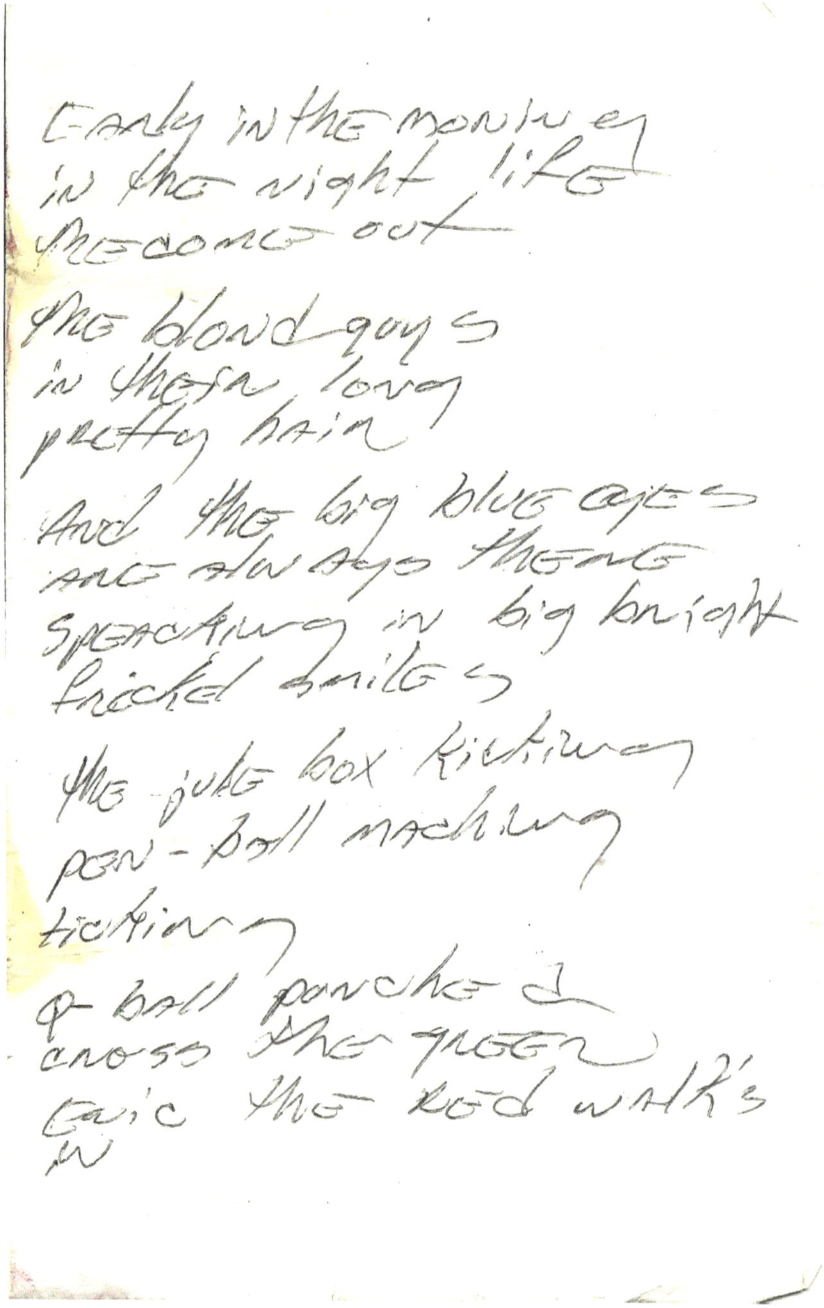

Early in the morning
in the night life
they come out

the blond guys
in there long
pretty hair

And the big blue eyes
are always there
speaking in big bright
tricked smiles

The juke box kicking
pin-ball machine
ticking

& ball punched
across the green
cue the red walk's
in

Early in the morning
In the night life
We come out

The blond guys
In their long
Pretty hair
And the big blue eyes
Are always there
Speaking in big bright
Freckled smiles

The juke box kicking
Pin-ball machine
Ticking
Q-ball punched
Across the green
Eric the Red walks
In

-You know Ali and Bill McGowan went up to DC there them last days.

-Yeah to see Herbie.

-Right, and Bill wrote all that down, you know. Story 'bout them being up there, and a bunch of other stories on Ali. I think he call it the ALI FILES.

-Oh yeah?

-Yeah, and that was his last big trip man, you know, going to Washington DC, going to the capital. Check it out man. Ali in the nation's capital. Man you gots to know that's a deal. And the peoples of the world see him there right, they get a load a him man, and anybody who see him know they seeing somebody (right). And the thing is Ali on his last leg man. You know what I'm saying?

-Yeah, that was near the end.

-He movin in the shadows man, he know his time comin. And it only make him more alive man, make him more alive with all the peoples. And Bill man he tellin me all 'bout that trip. He wrote it down. He say Ali greet everbody on the street that he passes, EVERBODY, and everbody know he alive.

-Know he more alive than they are.

-And they love him. Yeah, even though they might not know they do HA! I mean SOME people know, but even the ones who don't, they know something. They know they just seen someone who alive and livin it man.

-Oh yeah.

-And that was his last big trip out.

-Yeah.

-It's like Ali will now come to the capital.

-Yeah.

-Like here he is, and welcome him in.

-Yeah.

-Like they be givin somebody awards at the Kennedy Center, right?

-Right.

-But here Ali is on the street with the peoples and talkin to everone he meet, everone who go by (yeah), all the peoples, and he is the *Artiste*.

-Yeah, he de man.

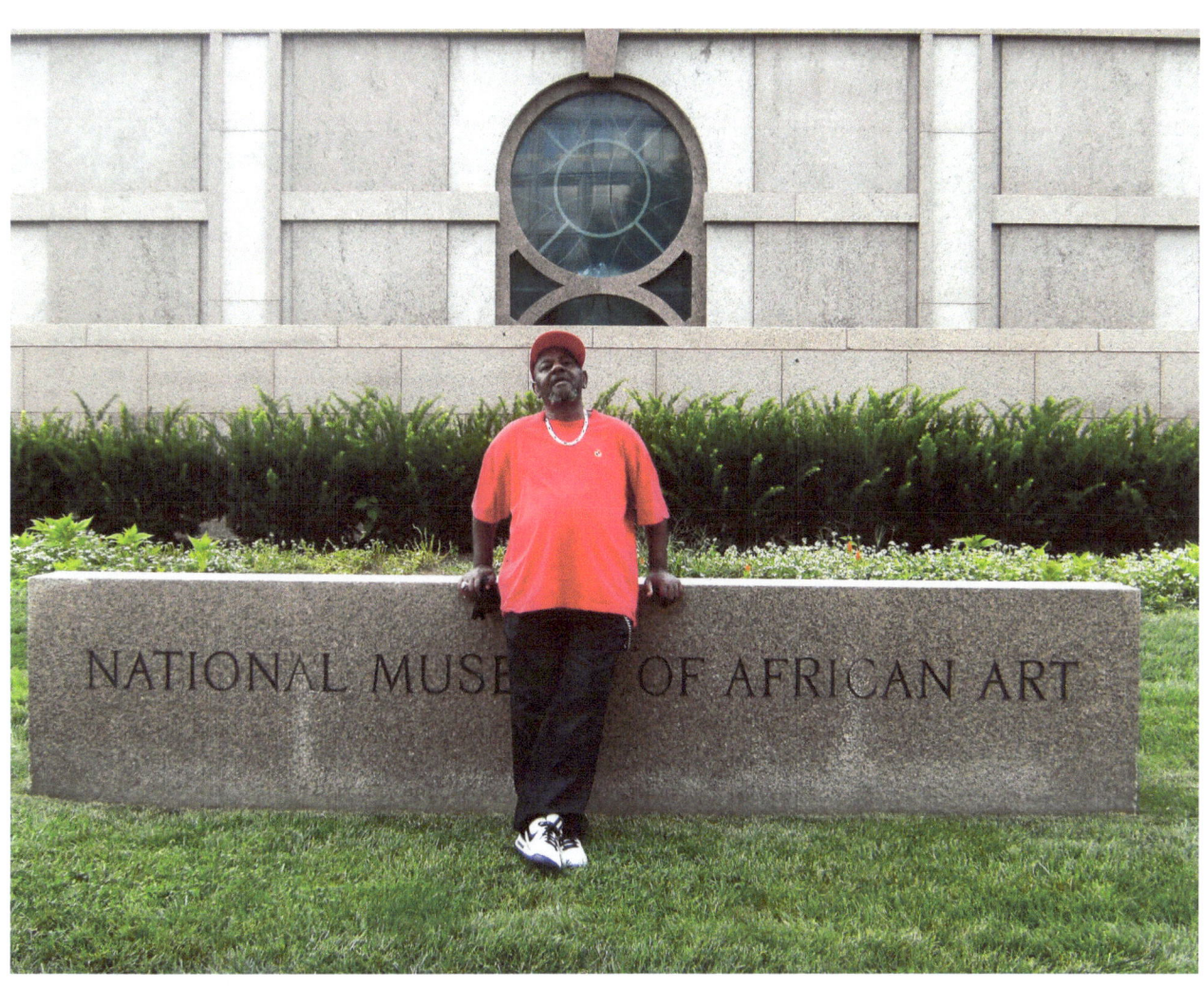

we all me dyeing
but i am not dyeing
to death
just cause
you know nowhere else
once taking that last
breath

Ah me man, I tired.
Y'all go on ahead.
Go on now, I catch up wid ya.
Yeah. In a minute.
I just gonna lay back here
In my crib take it easy.
Yeah. But I got my eye on you,
Yeah I do.
Y'all go on now.
Be cool. Be cool.
Hey don't let none them git ya down now.
They gots nothing on you,
And you know that.
Yeah, you know that.
I be with you,
I be with you.
Peace be upon you.
Just gonna rest a while see.
Oh yeah.

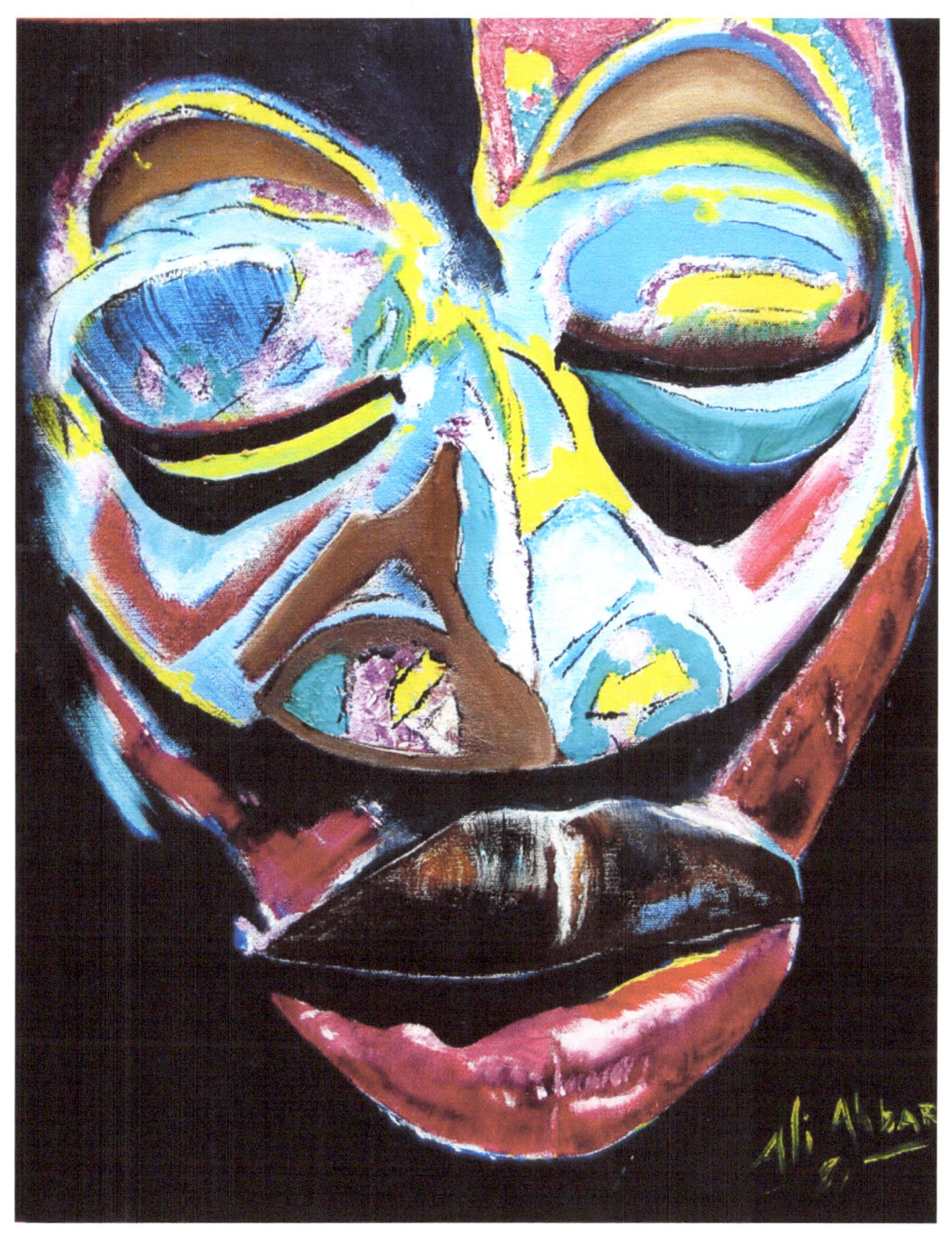

163

Ali Akbar
525 Renford Dr.
Apt. 606-A
Knoxville, TN 37919

Peacefully surrendering

In my loneliness
I surrender to peace
Where I recline happily
Resting in the nest
of my solitude

Where my worries abandon me
Where my worries take wings
Fly

I am an excited bride
Anxiously awaiting to be wedded
In union with the groom
I await death

Love crying in my tears
Love bleeding in my veins
Love undressing my heart
and no trace of me remains

GRAPHIC INDEX

Most of the art of Ali Akbar, a.k.a. Horace Pittman, has been lost to time, sold, traded, or given away. A certain amount of his art was 'street art' or 'guerrilla art', which he posted or hung in various places in the city and was destroyed or taken by people. What has been collected of his art often is without titles or dates, and in some cases where the work exists for us only in photograph or video reproductions, we can't be certain of all the mediums. Ali Akbar did title his work, and he worked in various mediums of drawing, painting, sculpture, installation, poetry, and performance. This index gives what information we have on the art as well as the photographs presented. The images are listed according to the page numbers where they occur.

Page 29 – Photograph of Ali Akbar. Photographer and date unknown.

Page 31 – Rhythm & Blues (no date), by Ali Akbar. Paint, colored pencil, crayon, possible application of materials into the paint.

Page 32 – No titles or dates, by Ali Akbar. Two charcoal pencil drawings.

Page 33 – No title or date, by Ali Akbar. Charcoal pencil drawing.

Page 34 – Woman Form (no date), by Ali Akbar. Paint with possible cut up canvas.

Page 36,37 – Photograph, photographer and date unknown.

Page 38- Photograph of Ali Akbar. Photographer and date unknown.

Page 40,41 – No title or date, by Ali Akbar. Detail #2 from African Collage. Cut up paper with paint applied and markers.

Page 42 – No title or date, by Ali Akbar. Detail #3 from African Collage. Cut up paper with paint applied and markers.

Page 44 – Photograph of Ali Akbar. Photographer and date unknown.

Page 45 – "What type person am I" lines by Ali Akbar, from his notebooks.

Page 47 – No title or date, by Ali Akbar. Paint, colored pencil, crayon.

Page 48 – "Before the gods took flight" poem by Ali Akbar, originally published in the Hard Knoxville Review #5, 1984.

Page 49 – Photograph of Ali Akbar. Photographer and date unknown.

Page 50,51 – Photographs from the first 200 East exhibition on Halloween night 1982, photographer unknown.

Page 52 – Poster by 200 East for the 2nd 200 East exhibition, Nov.-Dec., 1982.

Page 53 – Photograph of Ali Akbar. Photographer and date unknown.

Pages 54, 55 – Covers for the Hard Knoxville Review, issues #2-5, 1982-1984.

Page 56 – "The Walking Man," graphite drawing by Eric Sublett, with the Hard Knoxville Review logo by R.B. Morris. A poster announcing the music and poetry reading at 200 East gallery on Nov. 20, 1982.

Page 59 – "Black starrs" poem from Ali Akbar's notebooks.

Page 60 – Drawing by Roger Smith from the inside cover of Hard Knoxville Review #4, The Acts Man issue.

Pages 62, 64, 65 - Photographs by Don Tritt of Ali Akbar from the Alley des Refuses (Knoxville, TN), circa 1983.

Page 67 – Poteau des Refuses by Eric Sublett, from the 200 East exhibition Nov.-Dec. 1982.

Page 68 – Poster for the Glorious Gorilla Gala by Ali Akbar, May of 1983.

Page 70 – Poster by Eric Sublett for the art and performance event at The Place, June 22, 1983.

Page 71 – Poster by R.B. Morris for the art and performance event at The Place, June 22, 1983.

Page 72 – Jazz Muse (2008), by Ali Akbar. Paint, chalk, colored pencil, crayon.

Page 74 – "I rip off the days" poem by Ali Akbar from his notebooks. Photograph of Ali with his artwork in the Alley des Refuses circa 1983 with the Hard Knoxville Review #4 (1983) posted as well. Photographer unknown.

Page 75 – "Between zero and one" poem by Ali Akbar from his notebooks. No title or date, by Ali Akbar. Paint

Page 76 – Photograph of Peter Artin and Ali Akbar, circa mid 1980's. Photographer unknown.

Page 77 – Two paintings from the Alley des Refuses, circa 1983. On left, Guerrilla Artist by Peter Artin. Paint and marker. On right, no title, by Ali Akbar. Paint.

Page 79 – No title or date, by Ali Akbar. Charcoal pencil drawing.

Page 80 – "Neither are oceans divorced" poem by Ali Akbar from his notebooks.

Page 81 – Two paintings from an Alley des Refuses show circa 1983. On left, Dreams of Matisse by Ali Akbar. Paint. On right, a variation of The Enthusiasts by Ali Akbar. Paint.

Page 82 – Photograph of Ali Akbar with an unidentified woman, circa 1983. Photographer, Don Tritt.

Page 85 – Photograph of the Sublett Gallery by Eric Sublett, circa 1984.

Page 86 – Photograph of the Sublett Gallery by Eric Sublett, circa 1984.

Page 89 – Three photographs of the World's Fair Park crew taking down the 12' fence in front of the Artists Colony, circa 1986. Photographer, Eric Sublett.

Page 91 – Photograph of the Sublett Gallery by Eric Sublett, circa 1984.

Page 92 – No title or date, by Ali Akbar. Detail #4 from African Collage. Cut up paper, paint and markers.

Page 95 –Poster for Knoxragous event at the Bijou Theater in Knoxville, February 1992, by Kathi Freeman.

Page 96 – Photograph of Ali Akbar by Owen Weston, date unknown.

Page 98 – No title or date, by Ali Akbar. Found object, steel sculpture.

Page 99 – Four photographs of Ali Akbar (no date). Photographer, Birgitta Barth.

Page 100 – No title or date, by Ali Akbar. Sculpture of a musical instrument with a diagram for construction from his notebooks. Photographer, Bill McGowan.

Page 101 – No title or date. Detail of the sculpture from page 91. Photographer, Bill McGowan.

Page 105 - Photograph of Ali Akbar playing a kalimba, next to him Jerry Freeman playing a crosscut saw, and other artists on the world's fair park grounds with the U.S. Pavillion in the background. Photographer Eric Sublett.

Page 108 – No title or date, by Ali Akbar. Colored pencil drawing.

Page 109 – Geometric (no date), by Ali Akbar. Colored pencil drawing.

Page 113 – No title (2008), by Ali Akbar. For this book Collage 2. Cut up paper, colored pencil and marker or paint.

Page 114 – No title (2008), by Ali Akbar. Detail #1 of Collage 3. Cut up paper, paint and markers.

Page 117 – Inside page of Hard Knoxville Review #5 (1984), poem by R.B. Morris.

Page 119 – To Mike (no date), by Ali Akbar. Chalk or colored pencil.

Page 120 – No title (2008), by Ali Akbar. Detail #2 from Collage 3.

Page 122 – Triptych by Eric Sublett (1983), a portrait of Ali Akbar. Far left, a water color wash with Ali Akbar as model. The center and far right are zerox art of the original worked back into by the artist with pencil. The far right was used as the cover for Hard Knoxville Review #6 (1984).

Page 123 – "I garbage my silly ego" poem by Ali Akbar, from his notebooks.

Page 124 – Photograph of Ali Akbar. Photographer and date unknown.

Page 125 – "No longer" poem by Ali Akbar, from his notebooks.

Page 126 – "Through Islam I've become" poem by Ali Akbar, from his notebooks.

Page 127 – "The worst sin I committed in life" poem by Ali Akbar, from his notebooks.

Page 130 – "Love: this compulsive serial killer" poem by Ali Akbar, from his notebooks.

Page 131 – No title (1991), by Ali Akbar. Paint.

Page 132 – "I felt this horrible feeling in my gut" lines by Ali Akbar, from his notebooks.

Page 133 – ALLAH, by Ali Akbar (early to mid 1990's at Pellissippi State). Computer generated art and design.

Page 134 – Brochure cover for the Ali Akbar, Image Master exhibition at Pellissippi State, In Celebration of Black History Month, February 13-24, 1995.

Page 135 – "In heaven" poem by Ali Akbar, from his notebooks.

Page 136 – Three photographs of Ali Akbar while at Pellissippi State. Photographer unknown.

Page 137 – "Color has its own unique language, it's universal", three statements on 'color' by Ali Akbar, from his notebooks.

Page 138 – "My art is universal for all minds who are trying" statement from the Ali Akbar, Image Master exhibition at Pellissippi State, 1995.

Page 139 – Blues Man (1992), by Ali Akbar. Paint, colored pencil or chalk.

Page 140 – "The bartender serves the wine" lines by Ali Akbar, from his notebooks.

Page 141 – "In our minds we are not" lines by Ali Akbar, from his notebooks.

Page 142 – Photograph of Ali Akbar w/R.B. Morris performing at the Laurel Theater, by Ric Brooks, date unknown.

Page 143 – "This music" lines by Ali Akbar, from his notebooks.

Page 145 – No title (2008), by Ali Akbar. Detail #3 from Collage 3.

Page 149 – African Collage (circa 2008-09), by Ali Akbar. Cut paper, paint and markers.

Page 151 – Photograph of Ali Akbar and shadow (no date). Photographer, Birgitta Barth.

Page 152 – Poster for ALI AKBAR EXHALES exhibition at Eden gallery in Knoxville, April 6-30, circa 1997-99.

Page 153 – Poster for The Good Ol' Boys group exhibition at the Longbranch Saloon, Oct 7, 2006.

Page 154 – Still shot of Ali Akbar from a film taken at the Mexico City Blues music and spoken-word performance at the Pilot Light in Knoxville, 2009. Filmmaker, Eric Sublett. Note: The painting above the bar is by Steven Pogue. It also hung above the bar at the Snakesnatch Lodge on Market Square in Knoxville.

Page 155 – Photograph of Ali Akbar at the Longbranch Saloon by Josh Fodor, 2009.

Page 156 – The piece of paper which was folded to carry in his pocket, with the "Early in the morning" lines by Ali Akbar, circa 2008-2009.

Page 157 – "Early in the morning" lines by Ali Akbar, from a piece of paper found in his notebooks, circa 2008-2009.

Page 159 – Photograph of Ali Akbar at the National Museum of African Art in Washington, DC, 2009. Photographer, Bill McGowan.

Page 161 – "We all are dyeing" lines by Ali Akbar, from his notebooks.

Page 163 – No title or date, by Ali Akbar. Paint.

Page 164 – "Ali Akbar…Peacefully surrendering" lines by Ali Akbar, from his notebooks.

Page 165 – "I am an excited bride" lines by Ali Akbar, from his notebooks.

Page 166 – "Love crying in my tears" lines by Ali Akbar, from his notebooks.

Page 179 – Photograph of Ali Akbar, 2008. Photographer, Tynah Utsman.

Page 181 – Photograph of R.B. Morris, 1984. Photographer, Eric Sublett.

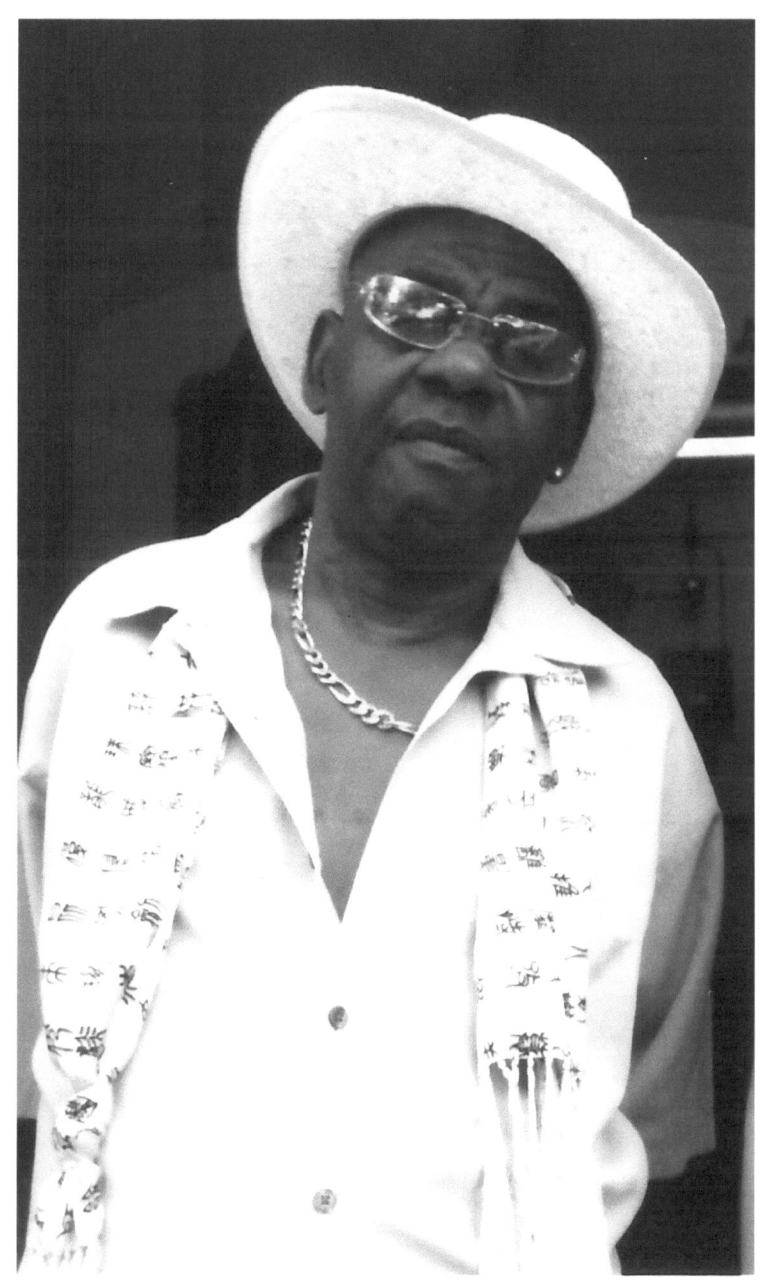

Ali Akbar a.k.a. Horace Pittman (1945-2009) was an artist all his life. Originally from Rock Hill, South Carolina, he served in the US military during the Vietnam War where he suffered a shrapnel wound and subsequent stroke. He moved to Knoxville, Tennessee around 1982 when the city was hosting a world's fair exposition and lived there for the rest of his life. He became a significant artist in the underground art movement of Knoxville, utilizing 'street art' and 'guerrilla art', and was a well known figure in the music and art scenes of the city. A 1992 graduate of Pellissippi State in Computer Integrated Drafting and Design, he also studied at Newark (New Jersey) School of Fine and Industrial Arts and at San Francisco State. He participated in numerous workshops primarily in Northern California, and his exhibitions include showings at galleries, libraries and colleges in Tennessee, South Carolina and California. He was also a poet, sometimes sculptor and performance artist.

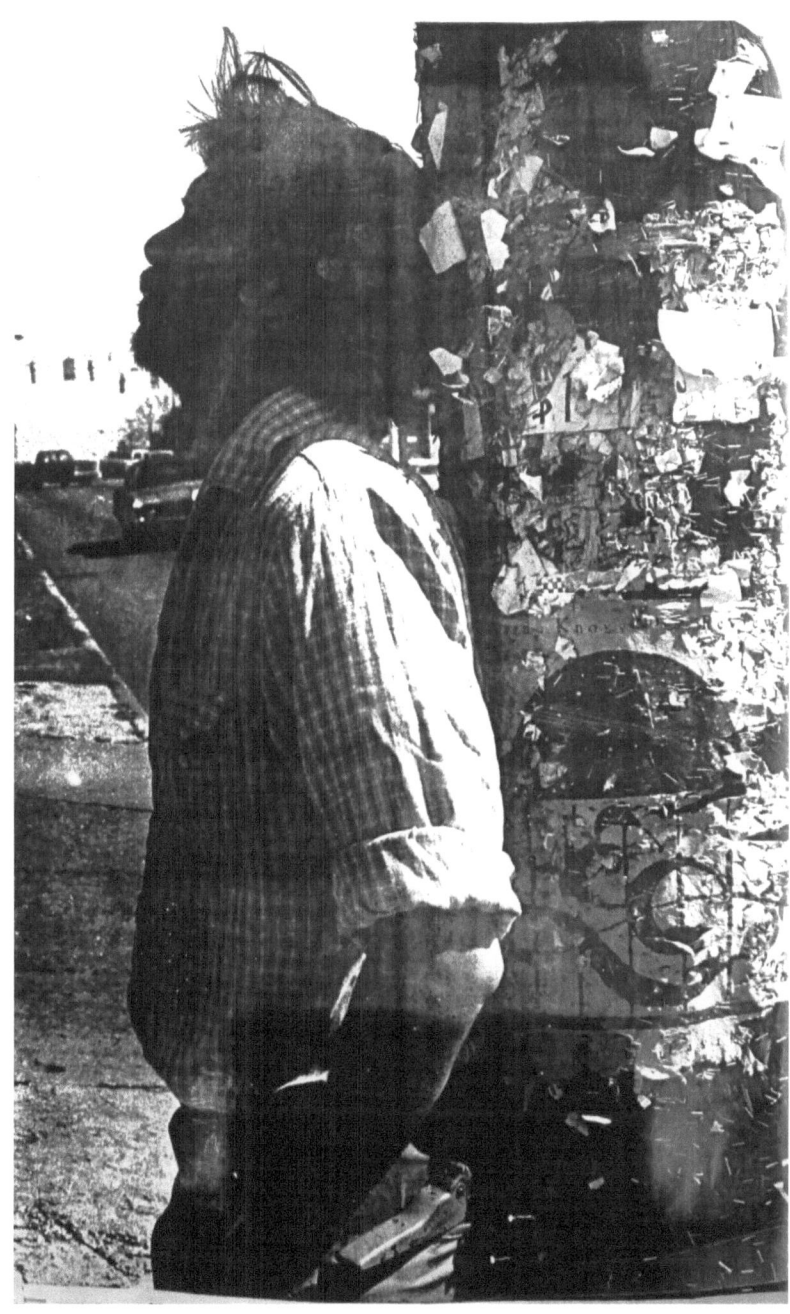

RB Morris is a poet and songwriter and performer from Knoxville, Tennessee. He has published books of poetry, including THE MOCKINGBIRD POEMS (Rich Mountain Bound) and EARLY FIRES (Iris Press), and music albums including SPIES LIES AND BURNING EYES and his most recent solo project RICH MOUNTAIN BOUND. He wrote and acted in THE MAN WHO LIVES HERE IS LOONY, a one-man play taken from the life and work of James Agee, and was instrumental in founding a park dedicated to Agee in Knoxville. Morris served as the Jack E. Reese Writer-in-Residence at the University of Tennessee from 2004-2008, and was inducted into the East Tennessee Writers Hall of Fame in 2009. He lives in Knoxville.

www.ingramcontent.com/pod-product-compliance
Lightning Source LLC
Chambersburg PA
CBHW050847180526
45159CB00007B/2605